IT INFRASTRUCTURE AND ITS MANAGEMENT

About the Authors

Phalguni Gupta is a professor in the Department of Computer Science and Engineering, IIT Kanpur, UP. He received his PhD degree from IIT Kharagpur, West Bengal in 1986. Prior to joining IIT Kanpur, he was with Image Processing and Data Product Group of the Space Applications Centre (ISRO), Ahmedabad, Gujarat (1983–1987) and was involved in developing a system for correcting image data received from first Indian Remote Sensing Satellite.

His research interest includes sequential algorithms, parallel algorithms, online algorithms, image processing, biometrics, and identity and infrastructure management. Currently, he is responsible for several research projects in the area of image processing, biometrics and parallel processing. Over the last 26 years, he has published over 150 peer-reviewed journals and conference papers. He is also the co-author of a book and six book chapters. He is a recipient of 2007 IBM Faculty Award.

Surya Prakash is currently a PhD scholar in the Department of Computer Science and Engineering, IIT Kanpur, UP. He received his MS degree in computer science and engineering from IIT Madras, Tamil Nadu. His research interest includes image processing, computer vision, biometrics, and identity and infrastructure management. He has published two journals and nine conference papers.

Umarani Jayaraman is currently a PhD scholar in the Department of Computer Science and Engineering, IIT Kanpur, UP. She received her MTech degree in computer science and engineering from Arulmigu Meenakshi Amman Engineering College, Tamil Nadu. Her research interest includes pattern recognition, biometrics, high dimensional data structures and infrastructure management.

IT INFRASTRUCTURE AND ITS MANAGEMENT

Phalguni Gupta
Professor
Department of Computer Science & Engineering
Indian Institute of Technology Kanpur

Surya Prakash
Ph.D Scholar
Department of Computer Science & Engineering
Indian Institute of Technology Kanpur

Umarani Jayaraman
Ph.D Scholar
Department of Computer Science & Engineering
Indian Institute of Technology Kanpur

Tata McGraw Hill Education Private Limited
NEW DELHI

McGraw-Hill Offices

New Delhi New York St Louis San Francisco Auckland Bogotá Caracas
Kuala Lumpur Lisbon London Madrid Mexico City Milan Montreal
San Juan Santiago Singapore Sydney Tokyo Toronto

Tata McGraw Hill

Published by the Tata McGraw Hill Education Private Limited,
7 West Patel Nagar, New Delhi 110 008.

IT Infrastructure and its Management

ISBN 13: 978-0-07-069979-3
ISBN 10: 0-07-069979-8

Managing Director: *Ajay Shukla*

Head—Higher Education Publishing: *Vibha Mahajan*
Manager: Sponsoring—SEM & Tech Ed: *Shalini Jha*
Editorial Executive: *Surabhi Shukla*
Jr Executive—Editorial Services: *Dipika Dey*
Jr Manager—Production: *Anjali Razdan*

General Manager: Marketing—Higher Education: *Michael J Cruz*
Sr Product Manager—SEM & Tech Ed: *Biju Ganesan*
Asst Product Manager—SEM & Tech Ed: *Amit Paranjpe*

General Manager—Production: *Rajender P Ghansela*
Asst General Manager—Production: *B L Dogra*

Typeset at Bukprint India, B-180A, Guru Nanak Pura, Laxmi Nagar-110 092 and printed at Adarsh Printers, C-50-51, Mohan Park, Naveen Shahdara, Delhi - 110 032

Cover Printer: SDR Printers

RALDRDRZRZLRA

The McGraw·Hill Companies

Contents

Preface

In the current competitive world, business enterprises face great challenges in scaling and managing their IT infrastructure. To handle these challenges, IT infrastructure management offers focused and efficient solutions in important infrastructure areas for developing and managing the organisational IT infrastructure. Business organisations can achieve cost-effective and quick time-to-delivery by using proven delivery models, mature techniques, standardised tools and robust processes offered by IT infrastructure management. IT infrastructure management guarantees high reliability, round-the-clock availability of services, efficient manageability and optimum scalability. IT infrastructure service delivery helps in achieving proactive and cost-effective solutions and gaining fast return on IT infrastructure investments.

INTENT

This book is aimed to help the undergraduate and postgraduate students of professional courses by familiarising them with the concept of IT infrastructure and its management, and providing them requisite expertise in this area. It is intended to impart knowledge of IT infrastructure management topics and issues, while keeping technical words at its minimum.

KEY FEATURES

The book emphasises on the following:

- *Basics of Information Technology (IT), IT infrastructure and its management*
- *Service delivery and service support processes*
- *Storage and security management in the context of IT infrastructure management*
- *Important security practices, threats and challenges in the field of computer security*
- *IT ethics*
- *Emerging trends in IT sector*
- *Case study*

ORGANISATION

The book contains nine chapters and starts with an introduction on the basics of Information Technology (IT), IT infrastructure and its management (*Chapter 1*). Subsequently, it provides a detailed overview of IT service and IT system management processes. Challenges in IT infrastructure management, IT system and service management process, information system design process, patterns for IT system management and IT infrastructure library are some of key concepts covered in *Chapter 2*.

The book gives a comprehensive discussion on service delivery and service support processes (*Chapters 3 and 4*) which are the most essential parts of IT infrastructure management. It provides an elaborate discussion on important service delivery processes such as service level management, financial management, service continuity management, capacity management and availability management. It also talks about service support processes such as configuration management, incident management, problem management, change management and release management.

Storage management is an important component of IT infrastructure management. It protects the organisation from the risks of data loss, helps in reducing complexity, manages cost, and provides compliance with data retention and availability requirements. It improves service continuity by reducing backup and recovery time, and improving application availability with data recovery and management technologies. It helps in adapting changes within the IT infrastructure to minimise service interruptions and generates fast restorations and backups. Chapter 5 is dedicated to Storage Management and discusses all its aspects.

Security management is an important area of management. It helps in realisation of the security and other external requirements which are specified in internal or external policies of an organisation. It also helps in accomplishing the basic level of security which is necessary to guarantee the continuity of the management organistion. Chapter 6 on Security Management provides an elaborate discussion on many important aspects of security in context to IT infrastructure management. Normal security practices, threats and challenges in the field of computer security are covered in depth.

IT ethics, which has become very important in current scenario, is discussed in Chapter 7. Chapter 8 delves into the emerging trends in IT sector, namely e-commerce, electronic data interchange, global system for mobile communications, Bluetooth and infrared technology. Chapter 9 focuses on a Case Study that elucidates the functioning of an IT organisation and studies various aspects of its activities and infrastructure management.

ACKNOWLEDGEMENTS

Several people have helped in the preparation of this book. We have been benefited from various existing text and reference material on IT infrastructure management, specifically from IBM India and Microsoft. We wish to extend our appreciation to Mr Vivek Manoria and Mr Devkant Aggrawal of IBM India for providing their support to complete this book. Mr Pradeep Nayak has helped us in printing the rough draft of the book and typesetting. We express our special thanks to him. The Tata McGraw-Hill team specially Vibha Mahajan, Shalini Jha, Surabhi Shukla, Dipika Dey, and Anjali Razdan have provided necessary assistance to bring out a quality product. Earnest thanks to all of them.

A note of acknowledgement is also due to the following reviewers for their valuable suggestions:

Girish Chandra
Department of Computer Science and Engineering
Institute of Engineering and Technology, Lucknow, UP

Udai Shanker
Department of Computer Science and Engineering
MMM Engineering College, Gorakhpur, UP

Pabitra Mitra
Department of Computer Science and Engineering,
Indian Institute of Technology Kharagpur, Kharagpur, West Bengal

Vinay Pathak
Computer Science & Engineering Department,
Harcourt Butler Technical Institute, Kanpur, UP

—Authors

Publisher's Note

Tata McGraw Hill Education looks forward to receiving from teachers and students their valuable views, comments and suggestions for improvements, all of which may be sent to tmh.csefeedback@gmail.com (*mentioning the title and author's name*). Also, please inform any observations on piracy related issues.

Introduction

Chapter 1

1.1 EVOLUTION OF COMPUTER

At the start of civilisation, any computation was done with the help of fingers, counting boards, pebbles and by putting rope knots. As people became more and more civilised, computing demand also grew and led to the development of modern high speed computers.

The evolution of computers started in late 1930s. Its history goes back to the invention of the first mechanical computing device for addition, called Abacus. Figure 1.1 shows the picture of an early *Chinese Abacus*. John Napier's invention of logarithm and William Oughtred's invention of slide rules are also considered as significant developments in the evolution of computers from the early computing devices such as Abacus. Binary arithmetic has always remained at the core of the computers.

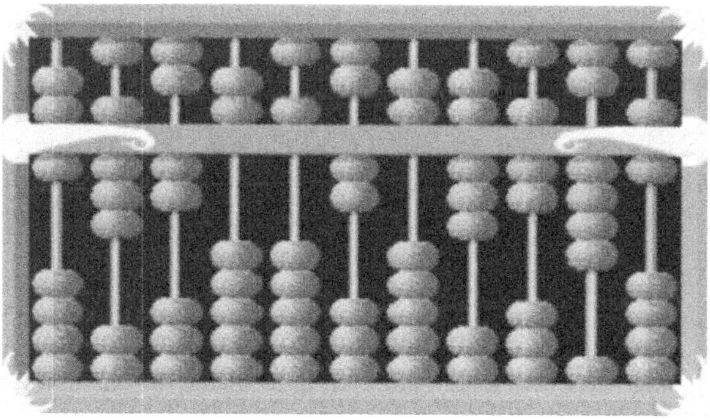

Fig. 1.1 *Chinese Abacus*[1]*, an early time mechanical computing machine*

[1]source: http://www.brianmicklethwait.com/education/archives/maths/

The journey of modern computer began in 1937 when Alan Turing invented *Turing Machine*, which paved the way to the idea of machines that could complete a defined task by being supplied with programs. In subsequent years, great development happened in the field of computing. Konrad Zuse in 1938 designed the first binary digital relay computer. In 1943, the first general-purpose digital computer—ENIAC—was developed. World's first stored-program electronic digital computer—Manchester Baby—was successfully built in 1948. This type of digital computer included the stored-program concept to utilise Random Access Memory, not only to hold the data involved in calculations but also to hold the program instructions. This enabled the instructions to be read successively at electronic speed. Also, the execution of a different program was possible in this computer only by resetting part of the memory, using a simple keyboard rather than reconfiguring the electronic circuitry, which typically took days on ENIAC machine.

First real-time processing computer was built by MIT in 1955, while in the next year, IBM developed the disk memory system. The integrated circuit chip was introduced in the following year. In 1959, IBM introduced the first desktop computer. This led to the development of first real microcomputer of Digital Equipment Corporation (DEC) in 1965.

In the computer evolution, first generation computers were characterised by the use of vacuum tubes[2]. These computers were very bulky and expensive. They were based on machine language and were capable of solving only one problem at a given point of time. There was no concept of multitasking. Second generation of computers were based on transistors. In the 1960s, vacuum tubes-based machines were replaced by transistor-based computers. This brought significant advancement in computers and made them cheaper, smaller and lighter. This also made computers efficient in terms of power consumption. However, there was a problem with these computers. They used to emit large amounts of heat from their circuitry because of which they were subjected to damage. Second generation computers used punched cards for taking input and assembly language for programming.

The integrated circuits led to the third generation of computers which used small transistors called semiconductors on silicon chips. Use of semiconductors improved the speed as well as efficiency of computers. In the third generation computers, operating systems became the human interface for computing, while keyboards and monitors were used as the input and output devices respectively. Introduction of microprocessors was the characteristic of fourth generation computers. In these computers, thousands of integrated circuits were put on a silicon chip, building a microprocessor.

The fifth generation computers are intended to use the concepts of artificial intelligence and natural language processing. These computers are in the development stage and developers are aiming to make these computers capable of organising themselves.

---

[2]Vacuum tubes are cathode ray tubes that emit electron rays.

1.2 COMPUTER BASICS

A computer is an information processing machine. It manipulates data based on the set of instructions supplied to it. Set of instructions to solve a problem is commonly referred as a program, and is provided by the programmer. Although there exist mechanical computers since long in human history, the first electronic computer could only be developed in 1940s. These computers were very large in size and used to consume huge amount of power. Modern computers are based on integrated circuits, take very little space and are much faster than the earlier machines.

1.2.1 Computer Hardware

A computer can be divided into two components, namely hardware and software. Hardware does all the physical work of computers. The second component, software, dictates to the hardware what is to be done and how it is to be done. Modern computers are based on Von-Neumann architecture, which follows stored program concept and defines a computing model that uses a processing unit and a storage unit. The processing unit is used to carry out the execution of instructions while storage unit is used to keep the instructions and data. Von-Neumann architecture implements a universal *Turing Machine* and follows a sequential architecture. Figure 1.2 shows the design of the Von-Neumann architecture with various components. These components are explained below.

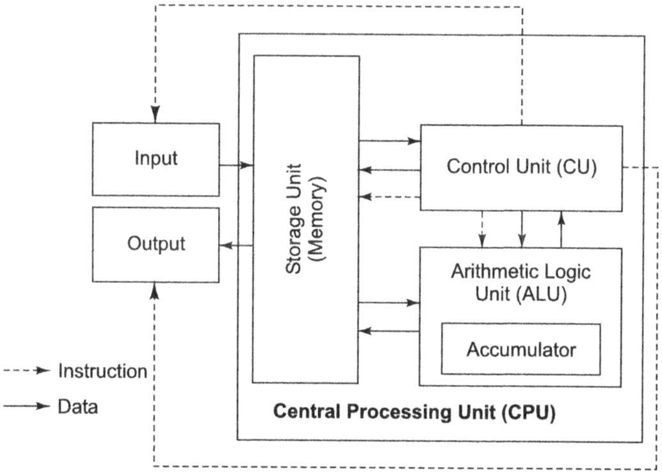

Fig. 1.2 *Von-Neumann architecture design of computer*

Central Processing Unit (CPU) It is an electronic circuit that can execute computer programs and is considered as the brain of the computer. It is responsible for reading the instructions from the memory and executing them. CPU performs most of the computation enabling a computer to function. It has three main components:

Control Unit (CU) It is responsible for fetching the instructions from the primary memory and for decoding them to find out the operations to be performed. After decoding, it instructs arithmetic and logic unit to perform the desired operation. It also controls input and output devices and monitors the overall functioning of the other units of the computer.

Arithmetic Logic Unit (ALU) It is responsible for the actual execution of instructions. It performs the arithmetic and logic operations on data. It gets the signals from the CU regarding the type of operations to be done, then it takes the data from the memory and executes that operation, and stores the results either in the internal storage or transfers it to the primary memory. ALU also has internal storage in the form of registers to store the intermediate results during the course of calculation.

Memory This unit holds the running program and the data. It is sometimes referred to as the primary memory or main memory. The task of memory is to take the data from input device and to store it until the computer is ready to process it. It is also used to hold the intermediate and final computing results. Once the processing is over, data from memory can be transferred to an output device.

Input-Output Unit It is used to input instructions and data from the user and to communicate the results to user. Input-output devices are the medium of communication between user and computer. Some of the common input devices are keyboard, mouse and light pen, while output devices are printer, monitor, plotter, etc.

Permanent Storage With above mentioned components, computers also have permanent storage—usually called *secondary storage*—for storing the information and data permanently. Permanent storage provides stored information to other units as and when required. Some common permanent storage devices are hard disk, floppy disk, CD, DVD, pen drive, etc.

1.2.2 Computer Software

Computer software is a program which instructs computer hardware regarding the steps to be carried out. It is usually developed by computer programmers with the help of a programming language. Software is often used in a broader context and it refers to anything which is not hardware but which is used with hardware such as tapes, films, and records. Computer software can be divided into three primary categories: system softwares, programming software and application software.

System Software They are the programs which allow the hardware to run properly. Typical example of system software is an operating system which interfaces with hardware to provide the necessary services for application software. Other examples of system softwares are device drivers, utilities, windowing systems, etc.

Programming Software It includes tools that help a programmer in writing a computer program or software, using different programming languages in a convenient way. These tools commonly include compilers, debuggers, linker, editors, etc.

Application Software It represents any program which allows users to create some application, in addition to simply running the hardware. Some examples of application software are word processors, graphics tools, medical softwares, database packages, computer games, business softwares, etc.

Figure 1.3 shows a layered architecture presenting the relative positions of hardware, operating system (system software), application software and user.

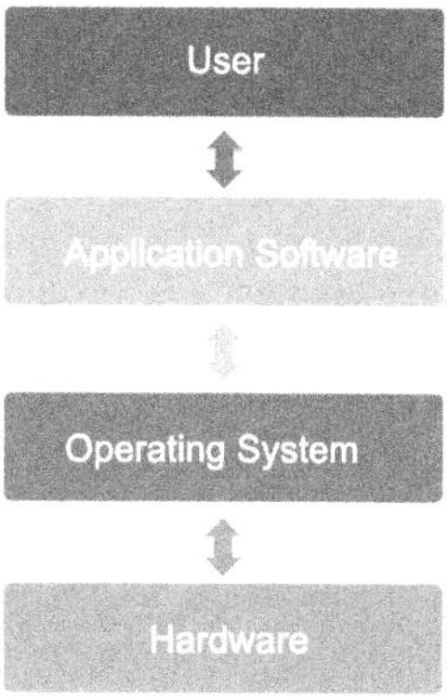

Fig. 1.3 *Relative positions of various software and hardware components*

1.3 NETWORK AND INTERNET

A computer network is a group of interconnected computers. The internet refers to a worldwide system of interconnected computer networks. As technological developments are taking place, they are causing a revolution in our society, economy and technological systems. Internet came into existence in late 1970s as a development of the ARPANET[3], a Department of Defence project. This network employed a new packet-switching concept for interconnecting computers and was initially deployed to link computers at universities and other institutions in the United States of America and in some other countries. At that point of time, the ARPANET was the only wide-area computer network with a base of several organisations. Most of the growth of internet took place in 1990s and it rapidly spread to most of the countries in the world during this time.

Internet, which is a network of networks, consists of millions of private and public networks of local as well as global scope from academic, business, and government arenas. Usually, communication between two computers in the internet uses a standardised Internet Protocol called TCP/IP. Connection between computers on the internet is commonly provided using transmission mediums such as copper wires, fiber-optic cables and wireless connections.

1.3.1 Internet Applications

The internet provides a huge amount of information resources and services. Some of them are discussed here.

Hypertext Documents Among the various services provided by the internet, hosting of inter-linked hypertext documents over the World Wide Web (WWW)

[3]ARPANET stands for Advanced Research Projects Agency NETwork

is the most noted one. Hypertext is the text which appears on computer with references (called hyperlinks) to other documents that a reader can access with a mouse click or by pressing keys. Hypertext documents, often called as web pages, provide a convenient way to gather related pages together and to consider them as a single multi-page hypertext document. Hypertext Transfer Protocol (HTTP) is typically used to transfer displayable web pages and related files.

Electronic Mail Often abbreviated as e-mail, it refers to the transmission of messages over networks. The messages can be notes entered through keyboard or electronic files already available in the computer. Generally, it takes very little time for an e-mail to reach its destination. E-mail serves a very effective means to communicate within a group since it can broadcast a message or document to everyone in the group since once. Almost all online services and Internet Service Providers (ISPs) offer e-mail service, and most of them also support gateways which allow users to communicate with the users of other systems. Simple Mail Transfer Protocol (SMTP) is generally used to transfer e-mail.

Telnet It is a communication program which enables a computer to function as a terminal program in a TCP/IP network. The telnet program runs on a user's computer and connects his personal computer to a server on the network. Once a connection between a personal computer and a server is established, commands can be entered through the telnet program and can be executed as if they are entered directly on the server console. This utility enables the remote control of servers. Usually in the beginning of a telnet session, a valid username and password are used to connect to remote server.

File Transfer Over Internet Usually, file transfer over internet is done using a standard internet protocol called File Transfer Protocol (FTP). It is the simplest way to exchange files between computers on the internet. Similar to other protocols like HTTP and SMTP, FTP is also an application protocol which runs on top of the TCP/IP protocols. It is usually used to download programs and other files from other servers. It is also used to transfer web pages and other related files from the user's computer to server, which makes pages visible to everyone on the internet.

Voice Over Internet Protocol (VOIP) It is a technology which allows voice calls to be made using an internet connection instead of a regular (or analog) phone line. VoIP service converts speaker's voice into a digital signal and transmits it over the internet. If the call is made to a regular analog phone, the signal is converted to an analog signal before it reaches the destination telephone. VoIP allows a call to be made directly from a computer, a special VoIP phone, or a traditional phone connected to a special adapter.

Miscellaneous Other services provided by internet include online text chat, voice/video chat, electronic trading, news groups, mailing lists, etc.

1.3.2 Size of the Internet

It is determined by the number of machines currently *on the internet*. By *on the internet*, we mean that there is a listing for a hostname and IP address on a domain name server (DNS). The machine does not need to exist. It is counted by the virtue of its mention on a DNS. Sometimes, by *on the internet*, we also mean that the machine is both listed on a DNS and is running, and responding to *ping* (an internet utility which is used to determine if a machine is alive and connected to the network or not). It should be noted that this excludes the machines which are behind firewalls (a utility used to increase network security) or machines that are not up at the time of the pinging.

1.4 COMPUTING RESOURCES

Great developments have been observed in computing since 1960. The recent development in microprocessor performance provides an appealing vehicle for improved computing. The availability of high speed networks and fast microprocessors makes clustered workstations a cost-effective choice for computing. Some of the current computing technologies are Client-Server based computing, Supercomputing, Cluster computing, Grid computing and Cloud computing.

1.4.1 Client-Server Based Computing

Several years ago, most organisations had mainframe-based computing, in which mainframe computers were connected to dumb terminals. These terminals were unable to do any independent computing and had to totally rely on the mainframe for data processing. As the years passed, development of personal computers led to the replacement of dumb terminals. However, the main processing work continued to be performed on the mainframe computer. The improved computing capability of personal computers was ignored to a great extent. After due course of time, many organisations started to realise the potential of personal computers and started to think about the possibility of using it either by sharing, or by splitting some of the processing demands between the mainframe and the personal computers. Client-server technology is the outcome of this development.

Client/server refers to a computing architecture in which software components interact with each other to provide a system that can be designed for and used by multiple users. It provides a way of separating the functions of an application into two or more different parts. Typically in client-server architecture, the client is a personal computer while the server is a high performance based mainframe machine; however, the same machine can work both as client and server. In practice, it is a very common practice to install a server at one end of a Local Area Network (LAN) and the clients at the other ends. The client is the requesting machine and the server works as a supplying machine. Client-server technology allows distributed computation, analysis and presentation between personal computers and one or more high computing machines on a network. In this architecture, each function of an application stays on the computer (client or server) which is more competent of managing that particular function. Many services used nowadays over the internet are based on client-server architecture. For example, File Transfer Protocol (FTP) uses client-server technology to exchange files between systems. In this, a FTP client requests a file (that exists on another computer) and FTP server (the system where the file exists) handles the request by supplying the file to the client.

Client-server architecture is generally of two types: 2-tier architecture and 3-tier architecture.

2-Tier Architecture Client-server applications initially started with 2-tiered architecture which composed of a client and an application server. Majority of first generation client-server systems are built on 2-tier architectures, where a client provides a front-end Graphical User Interface (GUI) to the user and works according to the user's actions to perform requests of a server running on a different machine. The window applications are generally developed using this technology. A common implementation of 2-tier client-server architecture is a *fat* client-*thin* server architecture, in which application logic resides in the client machine and server simply reports the results of queries.

For example, when a student wants to know his grades in 2-tier client-server architecture, the client application formulates a query and fires to the database server. The database server responds with the grades of all students. Now client application uses all this data to calculate the concerned student's grade, and displays it as per his request.

3-Tier Architecture 2-tier architecture works very well when database size is small but it performs very poorly in case of large database. This is due to the fact that, for every query generated by a client, the data server has to work out large queries for the client application to manipulate. This is a very large drain on network resources. The 3-tier architecture attempts to overcome some of the limitations (such as poor network utilisation) of the 2-tier schemes by making presentation, processing, and data separate and distinct entities.

The components of 3-tiered architecture can be thought of in the form of three tiers such as a presentation tier, functionality tier, and data tier which can be logically separated as shown in Fig. 1.4. Client sits at presentation tier and generates all requests. Functionality tier is the middle tier and implements protocols used for processing the request. Data tier implements back-end database and sends responses to the client. Typically, middle-tier functionality servers are multithreaded and can be accessed by multiple clients simultaneously even though the clients are running separate applications. Web applications are good examples of 3-tier architecture.

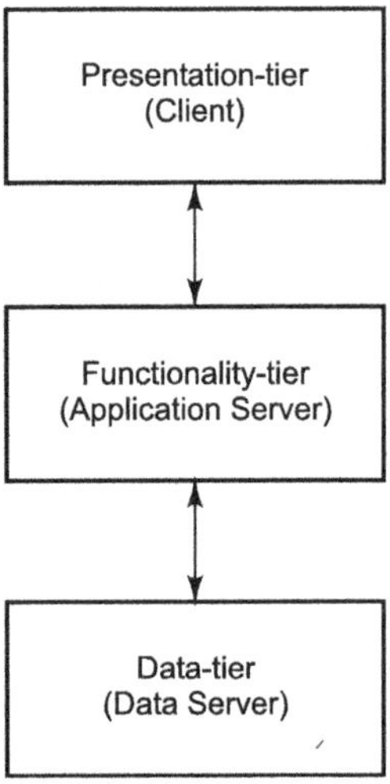

Fig. 1.4 *3-Tiered client-server architecture*

1.4.2 Supercomputing

It usually refers to the computation intensive software applications performed on the world's fastest computers called supercomputers. Supercomputers are very expensive and are typically employed for specialised applications that require large amount of mathematical computations. Some common applications where supercomputers are being used are weather forecasting, animated graphics, fluid dynamic calculations, nuclear energy research, petroleum exploration, molecular dynamics for drug design, and aero dynamics for car and aircraft design. Computing speed of supercomputers in usually measured in FLOPs[4]. As of May 2008, the 'IBM Roadrunner' is the fastest supercomputer in the world with 1.71 petaflops peak speed.

Sometimes supercomputers are confused with mainframes. The main difference between a supercomputer and a mainframe is that a supercomputer utilises all its computational power for executing a few programs as fast as possible, whereas a mainframe uses its power to execute many programs concurrently.

PARAM Padma Supercomputer It is India's next generation high performance scalable computing cluster with a peak computing power of one Teraflop and is developed by Centre for Development of Advance Computing (C-DAC). Figure 1.5 shows the picture of PARAM Padma super computer. The hardware environment of PARAM Padma is powered by compute nodes based on Power4 RISC processors. These nodes are connected using PARAMNet-II, a high performance System Area Network, designed and developed by C-DAC with a Gigabit Ethernet as a backup network. The PARAM Padma uses C-DAC's scalable HPCC software environment. The storage system of PARAM Padma has been designed to provide a primary storage of 5 terabytes, which is scalable up to 22 terabytes.

Fig. 1.5 *PARAM Padma supercomputer of India*

1.4.3 Cluster Computing

It refers to the use of a group of tightly coupled computer systems which work together closely to accomplish computational tasks. Clusters can be viewed as a single system with centralised management and scheduling system. Usually, computers participating in a cluster are connected to each other through a fast local area network. Cluster computing helps to improve the performance and availability of computing over that provided by a single computer and is more cost-effective compared to a single computer having similar speed. Figure 1.6 shows an example of Silicon Graphics computer cluster.

[4]FLOPs stands for Floating Point Operations Per Second

Fig. 1.6 *Silicon graphics computer cluster*[5]

Cluster Categorisation Central idea of cluster computing is that, to the outside world, the cluster appears to be a single system and it can be used for multiple purposes. Depending upon the type of computation and the purpose of use, clusters can be classified into following categories:

High Availability Clusters It is a group of independent computers (nodes) that work together to increase the availability of applications and services offered by the cluster. The clustered machines are connected by physical cables and by software. If one of the nodes in the cluster fails, another node begins to provide service, and users experience minimum disruption in service. This event is called 'failover.' Since these clusters are used to ensure the availability of the services all the time, they are also sometimes known as 'failover clusters.' To ensure availability, high availability cluster functions by having redundant nodes which are used to provide service when system components fail to work. The common size for a high availability cluster is two nodes, which is also the minimum need to provide redundancy.

Load Balancing Clusters These clusters are built using multiple computers by linking them together to share computational workload. These clusters receive workload from one or more load-balancing front-ends and then distribute it to a group of back-end machines forming the cluster. Though they are primarily built for improved performance, they also commonly include high availability features as well. These clusters are sometimes referred to as a server farm. Platform LSF HPC, Sun Grid Engine and Moab Cluster Suite are few examples of load balancing cluster.

[5]source: http://www.nas.nasa.gov/News/Images/columbia_3.html

High Performance Computing Clusters This type of cluster is implemented to provide increased performance by dividing a computational task across many different nodes in the cluster. These clusters run customised programs which are designed to exploit the parallelism available on high performance computing clusters. They are mostly used in scientific computations. Many software programs running on high performance computing clusters use libraries like MPI which are specially designed for writing applications for high performance computing clusters.

1.4.4 Grid Computing

It is a form of distributed computing and refers to the use of several computers to solve a single problem at the same time. It uses networked, loosely coupled computers acting simultaneously to perform very large tasks. In grid computing, a program is generally divided into many parts and these parts are allocated to several computers, often up to many thousands. Grid computing is used to solve scientific and technical problems which require a large amount of computing or access to large amounts of data. Grid computing can be considered as distributed and large-scale cluster computing. It can also be thought of as a distributed parallel processing system.

Grid computing may use small network of computer workstations confined within an organisation or it can use a large public collaboration across many companies and networks. This form of computing is largely used to solve computationally intensive scientific and mathematical problems through volunteer computing and has many commercial applications. Common applications where grid computing is used include drug discovery, economic forecasting and data processing in support of e-Commerce and web services. Functionally, grids can be classified into several types such as *computational grids* (which focus primarily on computationally-intensive operations) and *data grids* (which control sharing and management of large amounts of distributed data).

1.4.5 Difference between Grid Computing and Cluster Computing

Grid computing is often confused with cluster computing. It is focused on the supporting computation across the domains which make it different from traditional computer clusters or traditional distributed computing. The major differences are listed below:

Heterogeneous vs. Homogeneous The important difference between grid computing and cluster computing is that, in grid computing, grid is formed using heterogeneous computers. Moreover, grid is frequently built using general-purpose grid software libraries and middleware. In cluster computing, computer clusters are homogenous. The computers that are part of a grid can use different operating systems and have different hardware whereas the computers forming clusters should have the same hardware and operating system.

Loosely Coupled vs. Tightly Coupled Grid is formed using loosely coupled machines, and it can make use of spare computing power on a desktop computer while the machines in a cluster are tightly coupled and dedicated to work only as a single unit.

Global Positioning of the Machines Grids are inherently distributed in nature over a network and use geographically scattered machines. On the other hand, the computers in the cluster are normally present in a single location.

Resource Handling Another difference lies in the way that resources are managed. In case of grid computing, every node (machine) is autonomous, has its own resource manager and behaves like an independent unit whereas in case of cluster computing, all the nodes together behave like a single system, and resources are managed by a centralised resource manager.

1.4.6 Cloud Computing

Cloud computing is a term used for delivering hosted services over the internet. It is a style of computing where dynamically scalable and often virtualised computing resources are provided as a service over the internet. In many cases, cloud computing services provide common business applications online that can be accessed using a web browser while storing software and data on the servers. Figure 1.7 shows an example of cloud computing services followed by some companies. Cloud computing services are broadly categorised into three categories:

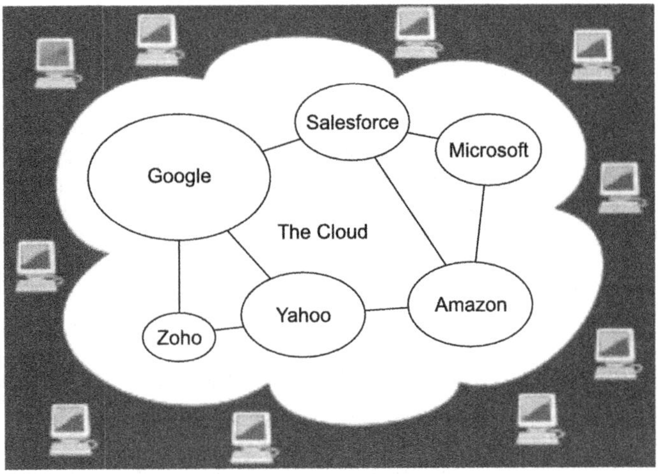

Fig. 1.7 *Some of the companies providing cloud computing services*[6]

Infrastructure-as-a-Service (IaaS) A good example of this kind of service is web service. For example, Amazon Web Services provides virtual server instances with unique IP addresses and blocks of storage on demand. In this kind of service, customers use the service provider's application program interface to control and configure their virtual servers and storage.

Platform-as-a-Service (PaaS) It is defined as a set of software and product development tools hosted on the service provider's infrastructure. Developers can create applications on the service provider's platform over the internet. GoogleApps is a good example of PaaS.

[6]source: http://en.wikipedia.org/

Software-as-a-Service (SaaS) In this model, service provider supplies the hardware infrastructure, software development tools and interacts with the user through a front-end. This type of service can range from web-based e-mail services to inventory control and database processing. Since this service hosts both application and data on the server, the service user can use the service from anywhere.

The name 'cloud computing' has been inspired by the typical cloud symbol which is frequently used to depict the internet in computer network diagrams and is an abstraction for the complex infrastructure that it conceals. In cloud computing, users need not have any knowledge of, expertise in, or control over the technology resources used in the *cloud* that supports them.

There are three basic characteristics that differentiate cloud computing services from traditional hosting. First one is that it is sold on demand. Cloud computing allows a user to pay only for required capacity and to bring more capacity online as soon as required. Second property is that this service is elastic and a user can have as much or as little of a service as they want at any given time. Third property of cloud computing service is that it is fully managed by the service provider. The user needs to have only a personal computer and internet access to use the service. Factors such as significant advancements in virtualisation, distributed computing and availability of high-speed internet have promoted the use of cloud computing in the slow economy. Since cloud computing model of pay-for-what-you-use resembles the way electricity, fuel and water are consumed, it is sometimes referred to as utility computing.

A cloud can be private as well as public. A public cloud offers services to anyone over the internet. A private cloud is a proprietary network or a data centre that offers hosted services to a limited number of users. Amazon Web Services is the largest public cloud provider in present time.

1.5 INFORMATION TECHNOLOGY

Information Technology (IT) is the branch of technology which is concerned with the dissemination, processing, and storage of information, particularly with the help of computers. It deals with the design, development, deployment, support and management of computer-based information systems, especially computer hardware and software programs. IT supports the use of computers to store, process, convert, transmit, protect and later retrieve information, if necessary. Due to the basic shift in computing technology and paperless workplaces, IT has become a popular phrase.

The term *Information Technology* in current time has become very recognisable, covering many fields. IT professionals are engaged in various kinds of tasks which include development of software applications, installation of softwares, designing large computer networks, development of reliable database systems, designing of security solutions, automation of machines, management computers, etc. Some of the other tasks performed by IT professionals include data management, designing computer hardware, web designing, etc.

1.5.1 History of Information Technology

Prior to 1970s, the term 'IT' was very little known and was used by only people working in places like banks and hospitals to describe the processes they carried out to store information. A single computer operator in the IT department of an organisation was sufficient to operate and manage computers. He was supposed to run the computers, mount the storage devices (like magnetic tape), store the data on tapes, put the tape in a box and physically store it somewhere. Computers were huge pieces of equipment that were kept in large, air-conditioned rooms, getting input from punch cards or paper tape.

The development in the field of IT has been fascinating. IT has become integral part of everyday activities. Many technological advances have been made in computing field and many new computing paradigms have been discovered in recent years. With the development of the personal computers in 1980s and its use in the home and the office, the world has evolved into the information age. IT departments have transformed from using storage tapes produced by a single computer operator to interconnected networks of workstations that often store information in a server kept at a remote site.

In today's time, in order to perform the complex tasks required by the organisation, IT departments have completely changed. A modern IT department uses computers, servers, database management systems, various application softwares, etc. The departments have several people required to keep the system up. For example, system administrators, database administrators, web administrators, network administrator, etc. have become an essential component of any IT department. Keeping in view the importance of activities of an IT department, organisations also maintain positions like IT managers and Chief Information Officer (CIO). In times to come, IT departments will become increasingly concerned with data storage and management, and information security would continue to be an important part of it.

1.5.2 Information Technology Management

Management is the act of managing and streamlining the resources of an organisation to accomplish desired goals and objectives. Management consists of many activities such as planning, staffing, organising, leading, controlling an organisation. Information Technology (IT) Management is related to the exploring, study and management of information technology as a technological resource. IT Management helps in designing, developing and deploying IT products and services which impart customer satisfaction, business productivity, profitability and competitiveness. There are many branches of IT Management. Some important branches are briefly discussed here:

IT Asset Management IT assets include all elements of software and hardware that are found in a business environment. Its management deals with managing these elements, and helps in understanding the true business values and analysing the improved business cost. It also helps in the process of procurement, cost optimisation, inventory control, ensuring accountability and compliance, strategic decision making, life cycle management and setting up IT credibility throughout the enterprise. It performs risk reduction through standardisation, proper documentation and loss detection. Depending upon the type of assets, asset management can be divided into two types: software asset management and hardware asset management.

IT Application Management It helps in managing the key aspects of an application. It deals with monitoring the availability of an application component and its performance. Good application management helps people such as system administrator, application administrators, database administrators, etc. to manage and achieve real-time availability and good performance of applications. It also assists in root cause analysis of any decline in application performance. At present, an organisation that does not manage availability of its key software applications cannot continue to remain competitive and is likely to suffer.

IT Infrastructure Management It refers to the management of essential components of an organisation which are necessary for providing services that it offers to its customers. Typically, these components include equipment, manpower, processes, data, applications and organisational policies.

IT Operations Management It focuses on efficiently managing the processes that are used to produce and distribute products and services of an organisation. A great deal of emphasis of operations management is on efficiency and effectiveness of the processes. Operations management often performs measurement and analysis of internal processes to assess their efficiency and effectiveness.

IT Performance Management It refers to the activities which ensure that the business goals set by an organisation are consistently being met in an effective and efficient manner. It includes the management of performance of the organisation, department and processes to build a product or provide a service.

IT Strategic Planning Strategy refers to an overall approach and plan. IT strategic planning deals with defining the strategy and direction of an organisation and making decisions on allocating its resources to carry out its strategy. Good IT strategic planning is an essential component to the success of an organisation. It allows an organisation to prioritise its projects, to optimise resource allocation, to monitor performance and to manage the value IT components.

IT Workforce Management In simplest terms, workforce management can be defined as the activity of assigning the right employees with the right skills to the right job at the right time. It is concerned with the assignment of the responsibilities in such a way that it helps in maintaining a productive and happy workforce. Its management has become an important strategic element in corporate management in all personnel intensive working areas.

1.6 IT INFRASTRUCTURE MANAGEMENT

In any information system, infrastructure refers to basic support system that is shared among all the users. Particularly, Information Technology (IT) infrastructure of an organisation is the basic set of components which are shared by all IT business applications. It not only refers to a set of hardware devices but also includes aspects such as software applications, information and its processing and working business practices. IT infrastructure management deals with the management of these essential components which are very necessary to run an organisation and in providing services to its customers. It includes components such as equipment, data, human resources, processes, organisational policies and external contacts.

IT infrastructure management process consists of two important parts viz. service delivery and service support. Service delivery includes processes such as IT service level management, financial management, IT service continuity management, service management, capacity management, and availability management. Common management processes involved in service support process are configuration management, incident management, problem management, change management, and release management. IT infrastructure management process also includes storage management and security management. Chapter 2 talks about the general overview of IT infrastructure and subsequent chapters discuss various management processes.

1.7 ORGANISATION OF THE BOOK

The book contains eight chapters. Chapter 2 elucidates the basics of IT infrastructure. It gives a detailed overview of IT service and IT system management processes. Chapter 3 and Chapter 4 discuss the service delivery and service support processes respectively, which are the main components of IT infrastructure management. Chapter 5 explains storage management in the context of IT infrastructure management. The next chapter deals with security management, and gives the details of normal security practices, threats and challenges in the field of computer security. In Chapter 7, IT ethics—which has become very important in current scenario—has been discussed. In the last chapter, emerging trends in IT are presented.

Review Questions

1. Briefly discuss computer evolution.
2. What do you understand by stored program concept? Discuss a computer architecture which is based on this concept.
3. Discuss Von-Neumann architecture of computers. How did it revolutionise the field of computers?
4. Explain the following:
    - Application Software
    - System Software
    - Programming software
    - Compiler
    - Debugger.
5. Briefly explain the development of internet.
6. Explain client-server architecture. How do 2-tier and 3-tier client-server architectures function?

7. What is cloud computing? Discuss various categories of services offered by cloud computing.
8. Explain cluster computing and grid computing. What are the applications of these technologies?
9. What is the difference between grid computing and cluster computing?
10. What is supercomputing? How is it different from cluster and grid computing?
11. What is the difference between a supercomputer and a mainframe computer?
12. Define following terms:
    - High availability clusters
    - High performance computing
    - Load balancing clusters.
13. Discuss following terms:
    - www
    - File Transfer Protocol (FTP)
    - Hyper Text Transfer Protocol (HTTP)
    - Telnet
    - Voice over IP (VoIP)
    - Electronic mail (E-mail).
14. How is telnet different from FTP? Explain.
15. What is the difference between FTP and HTTP? Give some examples of FTP and HTTP websites.
16. What is a firewall? What is its role in the internet?
17. Explain the difference between VoIP and normal analog voice telephony.
18. What is the meaning of Information Technology (IT)? How is it affecting the common life in current scenario?
19. Discuss various aspects of IT Management.
20. Write short notes on the following:
    - IT asset management
    - IT operations management
    - IT performance management
    - IT application management
    - IT workforce management
    - IT strategic planning.
21. What is IT infrastructure? What are the various components of IT infrastructure management?

IT Infrastructure

Chapter 2

2.1 INTRODUCTION—IT INFRASTRUCTURE MANAGEMENT

IT infrastructure of an organisation comprises of equipment, software, hardware, or any other components which are needed to deliver IT services to its customers. It also provides a base on top of which program or project-specific systems and capabilities of an organisation are created. IT infrastructure can be divided into several categories such as:

- Purchased softwares (e.g., ERP packages, RDBMS, operating systems, e-mail tools, office tools, financial applications, etc.)
- IT infrastructure hardware (e.g., machines, desktops, servers, switches, communication devices, etc.)
- Software development
- Software maintenance (corrective, perfective, adaptive, block changes)
- IT services (e.g., software setup, help desk, computer administration, etc.)
- Human resource (working staff).

IT infrastructure management aims to manage these components for effective utilisation in order to provide better services to customers. Almost all business activities of an organisation depend upon the infrastructure. Hence, its effective management is very essential. IT infrastructure needs to be developed and managed in an active manner to support the requirements of the organisation. This is usually done by IT department of an organisation in consultation with top management. A good and reliable IT infrastructure is the key to the successful operations and is the foundation of any viable IT organisation. IT infrastructure management creates an infrastructure management environment that reduces IT complicacies. It automates and supports required performance and service availability levels and resolves problems to ensure the business continuity. As an organisation scales its Information Technology (IT) infrastructure to support business growth, managing global networks, databases and applications becomes an important task. Among many other objectives, IT infrastructure management tries to:

- Decrease the duplication of effort and increase organisational productivity
- Decrease business risk
- Ensure the use of standards
- Ensure minimum downtime
- Improve adaptability necessary for a changeable environment
- Improve the information flow in information system
- Ensure interoperability among organisational and external entities
- Maintain effective change management policies and practices
- Reduce operational costs
- Increase service quality
- Increase business planning.

IT skills and managerial practices also play an important role in IT infrastructure management. Figure 2.1 presents a view of IT infrastructure highlighting the importance of human element in it. Three bottom layers of this figure show the IT infrastructure components where bottom—most layer depicts physical shared components such as computers and common technologies. The second bottom layer contains the commonly shared services such as database services and connections to internet. The components of these two layers are changed into IT infrastructure services by human element using its skills, experience and knowledge. The human element binds IT components into a reliable set of IT infrastructure services which are shared in business processes across the organisation. Good IT infrastructure management can avoid occurrence of IT infrastructure problems and resolve them before they impact business availability. The management aspect of IT infrastructure is very critical since management practices are developed over time and they are unique for each organisation.

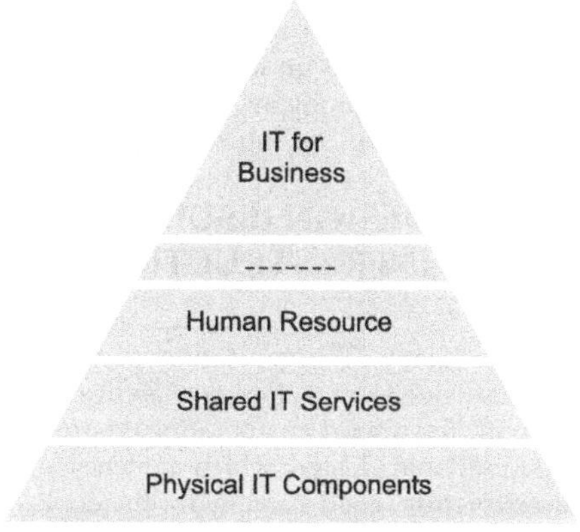

Fig. 2.1 *Relationship among various IT infrastructure elements*

2.2 CHALLENGES IN IT INFRASTRUCTURE MANAGEMENT

IT infrastructure consists of resources and capabilities which are built through the interaction between technology and people in the organisation. It consists of elements shared by different levels of users and processes, and provides platform to the people to share knowledge. Though IT infrastructure and its management are very essential for smooth running of an organisation, some challenges are faced in management and development of IT infrastructure. Few important challenges are listed below:

Suitability to the Organisation IT infrastructure management needs to develop and deploy management activities in such a way that they support operational and strategic goals of the organisation. The management activity consists of two parts: maintenance of existing systems and development of new infrastructure. Usually, information system development relies on existing hardware and software resources. However, vision is required in both business and IT in order to achieve what technology can do and how to make its best possible use.

Low Cost and High Quality Management activities should achieve low cost with high quality. Sometimes, interactions and partnership with outside IT service providers may provide solutions to this challenge.

Adaptability in Changeable Environment IT infrastructure should not only be reliable in operations today and but it should also be open for changes in the future, to incorporate future business requirements. All choices that are made in developing the infrastructure are important because the infrastructure is an organisational asset and meant to be used for an extended period.

Decrease Business Risk Infrastructure provides the foundation upon which business applications are built. Therefore, it is required to be managed in such a way that it does not fail under any circumstances. Since these challenges are related to IT management problems, IT managers should develop management procedures to match the current and future requirements.

2.3 DESIGN ISSUES OF IT ORGANISATIONS AND IT INFRASTRUCTURE

Success of any IT organisation depends on the suitability of its design with the business needs and the availability of effective and efficient IT infrastructure support. To support an operating environment smoothly, it is necessary to have good organisational design which matches with the business requirements, necessary infrastructure, good strategy for the deployment and technology, and clearly defined accountability plan for the use and application of technology.

2.3.1 Design of IT Organisation

Organisational design refers to the way in which an IT organisation divides its work force into different tasks and operates by coordinating these tasks. While carrying out design of an organisation, major factors influencing organisational design must be looked into carefully. Also, when the design is over, there should be some mechanism to estimate how the organisational design is effective and some way to identify strengths and weaknesses of the organisation. Designing an effective organisational structure is a real challenge. For IT organisational design, there is no single proven optimal design strategy which can be used but rather there is a set of practices that are conformed through learning and benchmarking processes for it. Keeping this challenge in mind, IT leaders always try to find out a perfect IT organisational model that addresses all problems in their current structure.

According to the people3, Inc[1] report "Structuring for Success: Building Blocks for IT Organisation Design", while designing an IT organisation, IT leaders should seek the answer of four questions: what works, what does not work, when will it work and why? Answers to these four questions provide the essence of a "best practice" for a specific organisational setting and help IT leaders in determining whether a specific "best practice" is appropriate for their organisation or not.

The report also recommends that IT and business leaders should follow the four basic steps of the organisational design process to increase the rate of success of their IT re-engineering initiatives. These four processes are as follows:

Business Driver Assessment This process identifies the business drivers that lead to the development of a re-engineering strategy.

Organisation Readiness Assessment It ensures that all the constraints and barriers to organisational re-engineering are evaluated and are taken into consideration during the design and implementation processes.

Structure Model Assessment This process understands the strengths and weaknesses of each IT structure model (centralised, decentralised or hybrid). It selects the organisational design that is not only aligned with business strategy but also fits to the culture of the organisation.

Business Impact Assessment This process conducts a series of "what if" business impact analyses during the organisational design phase. This helps in minimising any potentially negative impact on the business and evaluates how well the new structure achieves the business and IT objectives.

2.3.2 Design of IT Infrastructure

It starts with preparing a design document which contains the complete information about the IT infrastructure to be put in place. Generally, design document contains following information:

i. Design of Data Centre and Server Room
ii. Design of IT network
iii. Hardware and software specifications of Servers, Desktops and Laptops
iv. Specifications of Server and Client Operating systems
v. Details of access, controls to be implemented to access critical IT assets, etc
vi. Internet bandwidth, security devices and applications
vii. E-mail service to be setup
viii. Design of backup and disaster recovery mechanism.

An efficient and effective IT infrastructure requires continuous organisation and attention. IT infrastructure design should be able to take care of various tasks

[1] http://www.people3.com/

necessary to keep the business of an organisation running smoothly. A good IT infrastructure design needs extensive experience in designing and implementing infrastructure. Examples of some infrastructure services include:

Active Directory Design It explores the organisational structure and geographic spread of an organisation to assess the most effective deployment of active directory. It includes the design of the directory structure, deployment of domain controllers, global catalogue servers, bridgehead servers and single master role servers.

Migration to New Releases of Infrastructure Products This includes the review of implications to be incurred in migrating from old to new software releases (for example, from NT to Windows 2003, or Exchange 5.5 to Exchange 2003, etc.). It also prepares plans incorporating an assessment of the risks along with measures to be taken to reduce them.

Protecting the Enterprise Business managers need to understand the information assets, their values and then draw up a security risk assessment with countermeasures. Typical areas covered include operating system lockdown, application system development guidance, firewall placement and rule sets, intrusion detection requirements, user access controls and written policy documents for management and staff.

Local Area Network (LAN) and Wide Area Network (WAN) design and tuning It includes designing for LANs and WANs, including use of hubs, switches and routers; placement and configuration of DNS and DHCP servers.

2.4 DETERMINING CUSTOMER'S REQUIREMENTS

It is the process of identifying customers' requirements to include voice of the customer, data, and expectations of the customer in designing a process strategy. To incorporate customers' expectations effectively, they are usually converted into a measurable expression and then are used to ensure process compliance with the customers' needs.

Determination of customers' requirement is not static and is an ongoing matter; and needs to be updated as the customers' requirements are changed. Very frequently, data in requirement determination is collected using customer surveys and the like. Six sigma program is a business management strategy used to improve the quality of process outputs by recognising and removing the causes of imperfection and variation in manufacturing and business processes. It emphasises the importance of customers and considers them as a separate department.

2.5 IT SYSTEMS MANAGEMENT

IT systems management helps in designing, implementing, and managing IT infrastructures. It commonly refers to enterprise-wide administration of distributed computer systems, etc. It assists in managing any IT infrastructure to achieve optimum efficiency, stability, reliability, availability and support. It also helps in leveraging any IT organisation in a great ways by understanding and utilising proven systems management techniques. IT system management includes complete details of how to implement each key discipline in the places such as mainframe data centers, mid-range shops, client-server environments and Web-enabled systems.

2.5.1 Common Tasks of IT System Management

Today, IT systems are interconnected into complex supply chains and extended onto the desktops of home and business users who are not known to the managers of the systems. In such environment, IT professionals are expected to have responsibility for maintaining the stability and responsiveness of IT production environments. IT systems management is designed to help them in designing, implementing and managing any part of an IT environment or the entire IT infrastructure. Some of the common tasks of IT systems management are listed below:

i. Maintaining hardware inventories
ii. Server availability monitoring and metrics
iii. Software inventory and installation task
iv. Anti-virus and anti-malware management
v. User's activities monitoring
vi. Capacity monitoring
vii. Security management
viii. Storage management
ix. Network capacity and utilisation monitoring.

2.5.2 Organisational Management Approaches

There are many approaches which are followed for organisational management. The popular ones are—People-Process-Technology and Strategy-Tactics-Operations approaches.

People-Process-Technology Approach

This approach considers that an IT systems management is based on the fundamental belief that People, Process, and Technology (commonly known by acronym 'PPT') are the three key components of any successful IT organisation (Fig. 2.2). This is a widely accepted model for defining the core focus areas in managing organisational improvement. There is a need for these three areas to be addressed while considering organisational improvement. These three components are greatly related to each other.

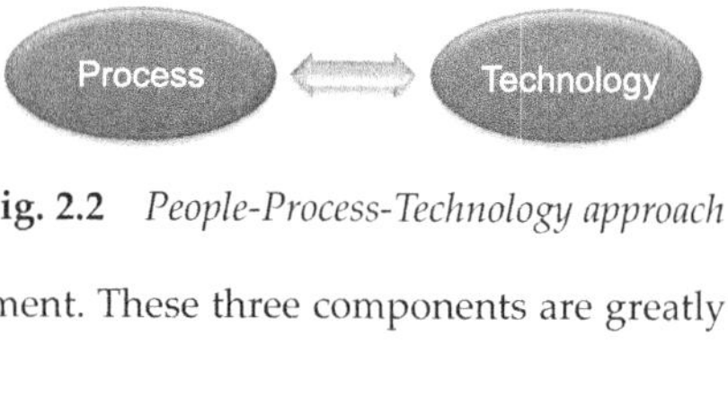

Fig. 2.2 *People-Process-Technology approach*

People It refers to the human resource involved in IT system management process at higher level. It generally includes infrastructure managers, directors and CIOs.

Process People involved at this level are system analysts, senior systems administrators and supervisors, who are typically involved with designing and implementing systems management processes and procedures.

Technology This component deals with technical professionals such as systems programmers, database administrators, operations analysts, network administrators and systems administrators, who are responsible for installing and maintaining systems.

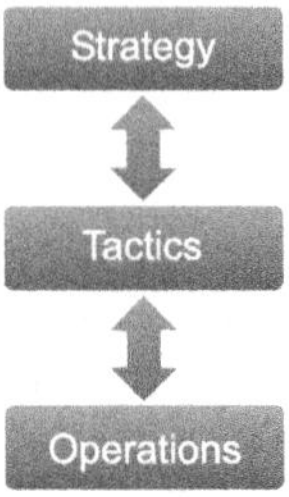

Fig. 2.3 *Strategy-Tactics-Operations approach*

Strategy-Tactics-Operations Approach This is another commonly used approach for organisational management. It consists of three important components, namely Strategy, Tactics and Operations (Fig. 2.3) and commonly identified by acronym 'STO'.

Strategy Long terms objectives of an organisation are managed at strategic level. These objectives are defined in terms of value, identity, relations prerequisite, choices, etc.

Tactics Objectives set at strategy level are translated into specific goals at this level.

Operations Goals are translated into action plans at operational level. Actual realisation of goals happens at this level.

2.6 IT SERVICE MANAGEMENT PROCESS

IT service refers to the delivery of information processing capabilities at an agreed quality level using a combination of software, hardware, people, networks, etc. The way IT organisations serve their customers, and the quality and value of the services they offer to their customers, continues to be a focus for companies worldwide. Quality can be defined in terms of capacity, security, availability of services, performance, etc. To deliver the IT services to the end user at agreed quality level, it is required that all processes engaged in providing services should be managed properly.

IT service management is the overall methodology for linking the various management processes necessary to ensure consistent supply of quality IT services. It emphasises customer-centric approach of IT management and business interaction in contrast to the technology-centric approaches. IT service management focuses on the quality of services that an organisation offers and concentrates on the relationship of the organisation with the customers rather than only focusing on technology and organisational issues. In the current business scenario, it has become an integral part of an organisation and is seen as an innovative way which can be used to prove the business value of IT services, to cut costs and improve service quality. IT service management needs an effective mechanism which allows the effective interaction of IT personnel with users of their services. The main goals of

IT service management is to align IT services with the critical needs of the business, to manage services to ensure appropriate IT support for critical business priorities, to minimise Total Cost of Ownership (TCO)[2] and to improve Return On Investment (ROI)[3]. These goals of are summarised below:

Customer Centric IT service management tries to align IT services with the needs of the business and its customers. It is intended to ensure that IT services offered by an organisation are aligned with the needs of customers and users. It is the management of all people, processes and technology that cooperates to ensure the quality of IT services, according to the levels of service agreed with the customer.

Availability and Stability of Services It also deals with improving the availability and stability of the services. It consistently tries to improve the quality of the services delivered.

Improved Communication For a business to grow, customer satisfaction is very necessary. IT service management puts a support system which allows the effective interaction of IT personnel within IT organisation and with its users.

Efficiency of Internal Processes IT service management works towards improving the efficiency of internal processes.

Cost of Services IT service management makes the offered services cost effective. It persistently tries to reduce the cost of the services and improve the quality of services provided by the organisation.

IT service management is divided into two parts: service delivery and service support. Figure 2.4 shows various parts and subparts of it.

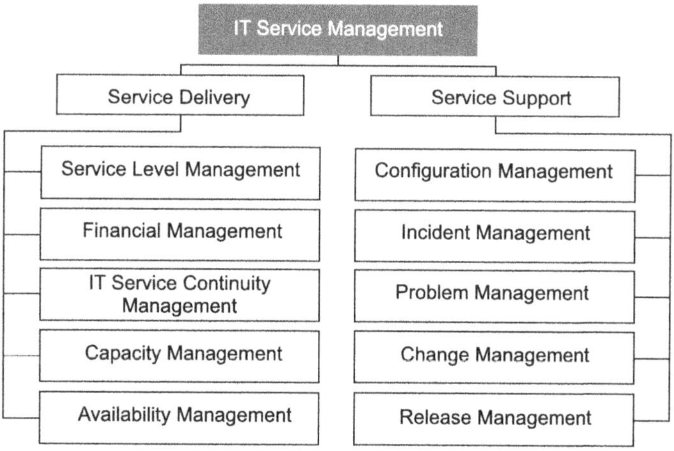

Fig. 2.4 *Parts of IT service management process*

[2] TCO is defined as the total cost of an IT asset throughout its lifecycle, right from its acquisition to its disposal.

[3] ROI is a performance measure used to evaluate the efficiency of an investment.

2.6.1 Service Delivery

Service delivery refers to the management of the IT services. It involves a number of management practices to ensure that IT services are actually provided as agreed between the service provider and the customer. These management practices are discussed briefly here.

Service Level Management It offers service-delivery management across business units and helps in successfully delivering, maintaining and improving IT services up to the expected level through a constant cycle of agreeing, monitoring and reporting to meet the customers' requirements and objectives. Major steps that are followed in implementation of service level management are preparing service catalogue, defining service and operational level agreements and formulating service quality plan.

Financial Management Its main emphasis is on managing the monetary resources of an IT organisation to achieve organisational goals. It offers cost-effective management of the IT assets and resources used in providing IT services. A good financial management process greatly helps IT managers in making decisions for planning and investment. Usually, financial management activities includes IT cost accounting, budgeting for IT services and activities, project investment appraisal, cost recovery and IT charging and billing activities.

IT Service Continuity Management Business organisations are expected to continue to operate and provide services in an uninterrupted fashion. IT service continuity management process helps them in this regard and ensures that all IT services are capable of providing value to the customer in an event when normal availability of solutions fails. It manages risks and ensures that an IT infrastructure of an organisation can continue to provide services in an unlikely or unexpected event. Major processes involved in IT service continuity management are collection of service level requirements, proposing contingent solution, formalising operation level agreement and formalising contingency plan.

Capacity Management Prime objective of capacity management is to ensure that IT capacity meets current and future business requirements of an organisation in a cost-effective manner, and IT infrastructure of the organisation is used in an efficient manner. Capacity management involves planning, analysing, sizing and optimising capacity to fulfill the demand in a timely manner and at a reasonable cost.

Availability Management The goal of availability management is to ensure that all IT services deliver the level of availability that the customer requires consistently and cost-effectively. It optimises the capability of the IT infrastructure, services and supporting organisation to deliver a cost effective and sustainable service availability that meets stringent business objectives. Processes involved in availability management are defining service level requirements, proposing availability solutions and formalising operational level agreements.

2.6.2 Service Support

It talks about a framework that enables effective IT Services. Various management practices involved in service support are discussed here briefly.

Configuration Management It deals with identifying and defining configuration items in a system and further monitoring the status of these items, processing requests for change and verifying the completeness and correctness of configuration items. Configuration management offers a logical model of the IT infrastructure by identifying, maintaining and verifying the version of all configuration items. Configuration management is mainly responsible for identifying Configuration items, finding relationship among configuration items and planning, designing and managing a Configuration Management Database (CMDB).

Incident Management The goal of incident management is to ensure that restoration of normal service operations is done as quickly as possible with the least possible impact on either the business or the user and minimum interruption in services, in a cost-effective way. It helps in maintaining continuity of the service levels and underlying service desk function.

Problem Management It ensures that all possible problems and known errors affecting the IT infrastructure are identified and recorded properly. It investigates and resolves the underlying root causes of incidents and prevents similar incidents from happening again. Problem management also provides valuable inputs such as recording problems and known errors to other service management processes like incident management, change management and service desk. The major activities of problem management includes problem control, error control and report generation.

Change Management The goal of change management is to ensure standardisation of methods and procedures so that it minimises the impact of any change on service quality. It offers a way to introduce the required changes to the IT environment with minimal disruption to ongoing operations. Change management offers reduced impact of changes, better cost estimation of changes, better information management of changes and improved personnel productivity.

Release Management The objective of release management is to formulate efficient mechanisms of building and releasing new software versions. Release management ensures the quality of the production environment by using formal procedures and checks while implementing new versions. Release management is responsible for activities such as planning, coordination and implementation, designing and implementation of efficient procedures for the distribution and installation of changes to IT systems, management of release of software into the live environment and its distribution, gathering users' feedback and maintaining Definitive Software Library (DSL) and Configuration Management Database (CMDB).

2.7 INFORMATION SYSTEM DESIGN PROCESS

The basic objective of the information system design is to create a customised instance of the IT system architecture from a basic model. A commonly accepted practice for designing an IT system architecture is to use a model of the business processes as the starting point and then subsequently to refine it using a step-by-step process by following selected computing paradigms, such as custom client-server, internet computing and so on. This kind of design process is commonly known as business-process centric design processes. This design process has two types of requirements: functional and non-functional. Functional requirements describe the behaviours (functions and services) of the system that support user goals, tasks or activities. Non-functional requirements consist of those requirements that specify criterion that can be employed to judge the operation of a system, rather than specific behaviours. These requirements include those for systems management to include performance, availability and security. These requirements are often treated as secondary considerations while designing. It is thought that they influence, but do not overly constrain the design or deployment of the IT solution. Due to this, the business process may not comprise adequate operational support for systems management.

To have a good design, there is a need to develop views and visualisation techniques to combine the design requirements for business processes and system management involved in those processes.

2.7.1 Design Models

Models in IT system design can be represented in many ways. There are three popular and relevant system models discussed below:

- **Business processes based model:** It is a business system model that represents the business processes. These models deal with the representation of processes involved in a business. The main goal behind business process modeling is to analyse the current processes and suggest future improvements. It is usually performed by business analysts and managers who are looking for improvements in process quality and efficiency.
- **Management activities based model:** It is a business system model that represents the management activities which support the business processes.
- **Hybrid model:** It is a business system model that combines both business processes and IT management processes.

2.7.2 System Context Diagram

A system context diagram provides the highest level view of a system and is used to specify details of a system design. It is used in systems design to represent all external entities that may interact with a system. It gives a convenient representation for a system model. System context diagram is similar to block diagram and normally shows a software-based system as a whole, and its inputs and outputs from/to external factors. System context diagrams are also related to data flow diagrams and help in understanding the context in which the system is part of.

System Context Diagrams are typically drawn using labelled boxes to represent each of the external entities and an additional labelled box to represent the system being developed. The relationship between entities and the developed system is shown using lines. The main system in system context diagram is kept at its centre with no details of its interior structure and all its interacting systems, environment and activities surrounding it. The relationships are labelled with a subject-verb-object format, for example, "customer places order". System context diagrams can also use many other different drawing types such as ovals, stick figures, pictures, clip art or any other representation to convey meaning and represent external entities.

Unified Modeling Language (UML) is a standardised formal visual specification language for object modeling and frequently used for drawing system context diagrams. It is a general-purpose modeling language which includes a graphical notation used to create an abstract model of a system, referred to as a UML model. UML defines several standard representations for architecture elaboration, to name a few—use-case diagrams, collaboration diagrams, class diagrams, sequence diagrams, component and deployment diagrams. A system context diagram follows the structure of use-case diagram.

Use-Case Diagram It is used to identify the primary elements and processes that form the system. The primary elements are called *actors* and the processes are called *use-cases*. The use-case diagram shows which actors interact with each use-case. It gives a graphical overview of the functionality provided by a system in terms of actors, their goals (depicted as use cases), and the dependencies between those use cases. When we adopt process view of system management, use-case diagram becomes a very important tool in explaining the workflow of business processes and activities associated with IT management.

Business System Context Diagrams It is used to identify a business system which involves a set of business processes. These business processes fall into four categories: self-service, collaboration, information aggregation, and extended enterprise. Figure 2.5 shows an example of a business system context diagram.

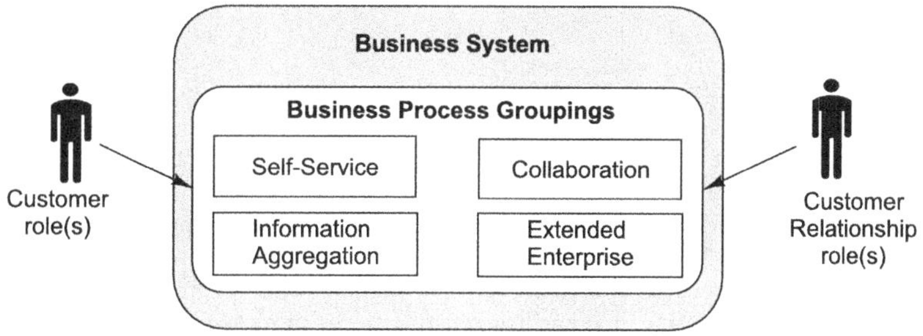

Fig. 2.5 *Example of business system context diagrams (Source: IBM RedPaper)*

This diagram can be used as a starting point on which more detailed elaboration for the subject business system can be built. For example, in a business environment, commerce portal can be considered as extended enterprise process, customer account management application can be considered as self-service process, e-mail system can be considered as collaboration process, and market support application can be considered as an information aggregation process. This business system model comprises of two roles: one for customers and other for customer relationship personnel.

IT Management System Context Diagram The concept of business system context diagram can be extended to define IT management system context diagram which identifies an IT system that contains a set of IT management processes. Figure 2.6 shows an example of IT management system context diagram where IT management processes are clubbed into eight groups. Similar to business system context diagram, IT management system context diagram can be used as a starting point based on which an elaboration can be developed for the subject IT management system. For example, IT management system context diagram can be used to identify the following:

- how systems' designs are developed, deployed, and operated
- how administration of an IT system is done
- how customer relationships are set up and sustained
- how the availability is maintained.

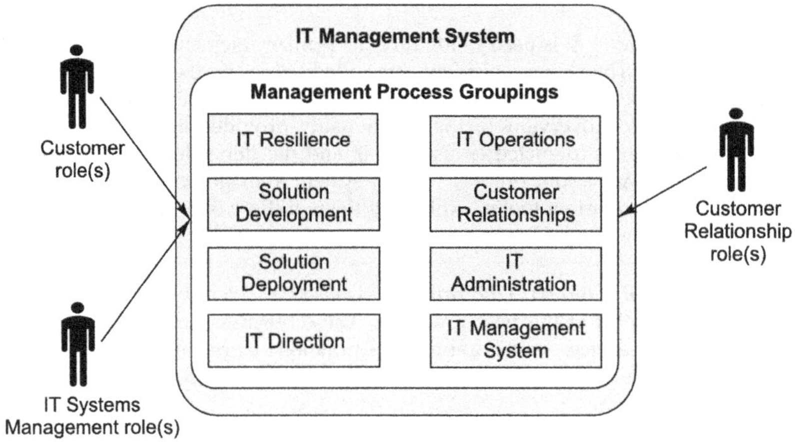

Fig. 2.6 *IT management system context diagram (Source: IBM RedPaper)*

Managed Business System Context Diagram There is a natural possibility of combining the business and IT management views of the system. The managed business system model integrates business and management aspects of the system. Managed business system context diagram is used to represent such business models. Business aspect is described as the functional view of the solution whereas management aspect is described as the non-functional view of the solution.

The combined process model shown in Fig. 2.7 is a composite view of the two previous models. It can be observed that the managed business system is divided into a business application domain and a management domain. In the business and IT management combined process model, there are three types of roles viz. one for customers, one for IT management personnel and other one for customer relationship personnel. Managed business systems can be very complex with respect to following aspects:

- All of the management activities and tasks required to support the operation
- Maintenance and management of the necessary business process
- Operation, maintenance and management of the IT infrastructure that supports the business process.

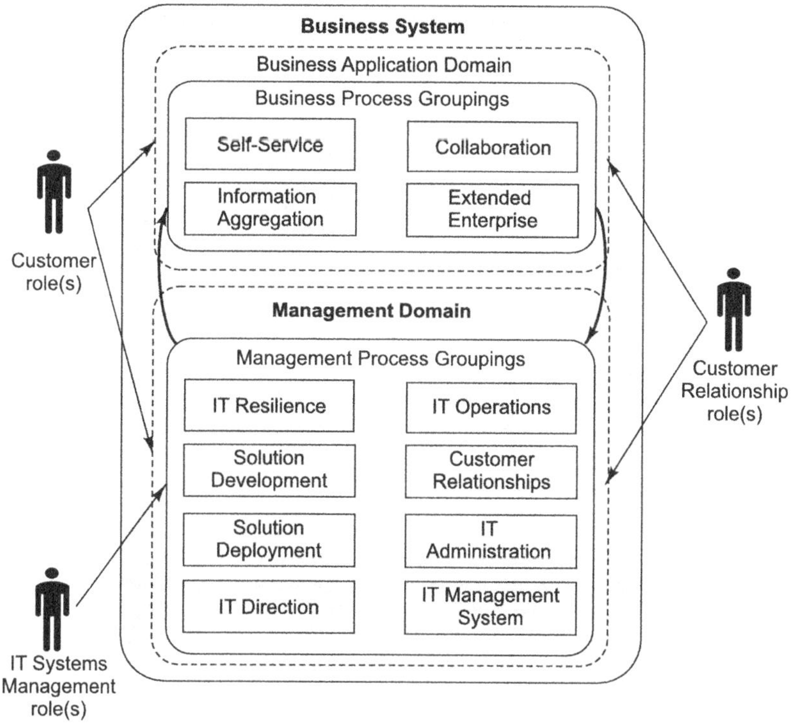

Fig. 2.7 *Managed business system context diagram (Source: IBM RedPaper)*

2.8 PATTERNS FOR IT SYSTEMS MANAGEMENT

In the field of IT, an architect evaluates a business problem to build a solution for it. The design of solution begins by gathering inputs about the problem, an outline of the desired solution and any special considerations that need to be taken care in the solution. The architect designs the solution considering these inputs. To improve the design over time, it is required to capture and reuse the experience of the IT architects so that future developments can be carried out in simpler and efficient way. It is usually done by capturing the knowledge gained from each past development and using it to build a repository of assets. IT architects can then build future solutions based on these proven assets. This reuse saves not only time, money and effort but also helps to ensure delivery of a solid and properly architected solution. A pattern helps to facilitate this reuse of assets that have been used, tested and proven to be successful.

The concept of patterns has been used extensively in the fields of design and architecture. Patterns have also been widely used in software engineering and object-oriented designing to provide efficient software solutions. Dr C Alexander in his book, *A Pattern Language, 1977*, has given a very simple and concise definition of patterns. According to him, each pattern describes a problem that occurs over and over again in our environment, and then describes the core of the solution to that problem in such a way that one can use this solution a million times over without ever doing it the same way twice.

Patterns for e-Business approach enables architects to implement successful e-Business solutions through the re-use of components and solutions from proven successful assets. Patterns approach is based on a set of layered assets that can be used by any existing development methodology to build a solution. These layered assets are organised in such a way that each level is built on the previous level.

An e-Business solution spans multiple business domains and is more complex to implement than traditional application systems. It requires a constant and clear exchange of ideas and information between the business owners driving the solution and the IT personnel responsible for its implementation. Though constructs such as design patterns are very useful in the development of the solution, they have minimal impact in the early phases of the solution design where key decisions are made on the overall structure of solution and end-to-end architecture.

2.8.1 Patterns for e-Business

The concept of patterns for e-Business, primarily introduced by IBM, extends the domain of software patterns to earlier phases of the application development life cycle. These patterns helps in understanding and analysing the complex business problems, and breaks them down into smaller, more manageable functions that can then be implemented using lower-level design patterns. There are four major types of patterns for e-Business:

Business Pattern It helps in identifying the interaction between users, businesses and data.

Integration Pattern It groups multiple business patterns together when a solution cannot be provided based on a single business pattern. The business and integration patterns have the same structure, as shown in Fig. 2.8.

Application Pattern This pattern provides a conceptual layout describing how the application components and data within a business pattern or integration pattern interact.

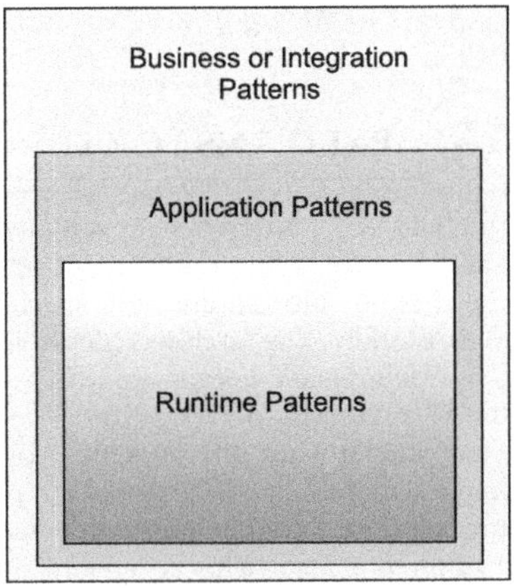

Fig. 2.8 *Structure of patterns for e-Business*

Runtime Pattern This pattern defines the logical middleware structure supporting an application pattern. A runtime pattern depicts the major middleware nodes, their roles and the interfaces between these nodes.

There is one more pattern for e-Business called ***Composite Pattern*** which represents commonly occurring combinations of business pattern and integration pattern. This pattern for e-Business represents a set of proven architectural solutions. IT systems management can also be integrated with these solutions using a patterned approach by linking business processes with IT management processes.

2.9 IT INFRASTRUCTURE LIBRARY

IT organisations are continuously enforced to deliver better IT services at lower cost. To provide guidelines to achieve this goal and cope up with the stringent challenges, several management frameworks have been developed; one of the best known frameworks is the Information Technology Infrastructure Library® (ITIL). It is the most widely accepted approach to IT service management worldwide. It is a customisable framework of best practices developed to promote quality services in the IT sector. Developed in the late 1980s by the CCTA[4] (now known as OGC[5]), it became popular worldwide and de facto standard in service management in mid 1990s. It was originally designed to serve as a set of standards to be followed by service providers to deliver IT services to the British government. After its inception, public companies have realised the benefits and implemented parts of ITIL in their internal IT departments. ITIL has now become acceptable to almost everyone as it is a public domain framework with scalable property.

As an IT service management framework, ITIL provides a systematic approach to manage IT services, from their inception through design, implementation, operation and continual improvement. The processes identified and described within ITIL are supplier and platform independent and apply to all aspects of IT infrastructure. ITIL consists of set of concepts, policies and practices used for managing IT infrastructure, development and operations. It provides a comprehensive description of a number of important IT practices with detailed catalogue, procedures and tasks that an IT organisation can adapt for its need. It provides business with a customisable framework of best practices to achieve quality service and overcome problems associated with the growth of IT systems.

ITIL is published in a series of books, each of which give details of an IT management topic. ITIL has grown up to three versions by now.

ITIL version 1 It is the initial version of IT infrastructure library which has expanded over 30 volumes. At the beginning, ITIL version 1 was projected as a set of formal methods, which was later changed and published as set of guidelines.

ITIL version 2 Originally, the ITIL was published as a collection of series of books, each of which covered a particular practice of IT service management. Number of books in the initial publication of ITIL (ITIL version 1) has grown up to 31 volumes. To make ITIL more approachable and financially manageable, ITIL version 2 consolidates the volumes of ITIL version 1 into logical sets by grouping the related process guidelines of IT management, applications, and services. The eight book volumes of ITIL version 2 are grouped into three parts as follows:

---

[4]CCTA: Central Computer and Telecommunications Agency
[5]OGC: Office of Government Commerce

1. The IT service management set
   - Service delivery
   - Service support
2. Operational guidance set
   - ICT infrastructure management
   - Security management
   - The business perspective
   - Application management
   - Software asset management
3. Implementation guidelines set
   - Planning to implement service management
4. Supplementary set
   - ITIL small-scale implementation (it has been published later, not part of original eight publications)

ITIL version 3 It updates the ITIL version 2 by expanding the scope of ITIL in the domain of service management. ITIL version 3 comprises of five key volumes which are listed below:

Service Strategy This volume is the main strength of the new ITIL library which focuses on helping IT organisations to improve and develop over the long term. It introduces the service lifecycle and encourages the development of a business perspective. This volume guides both the service provider as well as the business customer, through choices that they need to achieve service excellence. The key topics which are present in this volume include business case development, service assets, service value definition, market analysis and service provider types. The processes which are included are IT financial management, service portfolio management and demand management.

Service Design This volume provides good practice guidance on design of IT services and processes to create valuable IT service assets for an organisation within business constraints such as time and money. It gives a framework for service design which considers the customer's present and future requirements, while firmly maintaining the business view. Processes which are included in this volume are service level management, capacity management, availability management, IT service continuity management, supplier management, information security management and service catalogue management.

Service Transition This ITIL volume provides guidance on managing the many aspects of service changes, preventing undesired consequences while allowing for innovation. It is essential reading for anyone seeking to deliver IT change with the best possible benefit to the business. Topics covered in the volume are transition planning and support, service asset and configuration management and change management, release and deployment management and knowledge management. It also states the key roles and responsibilities of staff involved in service transition.

Service Operation This volume introduces delivery and control activities used to support high quality service operations. It covers best practices for balancing conflicting goals (such as reliability vs. cost), problem management, event management, incident management, service desk, asset management, technical and application management. It also defines the key roles and responsibilities for staff involved in service operation.

Continual Service Improvement Improvements in service quality enables the business to survive in a competitive environment and helps in achieving the best possible outcomes. This volume introduces the processes involved in identifying and introducing a cycle of service management improvements. The goal of continual service improvement is to align and realign IT services to changes in business needs by identifying and implementing improvements to the IT services (such as service quality, process effectiveness, efficiency and cost effectiveness) that support the business processes.

2.9.1 Alternatives to ITIL

Although ITIL is the most popular IT service management guideline, it is not the only approach which is available for standardising IT service operations. IT service management is a concept and though related to ITIL, it is not completely equivalent to ITIL. As we can see in ITIL version 2, only a subsection of it—entitled IT service management—talks about the IT service aspects. Moreover, ITIL version 3 volumes do not have any separate description on it. There are some other alternatives to ITIL such as Microsoft Operations Framework and ISO/IEC 20000. The following discussion provides brief discussion on them.

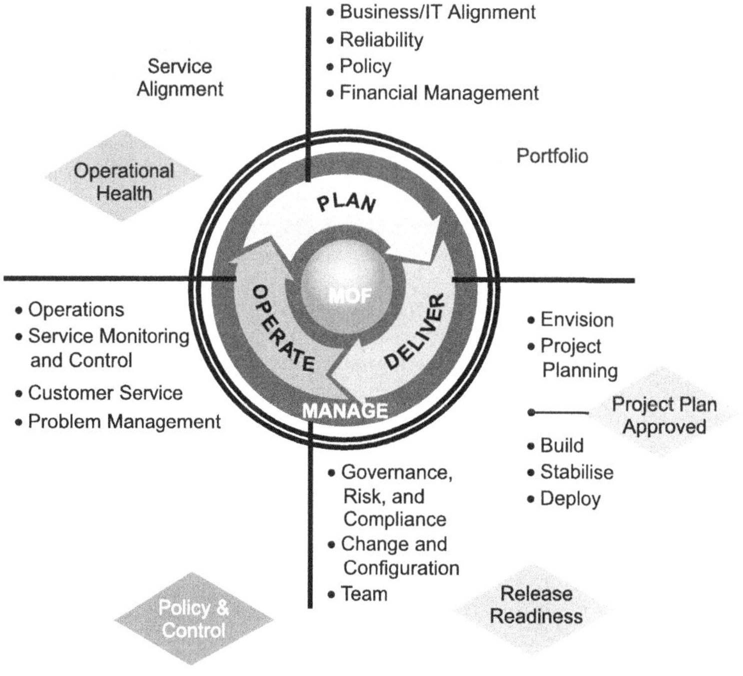

Fig. 2.9 *The MOF 4.0 IT service lifecycle (Source: MOF)*

Microsoft Operations Framework Goal of every business process is to provide better services at lower cost. The Microsoft Operations Framework (MOF) helps to achieve the same. It aims to help its customers in achieving operational excellence across the entire IT service lifecycle. Originally it was developed to provide IT professionals with knowledge and processes required to align their work in managing Microsoft platforms cost-effectively and with high reliability. Newer version of MOF (MOF 4.0) offers its customers new ways to cope up with the new challenges in providing better IT services. It provides practical guidelines for each and every day-to-day activity and helps in maintaining the regulatory requirements for enhancing organisational capabilities.

IT Service Lifecycle of MOF It is comprised of three phases and one manage layer as shown in Fig. 2.9. Manage layer operates throughout the cycle of other three phases and works as the foundation of IT service lifecycle and covers the components that apply to all lifecycle phases. These three phases and foundation layer are explained below.

Plan Phase The task of this phase is to plan and optimise an IT service strategy so that the set business objectives can be achieved.

- **Deliver phase:** It ensures that IT services are developed and deployed successfully and are ready for operations.
- **Operate phase:** This phase is responsible to ensure that IT services are operated, maintained and supported effectively to meet business objectives and expectations.
- **Manage layer:** This layer is the foundation of the IT service lifecycle, and processes in this layer apply to all phases of the lifecycle. It is responsible for IT governance, risk management, change management, configuration management, etc.

To align IT services to the business requirement, each phase of the IT service lifecycle contains Service Management Functions (SMFs). These SMFs define and structure the processes, people, and activities required. Each SMF has three to six key processes, and each process has one to six key activities.

ISO/IEC 20000 It is the first international standard for IT service management which is referred to as combination of service support and service delivery volumes of ITIL version 2. ISO/IEC 20000 was originally developed to reflect best practices of ITIL. It equally supports other IT service management frameworks such as Microsoft Operations Framework, components of ISACA's CobIT framework, etc. ISO/IEC 20000 IT service management standard consists of two parts—the first part contains a specification for IT service management whereas second one defines the code of practice for service management.

Review Questions

1. Define the term 'IT infrastructure'. What are the various components which are considered under IT infrastructure?

2. Why is it necessary to have IT infrastructure management activity?
3. What are the advantages of IT infrastructure management?
4. Discuss various challenges in IT infrastructure management.
5. Explain various issues involved in designing IT organisations and IT infrastructure.
6. List the various items that a design document contains in case of designing IT infrastructure.
7. Discuss four basic steps that are followed in an organisational design.
8. What are the common tasks of IT system management?
9. Discuss following organisational development approaches:
   a. People-Process-Technology Approach
   b. Strategy-Tactics-Operations Approach.
10. What are the sub-processes involved in IT service management? Explain them.
11. What are the goals of IT service management process?
12. Define the terms 'Total Cost of Ownership (TCO)' and 'Return on Investment' (ROI). What is the significance of these terms in context to IT service management?
13. List various sub-processes involved in service delivery process and service support process.
14. Discuss following design models:
    a. Business activities based model
    b. Management activities based model
    c. Hybrid model.
15. Write short notes on the following:
    a. System context diagram
    b. Business system context diagram
    c. IT management system context diagram
    d. Managed business system context diagram
    e. UML
    f. Use-case diagram
    g. IT system management case diagram
16. How does use-case diagram help in modeling IT system management process?
17. What is ITIL? Discuss various processes involved in ITIL.
18. What are the alternatives of ITIL?
19. Compare and contrast ITIL and MOF.

Service Delivery Process

Chapter 3

Service delivery process is concerned with the management of IT services and involves several management practices to ensure that IT services are provided as agreed between the service provider and the customer. It is one of the two important components of IT service management process. This chapter deals with service delivery process which involves five sub-processes. These sub-processes concentrate on long-term planning and improvement of IT services. Following sections discuss them one by one in detail.

3.1 SERVICE LEVEL MANAGEMENT

Service level management deals with various issues related to service delivery across business units and helps in the management of services that an organisation provides to its customers in a cost-effective manner. It assists in delivering, maintaining and improving IT services up to the desired level through a constant cycle of agreeing, monitoring and reporting to achieve the customers' requirements, expectations and objectives.

Main objectives of service level management are to align and manage IT services through a process of definition, agreement, operation measurement and review. An organisation which wishes to implement service level management must first analyse the types of services that it provides to the customers and finds out types of existing service contracts that are currently in place for these services. This exercise gives the full insight of the services that an organisation can provide to its customer and can help in developing a good service level management process. Before going into the implementation details of service level management into business, let us first define the two terms: service level agreement and operational level agreement.

Service Level Agreement The scope of service level management includes defining the IT services for the organisation and establishing service level agreements (SLA) for them. SLA is the written negotiated agreement documenting the required levels of services to be provided by the organisation to the customer. It is the part of service contract. It clearly states common understanding about services, priorities, unambiguous and measurable service targets, responsibilities, guarantees and warranties, IT service quality requirements (for example, performance and security) and communication structures. It usually includes elaborate definition of services, performance measures, problem management, disaster recovery, customer duties, warranties, termination of agreement, etc.

Each area of service scope should have the *level of service* defined for it. Level of Service (LOS) is a measure-of-effectiveness by which the quality of service on elements of IT infrastructure is determined. For example, SLA may clearly describe the levels of availability, serviceability, performance, operation, or other attributes of the service such as charges and billing.

Operational Level Agreement (OLA) The relationship between the internal parts of an organisation is defined in this type of agreement. It states the interdependent relationships among the internal support groups of an organisation working towards supporting a service level agreement. This agreement gives the description of the responsibilities of each internal support group towards the other support groups. It provides detailed description of the internal process including the timeframe for the delivery of their services. The focus of the OLA is to present a clear, concise and measurable description of the internal support relationships of service providing organisation.

Use of service level management in an organisation usually does not give an immediate improvement in the levels of services delivered. It is in fact a long-term commitment. Initially, the services are likely to change slightly but improvement can be observed over a period of time. This improvement happens as the targets are achieved and then exceeded. Service level management expects that the organisation fully understands the services that it offers to its customers to get the advantages of it. Major steps that are required to implement service level management are as follows:

Preparing Service Catalogue It provides the details of range of services that can be delivered and the levels of services that are available to the customers.

Developing Service Level Agreement (SLA) It consists of the negotiations agreed upon by the customer and the service provider to deliver the required levels of service support.

Operational Level Agreement (OLA) It is an agreement between two internal areas. It describes the delivery of one or more components of the end-to-end service.

Service Spreadsheet This is a detailed document identifying what is agreed in the SLA and the required technical specifications to deliver the service.

Service Quality Plan This contains the management information necessary for steering the organisation to meet its goals. For each process, target values are defined and solution time—with its impact level—is set.

3.1.1 Service Level Management Approaches

There are two main approaches which are followed in service level management and they are linear approach and cyclical approach.

Linear Approach Besides the process of defining service catalog and SLAs, linear approach of service level management follows four more processes. Figure 3.1 illustrates the block diagram of it. Each of these processes is explained below:

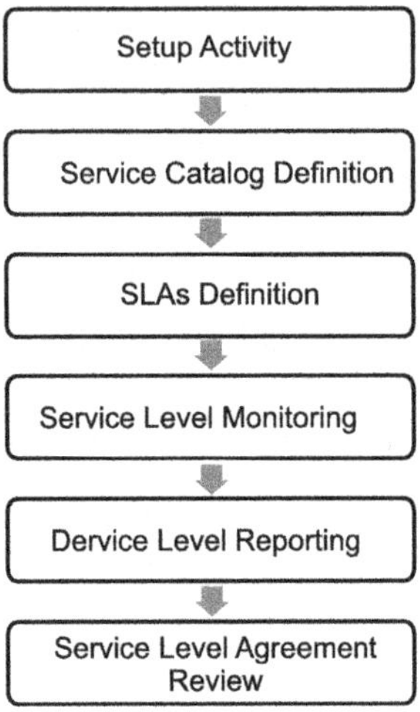

Fig. 3.1 *Linear approach of service level management* (*Source: MOF*[1])

Setup Activity It consists of a series of preliminary steps that are carried out at the starting phase for the assessment of service level management project. These early steps help the business in determining if there is a requirement for service level management and whether it possesses the resources for its implementation. To do this, the IT department sets up a baseline for the business by considering a quick view of the existing services and management activities.

Service Catalogue It is a guide to the services available to the business. It provides details of variety of services that can be delivered to the customer and their level of service. It gives end-to-end details of the service components used to deliver the services and the IT functionality used by the business.

Service Level Agreements It is a mutually agreed-on and negotiated agreement documenting the required levels of service. It is agreed on by the IT service provider and the business or the IT service provider and a third-party provider to deliver the required levels of support.

Service Level Monitoring Each service is monitored according to the agreed-on SLA criteria in order to ensure compliance with the SLA. Service level monitoring involves continual measurement of mutually agreed-on service-level thresholds and the initiation of corrective actions if the thresholds are broken.

Service Level Reporting It is an interface between an IT department of an organisation and the person responsible for a business process. Service level reports contain the monitoring data used to measure performance against objectives. This helps to quickly react to risks and continually improve the delivery of IT services.

Service Level Agreement Review It is conducted to formalise and renew service level agreements. It is a two-way communication between the IT department and the organisation. It ensures that the services are being delivered efficiently and are optimised to meet the organisation's requirements. SLA review is a time-based process and is a key management inspection which is carried out at specified intervals. For example, SLA reviews can be carried monthly, quarterly, or bi-annually. Figure 3.2 shows the various stages used in setting up and operating the SLA review.

[1] MOF stands for Microsoft Operations Framework

Cyclical Approach Figure 3.3 illustrates cyclical approach of service level management and shows the phases that IT department of an organisation can follow in implementing effective service level management. Cyclical approach is applied to each process in turn. It is considered at each stage and can be used to add value in the implementation of the elements of service level management.

This cycle does not stop after the service level management processes are implemented. It is subject to the service level reviews and changes are made according to the review outputs. Four steps of cyclical approach are discussed below.

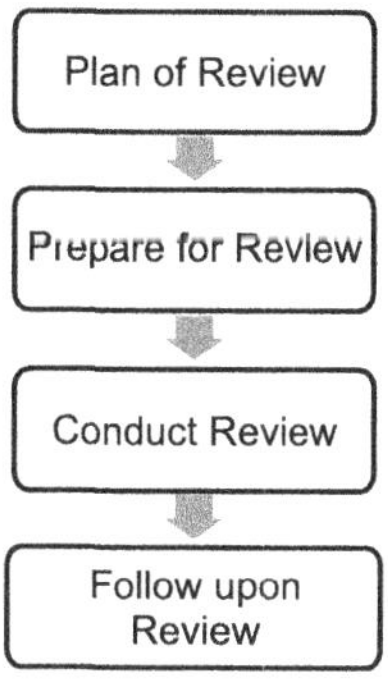

Fig. 3.2 *SLA review processes*

Defining Services This is a strategic step of service level management. Goal of this step is to define and document the services offered by the organisation.

Agree and Operate Mutual agreement is laid down in the form of SLA document between the IT service provider and the customer, or the IT service provider and a third-party service provider, to deliver the required levels of support.

Monitor and Report This phase includes monitoring of the services as per the terms and criterion mentioned in the SLA document. It also considers the report preparation based on observations.

Review and Optimise This step reviews the offered services based on the monitory report and ensures that the services are being delivered efficiently and are optimised to meet the requirement of the organisation.

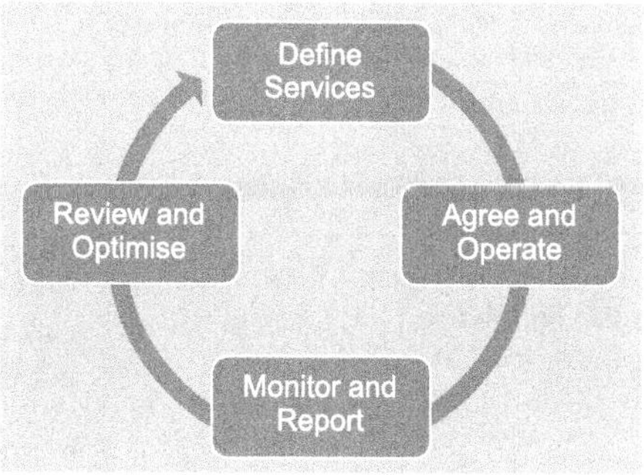

Fig. 3.3 *Cyclic approach of service level management*

3.1.2 Advantages of Service Level Management

To implement service level management, an organisation must first determine various services that its IT department can offer to its customers and should find out different service contracts that are currently in place for these services. This helps an IT service department in getting aware of the full range of services that can be offered. With the information gained through this exercise, the organisation can develop and implement the full advantage of the service level management process. service level management can be used to improve communication between IT service providers and their customers. There are many benefits that can be easily obtained by implementing service level management. Few major benefits are listed here:

Increased Service Quality Main objective of service level management is to improve the services available to the customers in the long term and resolve service provision issues that currently exist.

Reduced Cost In addition to the improvement of service, other benefit includes an increased knowledge of business expectations and improved cost management.

Improved Communication with the Customers Very often, management of an organisation finds dissatisfaction among its customers for the quality and cost of IT service delivery of the organisation. Usually dissatisfaction is due to one of the two factors—first is the bad quality of service delivery and second is the poor communication between IT service providers and their customers. Implementation of service level management can help to improve the communication. It includes use of appropriate SLAs, supported by an effective service catalogue that shows the full range of options available to the customers.

Improved Customer Satisfaction It can quickly affect the overall reputation and success of the organisation. Service level management allows the IT department to meet customers' expectations and opens a dialogue to confirm these expectations.

Other Advantages The main goal of service level management is to improve the services available to the customers in the long term and to resolve the existing service provision issues. It helps to improve the services, provides increased knowledge of customers' business expectations and helps to open a dialogue to confirm these expectations, and improves cost and quality management.

3.1.3 Cost of Service Level Management

Implementation cost of service level management can be divided into many components. Figure 3.4 shows the pictorial representation of these components. Following discussion provides more insights about them.

- **Personnel cost:** It includes the cost of staff such as service level managers and the project team. Cost comprises of personnel's salary, perks, etc.
- **Training cost:** It is the cost incurred by the training program to train the project members.

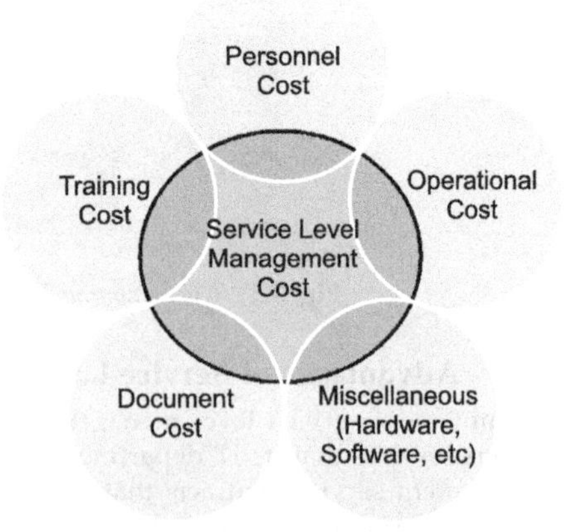

Fig. 3.4 *Service level management implementation cost*

- **Documentation cost:** It includes the cost of the documentation of related items such as service level agreements, service catalogue, etc.
- **Operational cost:** Costs of operational activities related to modification of the service quality plan, service level agreements and service catalogue.
- **Miscellaneous cost:** It includes costs of accommodation, hardware, software, etc.

3.1.4 Relationship with other Processes

Service level management is an important component of service delivery process and it is closely related to the other processes of service delivery. This section discusses the relationship of service level management with other service delivery processes. Brief description of the same is given in Fig. 3.5.

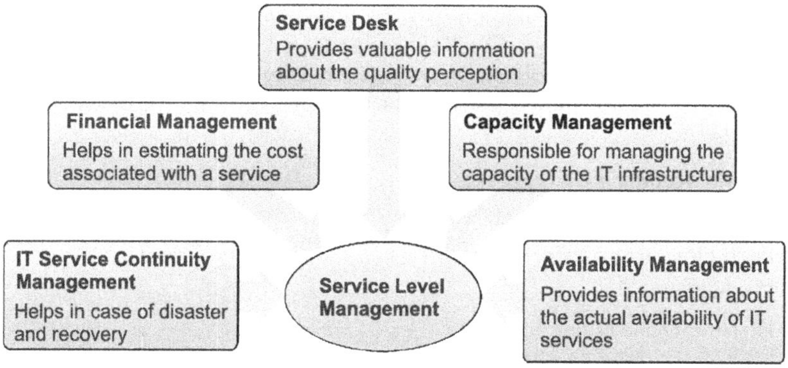

Fig. 3.5 *Relationship of service level management with other service delivery processes*

- **Service Desk:** Although it is not a process, the relationship between the service desk process and the service level management process is particularly of much importance. The service desk is the initial point of contact for users to any IT organisation and through incident management, it aims to recover the agreed service levels as soon as possible in the event of an error. Because of its direct contact with the users of the IT services, the service desk can often provide valuable information about the quality perception (user satisfaction, etc.) of service level management by the users.
- **Financial Management for IT Services:** It provides service level management with information about the costs associated with providing a service. It also provides information about charging methods and the rate that the customer may be charged to recover the costs of a service.
- **IT Service Continuity Management:** It is concerned with the rapid recovery of IT services in the event of a disaster and monitors the appropriate measures and procedures. The agreements about this with the customer are made within the service level management process.
- **Capacity Management:** It is responsible for managing the capacity of the IT infrastructure. It supports service level management by providing information about the impact of a new service on the overall capacity and also indicates

whether the use made of a service is within the agreed limits. Service level management provides information to capacity management about the expected current and future use which service level management has agreed—or is about to agree—with the customer.

- **Availability Management:** Service level management provides availability management with input about the required availability of the IT services and availability management provides information about the actual availability of IT services to service level management.

3.2 FINANCIAL MANAGEMENT

The objective of financial management is to manage the monetary resources of the organisation to achieve organisational goals. It provides cost-effective management of the IT assets and resources used to provide IT services. A properly functioning financial management process helps IT managers in making decisions for planning and investment. In common practice, financial management for IT includes the following:

- IT cost accounting
- Budgeting for IT services and activities
- Project investment appraisal
- Cost recovery
- IT charging and billing activities.

In short, financial management ensures that IT infrastructure is obtained at the most effective price and helps in estimating the cost of the services organisation offers to its customers. Various factors which are considered in financial management for estimating costs include equipment, software, personnel cost and costs of third party service providers. The cost is divided into two types—direct cost and indirect cost—and it can be capital or ongoing.

3.2.1 Components of Financial Management

Primary activities where financial management is used include cost accounting, budgeting, project investment appraisals, cost recovery and billing. Figure 3.6 gives an overall view of financial management.

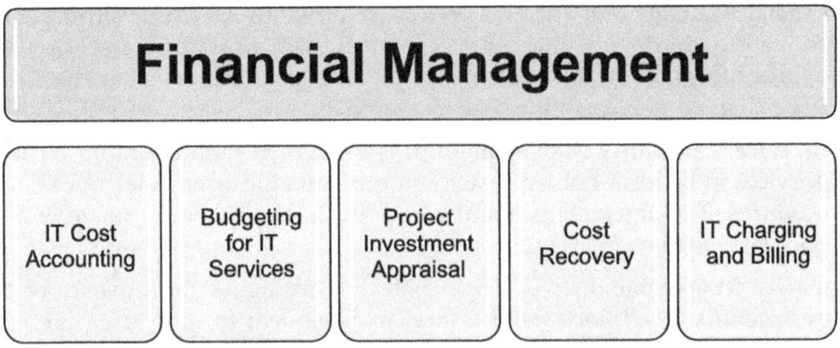

Fig. 3.6 *Components of the financial management process*

IT Cost Accounting It is an inward-looking activity which is used for monitoring the financial management process. It examines the actual costs of performing the IT activities of an organisation. It involves the identification of assets and the identification of the activities to which costs can be assigned. It is also responsible for the development of cost allocation schemes to each element. It breaks down the costs associated with a particular activity and may assign these costs to a project or customer. Cost accounting can also be used to measure the efficiency of the IT department. Major roles of the cost accounting are listed below:

- It allows IT departments to track costs and to make informed decisions about the best way to achieve cost savings related to IT activities.
- It enables IT departments to quantify and understand their costs.
- It helps users to feel in control of costs and understand the method of allocation of costs. This reduces customer frustration and confusion.
- It provides assistance to managers in planning and controlling the operation of the IT organisation.
- Cost accounting and cost management are very helpful in protecting IT departments from cost-based attacks from outside vendors.

An effective accounting system tracks the cost of life cycle of all IT assets and to have a system for recording and tracking these costs. Life cycle costs consist of costs for procurement, maintenance and disposal of IT components. To facilitate cost recording and tracking, the Configuration Management Database (CMDB) is usually used.

Budgeting of IT Services Budget includes a detailed plan which specifies the method followed to obtain specific resources and is used over a specified period of time. Budgeting is the planning activity of the financial management process. It includes planning of the future activities and assessment of the performance of current activities. It is the activity of foretelling the estimated expenditure to be incurred by an organisation during a specified period of time. It also involves controlling and distribution of money to the areas for which it has been originally budgeted. This ensures that sufficient funds are available throughout the entire period. Budgeting enables organisations to plan for routine operational costs as well as for important expenses such as purchasing a new group of servers, storage devices, etc.

While developing budgets, the financial manager must get information from various sources such as the organisational department that uses IT services and each Service Management Function (SMF) within the IT department. Some of the factors that must be considered at the time of developing a budget include:

(i) **Prior period trends** Financial manager should examine the trends of service levels over past budget periods and use the experience to approximate future requirements.

(ii) **Service Level Agreements (SLAs) with each organisational group** SLAs tell about the service levels that are provided to customers as well as the costs for providing those services, and these must be referred before making the budget.

(iii) **IT organisational requirements such as personnel training and system upgrades** Changes in IT environment may require significant resources, which must be planned in advance.

(iv) **Industry and economic trends** Industry or general economic trends affect the need for IT services; so they must be examined beforehand.

(v) **Special requirements such as developing "in-house" applications** There may be some special requirements in some cases. For example, depending on the scope of the applications to be developed, significant resources may be required.

(vi) **Customer satisfaction** Satisfaction of customer is very much important for an organisation to succeed. Customer survey can be used to find out the service performance from the previous budget. This will certainly help to determine if the correct levels of services are being provided to customers.

Methods Used for Preparing Budget There are many methods used for the preparation of budget. Two frequently used methods are previous year budgeting and zero-based budgeting.

- **Previous Year Budgeting** In this method, new budget is based on the previous year budget. The budget process begins with a copy of the previous year budget and any modification done to the budgeted amount is based on the actual cost incurred to date.
- **Zero-based Budgeting** In this technique, the budget planning process begins with a zero balance and each activity that is to be funded must provide a justifiable reason for its inclusion in the budget. Zero-based budgets are built from the ground up, with all funds appropriately justified before they are included in the budget.

  Zero-based budgeting method has an advantage over the previous year budgeting method because it is not simply a reworked version of the prior period's budget. Zero-based budgeting requires that all prior period costs be evaluated before they are included in the budget.

Project Investment Appraisal It is an analysing activity of the financial management process. It involves the evaluation of costs and benefits of proposed changes by the IT department and suggests for the investment. Methods used for analysing the financial impact of a change include payback period, net present value, return on investment, total cost of ownership and real cost of ownership. Each method has its own advantages and drawbacks and none is best for evaluating all kinds of changes.

Investment is a very crucial process and requires intensive analysis. IT manager should evaluate each investment to see if it is useful and worthwhile to the organisation. He should explore all available alternatives before finalizing one. Some metric can be used to compare the alternatives. Methods that are typically employed are as follows:

Net Present Value (NPV) It is defined as the total Present Value (PV) of a time series of cash flows. In other words, for an investment (or project), it is the difference between the sum of the discounted cash flows which are expected from the investment and the amount which is initially invested. It is a standard method for using the time value of money to appraise long-term projects. Computation of NPV comprises of following three steps:

1. Calculate the expected free cash flow (usually per year) that results out of the investment.
2. Subtract /discount for the cost of capital (an interest rate to adjust for time and risk). The intermediate result is called Present Value (PV).
3. Subtract the initial investments from PV to get Net Present Value (NPV).

More clearly, formula for the computation of NPV over the last n years can be given as follows:

$$NPV = (PV_1 + PV_2 + \cdots + PV_n) - \text{Initial Investment Cost}$$

where PV_i is the present value or the cash flow from the ith year (positive for cash inflows, negative for cash outflows).

Payback Period It is defined as the length of time required to recover the cost of an investment. It can be formulated as follows:

$$\text{Payback Period} = \frac{\text{Cost of Project}}{\text{Annual Cash Inflows}}$$

For example, if a project costs Rs 1,00,000 and is expected to return Rs 20,000 annually, the payback period will be 5 years.

There are two main drawbacks of payback period method:

1. It disregards any profit that occurs after the payback period and therefore, it does not measure profitability.
2. It also disregards the time value of money. Time value of money is defined as the value of money figuring in a given amount of interest for a given amount of time.

Because of these reasons, other methods of capital budgeting such as net present value are generally preferred over payback period method.

Return on Investment (ROI) It is a measure of the performance of any investment and sometimes referred as the Rate of Return (ROR). It is the ratio between the financial benefit or loss of an investment and the amount of money invested. To calculate ROI, the benefit (return) of an investment is divided by the cost of the investment and the result is expressed as a percentage or a ratio. The Return on Investment (ROI) can be obtained by:

$$\text{ROI} = \frac{\text{Return from Investment} - \text{Cost of Investment}}{\text{Cost of Investment}} \times 100$$

IT appraisal methods should be developed with the assistance of the finance department and approved by officials such as Chief Financial Officer (CFO) of the organisation. This often helps in building a better system as it can explore and exploit some preferred methods. It is important to note that making an investment decision should not only rely on investment appraisal methods. Other measures should also be considered in order to have a complete picture of the advantages and disadvantages of making a particular investment. For example, the financial measures may not take into account whether a project is intended to reduce the number of support personnel to actually accomplish its intended goal. In short, IT managers must consider many components in addition to financial measures and evaluate the role of each component to know its influence on any decision.

Cost Recovery It is also referred as charging. It is charge-back activity of the financial management process. It involves the development of charge-back methods and the billing of costs to customers. There are two key aspects that one should keep in mind while charging customers.

- First, the bill should be prepared in such a way that customer easily understands the costs included in the bill. Costs of those which are not easily understandable may lead to confusion and create distrust of the IT department.
- Second, cost should be tied to specific customer-perceived benefits that the customer realises through the use of the IT services.

The amount charged back to customers is referred to as the price of transfer or the charge-back. The prices that are charged to customers are generally negotiated on an annual basis as a part of the SLA negotiation process. It is very important to negotiate these prices so that customers are not surprised by the cost of the IT services that they have received.

IT Charging and Billing Financial management also performs charging and billing service. These activities involve deciding the charges for various services that IT department of an organisation provides, to prepare the bill and to send them to the concerned people.

3.2.2 Advantages of Financial Management

Financial management practices are becoming an integral part of the business operations in current scenario. A good financial management process generates benefits in many areas such as cost visibility, planning, optimisation and cost of recovery. An IT organisation with proper financial management can do the following effectively:

Cost Estimation of IT Services Financial management helps in determining the cost of the IT services. It assists in fair allocation of cost to IT services provided by the organisation to internal and external customers. It accurately and efficiently formulates charges and cost of recovery for IT services.

Revision of Cost Structure It identifies and classifies the cost structure of IT services. It checks the charges at regular interval to find out if they are still realistic or need to be revised. It periodically performs audit of IT financial information to ensure its accuracy.

Budget Planning Financial management helps in effective IT budget and planning activities. It does precise bookkeeping of IT expenditures and revenues and also maintains the costs and revenues on a regular basis.

3.2.3 Cost of Financial Management

The costs of this process can be divided into three heads: administrative cost, organisational cost and tools cost. Cost under first two heads is associated with planning, introducing and carrying out the process while that under the third head includes the cost of necessary tools, such as hardware cost, application softwares cost, etc.

3.2.4 Relationship with other Processes

Financial management involves the planning for the future of an organisation to ensure a positive cash flow. To achieve this, it works closely with the other service delivery processes. Figure 3.7 provides an overview of the relationship of financial management with other processes.

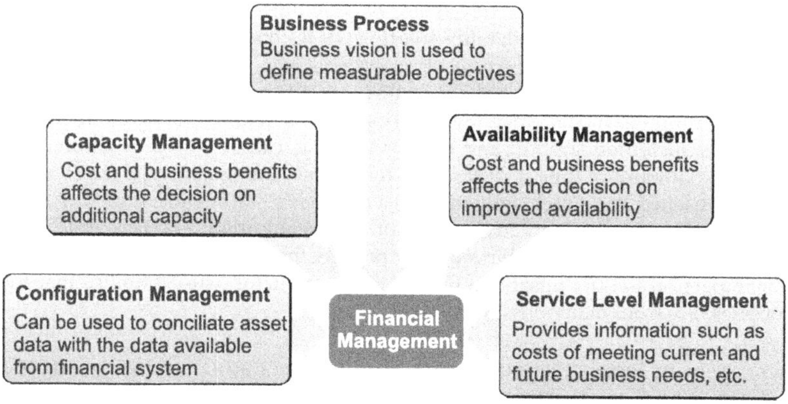

Fig. 3.7 *Financial management relationship with other service delivery processes*

Business Processes The work of service level management is to define the vision, strategy and planning in accordance with the business processes. Though the activities of business processes come outside the scope of financial management, they play an important role in this area. This is due to the fact that any business always has a vision of the future which is used to define various objectives for IT organisation affecting all business units. It is therefore important that IT strategy should be based on the business objectives.

Capacity Management Information on cost and business benefits may affect the decision on whether to buy additional capacity or not. It is important and very relevant to discuss the cost of any provision of increased capacity with the customer or the business as a whole.

Availability Management It is very similar to capacity management, and the decision on whether to buy improved availability may also be affected by the information on cost and business benefits. As in the case of capacity management, it also becomes very important and relevant to discuss the cost of any provision for improved availability with the customer.

Configuration Management It focuses on establishing and maintaining consistency of performance of a system or product. It specifies, identifies and records all changes to various IT infrastructure elements. Configuration management can be utilised to conciliate asset data with the data available from financial system.

Service Level Management The financial manager of an IT organisation consults with the service level manager about issues such as the costs of meeting current and future business requirements, the charging policy of the organisation and its effect on customers, and how the policy influences customer behaviour.

3·3 IT SERVICE CONTINUITY MANAGEMENT

In the current scenario, companies are expected to continue to operate and provide services at all times. The objective of the IT service continuity management is to help in ensuring that all IT services are capable of providing value to the customer at the time of failure of normal availability solutions. It is concerned with managing risks to ensure that an IT infrastructure of an organisation can continue by providing services in the event of an unlikely or unexpected event. It supports the overall business continuity management by ensuring that the required IT infrastructure and IT services, including support and the service desk, can be restored within desired and agreed amount of time if such a disaster happens. Availability of the IT services or their absence has much influence on customer's satisfaction and can quickly affect the overall reputation and success of the organisation. The task of IT service continuity management is achieved by a process that analyses business processes, their impact on the organisation and the IT infrastructure susceptibility that these processes face from many possible risks.

There are many factors that influence the availability of an IT service. Among them, hardware failure, environmental issues and human error are important. A hardware failure, such as a broken power supply or disk drive, is one of the most critical factors to consider. For example, mere failure of power supply to a server might cause the whole IT services to be discontinued. Dual redundant power supplies attached to the server can be employed to minimise some of these kinds of risks. If power to the whole computer room or data center is interrupted, battery backup systems can be used to cover the time it might take to start up a standby generator. These kinds of problems are referred to as availability risks, and the actions taken to minimise these problems are called countermeasures. If any of the countermeasures fails, more drastic actions must be taken. These actions are outlined in a document called the contingency plan. The need of a contingency plan can be understood by the following example. Consider an organisation having an arrangement that when power fails, generator should be used as a backup system. Now suppose normal power supply and generator both fail. The manager has to implement the contingency plan and has to move the service to another site.

3.3.1 Processes involved in IT Service Continuity Management

The process flowchart of IT service continuity management process is given in Figure 3.8. It consists of four major processes involved in IT service continuity management process.

Collection of Service Level Requirements Once risks are known, users take the help of IT to decide which risks are to be minimised and which ones are to be assumed. Since, in order to reduce a risk, one needs to handle many resources like people, time and money, IT management takes the necessary steps to determine a risk which is so small that it does not want to incur much cost to minimise it.

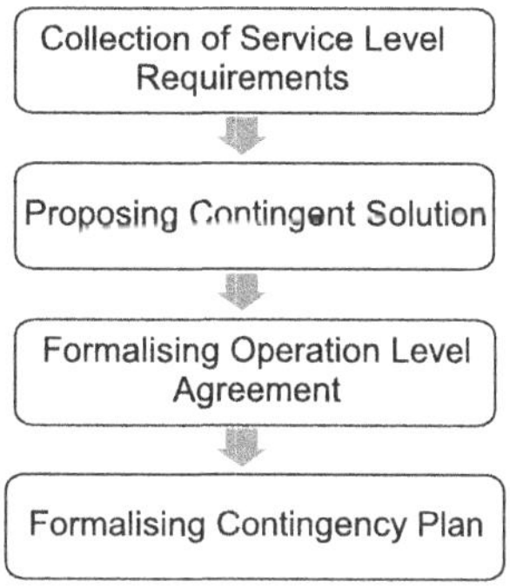

Fig. 3.8 *IT service continuity management process flow*

IT service continuity management begins by cautiously agreeing to availability targets with the customer and determining the cost of downtime or unavailability of the concerned IT service, so that a realistic and effective IT budget can be set up. It is also desirable that the negotiation contains realistic expectations of reduced system availability while the contingency plan is in place. This process needs an element of education and negotiation on both sides, i.e., the customer and the IT organisation.

To implement IT service continuity management effectively, customers need to understand the methods that they can use to define their availability requirements, and IT organisation needs to understand the functions required for providing IT services and which of them are the most critical. Effective implementation of IT service continuity management requires consideration of following two steps.

Identify Information Technology Service Layers To find out the probable places where risk may be introduced, IT environment needs to be broken down into some logical components. To do this, services provided by an organisation can be divided into layers. In the layered structure, an IT service can be delivered only if all the services underneath are functioning. Figure 3.9 presents an example of layers (IT stack) for the services provided by an IT department.

Identify Risk to Each Information Technology Service Layer Single point of failure can be iden-tified by inspecting possible risk vulnerabilities of each layer in the IT stack. Also, one can identify a single layer that may address risk on the layers above. An example of risk assessment is given in Table 3.1, which addresses the risk involved in some of the layers shown in Fig. 3.9. First column of this

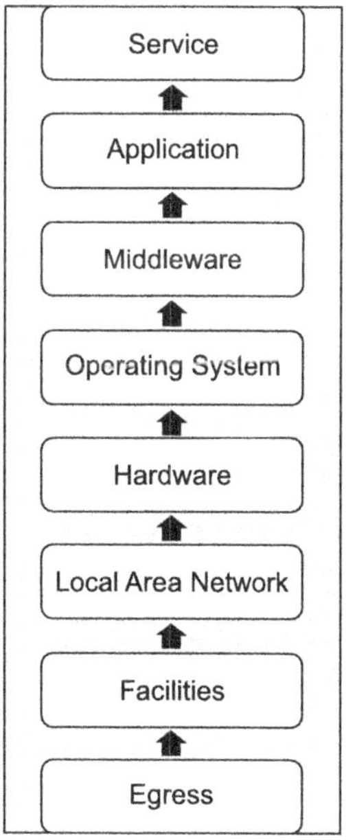

Fig. 3.9 *IT Stack (layers) for services provided by IT department of an organisation where lower layer provides service to upper layer*

table provides the names of various possible risks while rest of the columns give the level of risk present at various layers. Risk levels are categorised into three types, namely Low, Medium and High, representing low, medium and high level of risk respectively. Empty cell in the table shows that a risk does not affect that particular layer.

Table 3.1 *Risk Assessment (source: MOF)*

Risk	*Fire*	*Flood*	*Virus*	*Power outage*	*Logon failure*	*Lack of staff*	*Human error*
Egress				Medium			
Facilities	Medium	Low					Medium
Network					Medium	Medium	
Hardware			Low	High			Low
Operating System			High				
Middleware							
Application			High	Medium		Medium	
Service							

Proposing Contingent Solution Once the possible risk factors for the important business process have been recognized and their relative importance and financial implications are understood, one can start preparing its contingency plan. IT service continuity management ensures that the services are available in the case of a service interruption, irrespective of the cause of the disruption. Service continuity involves two main processes: failover and restoration.

Failover It is an act of automatic or manual movement of the operations of a component from its primary location to a secondary location. Following two examples illustrate automatic and manual failover.

Example 1 (Automatic failover): Assume that computer has dual redundant power supplies. At the time of normal operation, each supply provides half the load required by the system. When one of the supplies fails or goes off, the other automatically starts supplying all the power to the system. This is an example of automatic failover.

Example 2 (Manual failover): Consider a data center site which has got destroyed by a natural calamity. In this situation, the whole IT infrastructure must be recreated at a new place located at some distance away. This needs manual intervention and comes under manual failover.

Restoration It involves the act of bringing the operation of a component back from the secondary location to the primary location. This is an important activity and must be carefully dealt with while creating a contingency plan. Usually, it has been found that organisations have detailed plans for moving the service to a new location in case of an emergency, but they rarely have any plan to restore the service back to the original location when the time comes.

Formalising Operation Level Agreement Once IT department of an organisation and the customer agree on a cost-effective level of service continuity, an agreement needs to be formalised between various internal support groups of an organisation. This agreement is called an Operation Level Agreement (OLA). The OLA is an important building block for the Service Level Agreement (SLA) and defines the interdependent relationships among the internal support groups of an IT organisation working to support a service level agreement. The main objective of the OLA is to present a clear, concise and measurable description of the internal support relationships of the service provider.

While SLA is a legal document formalised between IT and its customers, OLA is an agreement between the IT entities within the organisation. It should be understood that OLA is not the substitute for SLA. OLA has to be considered as the basis of good practice and common agreement; however, some portions of it which may contribute to an SLA. Following are few important components that an OLA should include:

(i) Definition of the business processing

(ii) Impact of downtime or non-availability of IT services on business

(iii) The cost of downtime or non-availability and the way these costs can change over time

(iv) Minimum performance characteristics and hours of service required

(v) Critical periods of service, where downtime is intolerable

(vi) Less critical periods of service, where downtime is more tolerable

(vii) Scheduled downtime periods for planned maintenance

(viii) Amount of downtime can be tolerated before contingency plans should be invoked

(ix) Number of users.

The service level manager is ultimately responsible for the agreement and the documentation (SLA, OLA) of service levels with the customers.

Formalising the Contingency Plan The contingency plan is like a guide for the IT personnel which is to be used to failover and recover the service in case of a disaster. This document includes the information on escalation and notification procedure, start up and shut down procedures, communications methods and status reporting requirements. These procedures are discussed in detail below. It is also required that the document containing contingency plan should discuss the levels of contingency (level increases as the severity of the problem increases) and the procedure to be used to define the levels of contingency. This helps in taking the appropriate measures to handle any emergency situation.

Escalation and Notification Procedures This is the document which maintains the information about who can fix the problem at the time of contingency and who is affected by the break. This list may also include the relevant times when an individual can be contacted. Table 3.2 shows a sample notification list where each column represents one week day. Content of a cell shows the name of the person to be contacted, his or her area of expertise and availability timing.

Startup and Shutdown Procedures Startup and shutdown procedures are important for the data centre of any organisation. In case of any disaster, the sequence of the steps to be followed should be made available in advance. Startup and shutdown procedures can be grouped by technology and by dependency. In case of natural calamities, availability of this information helps in rebuilding and activating a recovered data centre with less time needed for resolving the dependencies. It is important to document startup and shutdown procedures properly so that there is no confusion in understanding these processes when required at a later time.

Communications Methods The contingency plan should describe clearly the methods of communications that are used by the repair staff to communicate with each other and with the affected process. Contingency plan should also be made for each communication type. For example, it should include the set of actions to be taken if communication media such as telephone, e-mails fails.

Status Reporting Requirements The contingency plan needs to be described clearly so that in case of any emergency, the list of people that need to be notified for each contingency level can be identified. It also needs to describe the frequency at which this communication is to take place.

Table 3.2 *Escalation and Notification List*

1	2	3	4	5
...	Jay Singh, IT	Jay Singh, IT	Jay Singh, IT	Jay Singh, IT
...	...	Meenu Roy Finance (7 am–7 pm)	Meenu Roy Finance (7 am–7 pm)	Meenu Roy Finance (24 hours)
...	...	...	Kiran Rao (7 pm–7 am)	Jitendra Singh, CIO (24 hrs)
...	...	...	...	Meenu Roy Public Relations (24 hrs)
...	...	...	...	Kiran Rao, Finance (7 pm–7 am)

3.3.2 Advantages of IT Service Continuity Management

IT service continuity management is the process by which plans are formulated and managed to ensure that IT services can recover and continue in case of a serious incident. The guidelines of IT service level management can be used to limit and manage the impact of disasters. If a disaster occurs, businesses with an IT service continuity management process have the following advantages:

- Organisations implementing service continuity management can manage the recovery of their systems.
- Organisations lose less time for service availability and offer better continuity to the users if they use IT service continuity management.
- It minimises the interruption to their business activities.
- It defines proactive measures to reduce the risk of a disaster in the first instance.
- It is regarded as the recovery of the IT Infrastructure used to deliver IT services.

3.3.3 Cost of IT Service Continuity Management

Major cost components associated with IT service continuity management implementation are as follows:

- Initial time and cost required to initiate, develop and implement IT service continuity management.
- Cost of hardware and software associated with the results of the introduction of risk management. These costs can be reduced if measures are considered within the limit of availability management.
- Cost required for continuing the recovery arrangements. For example, cost of making test arrangements and the period during which the recovery facilities are available.
- Ongoing operational costs of IT service continuity management. This includes cost of testing, auditing, and updating the plan.

3.3.4 Relationship with other Processes

Relationship of IT service continuity management with other processes is shown in Fig. 3.10.

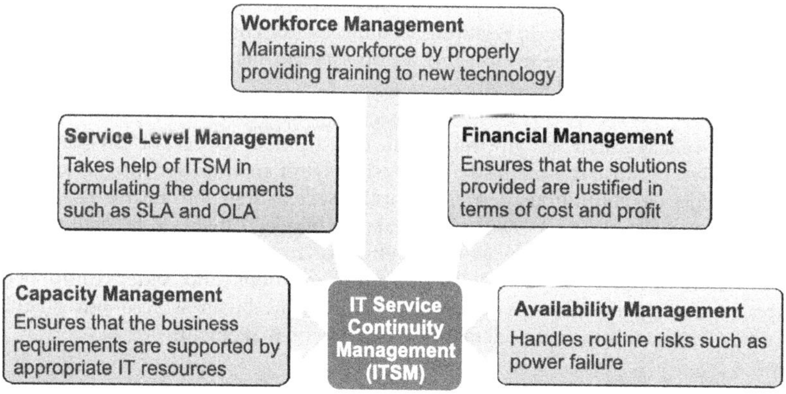

Fig. 3.10 *IT service continuity management relationship with other processes*

- **Service Level Management:** Service level management formulates and manages service level agreements (SLAs) and operating level agreements (OLAs). It provides information about the IT service obligations.

- **Financial Level Management:** Financial management ensures that the solutions proposed by capacity management, availability management and IT service continuity management are justifiable in terms of their cost of implementation against their profit to the customer. Financial management monitors, controls and recovers costs incurred by the IT organisation.
- **Workforce Management:** People need to be trained properly to any new technology which is introduced into the IT environment. Workforce management makes sure that existing personnel of the organisation are motivated, properly trained and ready to operate a new availability solution when it is ready.
- **Capacity Level Management:** It ensures that the business requirements are fully supported by the appropriate IT resources. Capacity management has a very close relation to IT service continuity management since the contingency plan may outline reduced capacity capabilities in the event of a disaster. These reduced capabilities should be clearly outlined in the OLAs that build the service.
- **Availability Management:** IT service continuity management is closely related to availability management and because both processes work to eliminate risks to the availability of IT services. The main focus of availability management is handling the routine risks to availability (such as power failure) that are expected on a day-to-day basis while IT service continuity management addresses the more extreme and relatively rare availability risks (such as fire and flood).

3.4 CAPACITY MANAGEMENT

The primary goal of capacity management is to ensure that IT capacity meets current and future business requirements of the organisation in a cost-effective way. It is the process of planning, analysing, sizing, and optimising capacity to satisfy demand in a timely manner and at a reasonable cost. It provides the required capacity for data processing and storage at the right time and in appropriate volume. It also ensures the efficient use of IT infrastructure. Improper planning for capacity may lead to wastage of resources, resulting in unnecessary cost or may lead to shortage of resources which may be responsible for poor performance or the unavailability of an IT service.

Capacity management is an important quantitative aspect of an IT service management because it includes both a business and an end-user focus on capacity requirements. It continuously tries to optimise existing and future IT resource demands and supply, and ensures the balance between them. It proactively adds components, space or people in a cost-effective manner while assuring that the performance is at acceptable level for new additions and older components. Capacity management is very much aligned with the business case and planning process. There are three main elements of capacity management:

- *Inputs* Usual inputs include business plans, processes, technology and related information used by each of the sub-processes.
- *Sub-processes* These are the levels of analysis where capacity is considered.
- *Outputs* Capacity plans, databases, reports, changes and recommendations are the main outputs of the sub-processes.

Capacity management is an iterative process. Figure 3.11 gives an overview of the various management tasks involved in capacity management process.

Monitoring It monitors utilisation of each resource and service on an ongoing basis to make sure that each hardware and software resource is being used optimally. It helps to ensure that everything is happening as agreed in service level agreement document.

Analysis Data collected during the monitoring phase need to be analysed and used to carry out tuning exercises and to establish profiles. Analysis activity helps in identifying the following issues:

(a) Contention in data, file, memory, processor

(b) Inappropriate distribution of workload across available resources

(c) Inappropriate locking strategy

(d) Inefficiencies in the application design.

Modelling Modelling is a central element of the capacity management process. It relies on the data obtained from other capacity management sub-processes and activities. Particularly, it gets data from forecasts of workloads and the use of resources by applications in development and associated hardware specifications. Modelling techniques with the effective use of simulation software helps in investigating capacity planning in order to build a model that simulates the desired outcome.

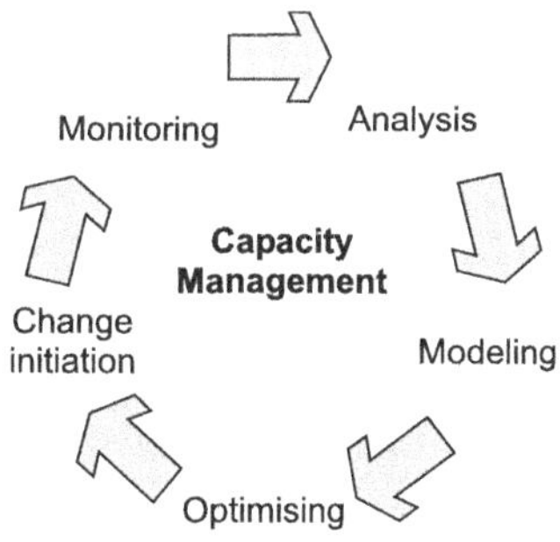

Fig. 3.11 *Capacity management as an iterative process (Source: MOF)*

Optimising Analysis of the monitored data may identify few important areas of the configuration that could be tuned and optimised to make better use of the system resources or to improve the performance of a particular service. Optimising techniques that are helpful include balancing workloads, balancing disk traffic, defining an accepted locking strategy and efficient use of memory.

Change Initiation It implements changes to the services that have been identified by the analysis and tuning activities. This activity also includes the identification of the necessary changes and subsequent generation and approval of change requests.

3.4.1 Process involved in Capacity Management

Capacity management aims to prevent surprises and rushed purchases by making better use of the available resources, and to increase capacity at the right time. Implementation of capacity management helps in preventing unnecessary investments and adhoc capacity changes. There are three main sub-processes involved in capacity management.

Business Capacity Management It is a part of capacity management activity which is responsible for ensuring that the future business requirements for IT services are well considered, planned and implemented in a cost effective and timely manner. Business capacity management is strongly connected to service level management and works jointly with the business planning efforts of the organisation.

Service Capacity Management Service capacity management addresses the issues of IT services. It is responsible for ensuring that the performance of all services is monitored and measured properly, as discussed in service level management.

Resource Capacity Management[2] Resource capacity management concentrates on the technology components and supports the service provisions. It ensures that all components with declared finite resources are monitored and measured accurately.

3.4.2 Advantages of Capacity Management

The implementation of capacity management in an organisation provides following advantages:

Reduced Risk As the capacity management effectively manages the resources, it reduces the risks associated with existing service and monitors the performance of the resources continuously.

Reduced Cost It helps in making the decision of any investment at the appropriate time, neither too early nor too late, which results in reduced service cost. Hence, purchasing process does not have to do last-minute purchases or over purchases of capacity too far in advance of need.

Greater Efficiency Since demand and supply are balanced at an early stage, this results in a greater degree of efficiency.

Reduced Business Disruption Capacity management has close connection with change management. So it reduces business disruptions by preventing urgent changes resulting from inadequate or incorrect capacity estimates.

Improved Customer Satisfaction Capacity management ensures better customer satisfaction. It consults the customers at an early stage and anticipates the requirements efficiently.

Better Validation of IT Spending Use of capacity management ensures avoidance of incorrect capacity sizing which results in appropriate use of resources and sufficient capacity availability in time to meet production workload needs.

Improvement of Relationship with Suppliers Further, purchasing, delivery, installation and maintenance agreements can also be planned more productively and effectively.

---

[2] Resource capacity management is referred as component capacity management in ITIL Version 3.

3.4.3 Cost of Capacity Management

The costs of setting up capacity management in an IT organisation must be estimated during the preparation. Following is the list of various components where investment is needed to be done:

Cost of Software and Hardware This includes the cost of purchase of hardware and software tools. Common tools needed are monitoring tools, trending and modelling tools for simulations and statistical analysis, reporting tools, capacity Management database etc.

Project Management Cost It is the cost associated with the implementation of the project management process.

Cost of Training This includes the cost incurred in providing personnel training and to develop support base.

Facilities and Services This includes the cost of facilities used and cost of services provided.

3.4.4 Relationship with Other Processes

Relationship of capacity management with other processes is pictorially shown in Fig. 3.12 and discussed below.

Service Level Management Capacity management helps service level management by advising about the feasibility of service levels, for example, for response times and service level requirements. It also helps in defining the OLA that results from service level requirements. It monitors and measures the performance levels and supplies information for checking and changing the agreed service levels where ever it is necessary. Capacity management works closely with service level, availability, service continuity and financial management personnel to formulate precautionary measures to improve the quality of the service at justified cost.

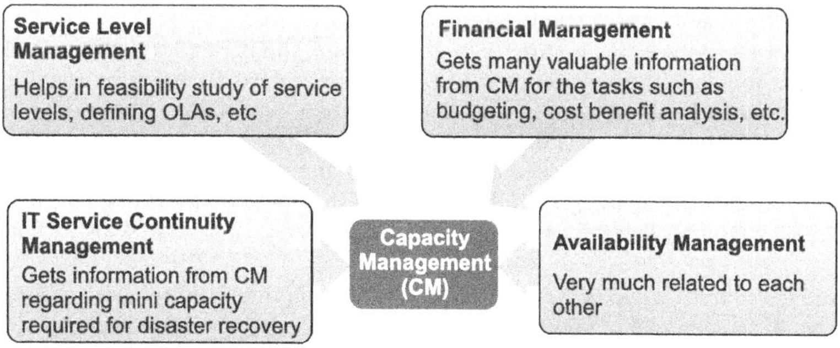

Fig. 3.12 *Relationship of capacity management with other service delivery processes*

Financial Management Capacity management provides valuable information to financial management activities such as investment budgeting, cost-benefit analysis and investment decisions. It also provides required information for charging capacity-related services, such as the usage of network capacity. Capacity management must ensure that the necessary resources are acquired and implemented in a cost-effective manner. It is essential that the capacity plan is consistent with all aspects of financial planning.

IT Service Continuity Management Capacity management informs about the minimum capacity required to continue the service or recover service in case of a disaster. Also, the capacity needs of IT service continuity management should be constantly reviewed to make sure that they reflect day-to-day changes in the operating environment. Capacity management helps service continuity management in judging the level of performance when countermeasures are executed.

Availability Management There is a close relation between capacity management and availability management processes. They both use many common tools and techniques to identify faults in the components. For example, component failure impact analysis and fault tree analysis are used by both of them. Moreover, same technology solution can often meet the needs of both the processes.

Since these two processes are very much dependent on each other, the availability plan needs to be coordinated with the capacity planning process and availability and capacity plans should be created in collaboration. Due to many dependencies with each other, these two processes should be coordinated effectively.

3.5 AVAILABILITY MANAGEMENT

Availability refers to the ability of a service or component to perform the function as desired at a stated instant or over a stated period of time. The goal of the availability management is to make sure that any given IT service delivers its functions consistently and cost-effectively at the level of service availability that the customer requires. It optimises the capability of the IT infrastructure, services and supporting organisation to deliver a cost effective and sustained level of service availability that meets stringent business objectives.

Availability management needs to ensure that the processes used for the support of critical IT services are mature enough and have the necessary personnel, skills, and tools to take effectively on their responsibilities. It also makes sure that, if there is a difference between supply and demand, then availability management may have to provide a solution. Furthermore, availability management ensures that the achieved availability levels are measured and, where ever necessary, are improved continuously. This means, the process needs to include both proactive and reactive activities to accomplish this. Availability management focuses on two distinct areas:

New IT Service It needs the clear definitions of complete requirements and design phases. The main goal of new IT services is to achieve the desired availability targets from the very beginning and to successfully manage the levels of availability in entire life cycle of the solution. New IT services also provide the best opportunity to an organisation for achieving desired availability targets in a cost-effective manner because availability considerations can be built from the earliest stages by selecting suitable technologies and an efficient IT support infrastructure.

Existing IT Service It may require considerable amount of short-term effort to improve levels of availability. Existing IT services can have their availability levels much improved and stabilised through the use of a formal availability management process. Then, they can benefit from a continuous improvement process and by careful managing the future changes.

3.5.1 Processes Involved in Availability Management

There are many different IT approaches that can be employed to deliver the required levels of availability, each having its own cost implications. However, in this section, most popular ones of these approaches are discussed in detail. Figure 3.13 illustrates the three major sub-processes involved in this approach of availability management process.

Defining Service Level Requirements Availability management is required to understand the availability targets of the customer before agreeing. It should also determine the cost of downtime or unavailability of the required IT service, so that a feasible IT budget can be set up.

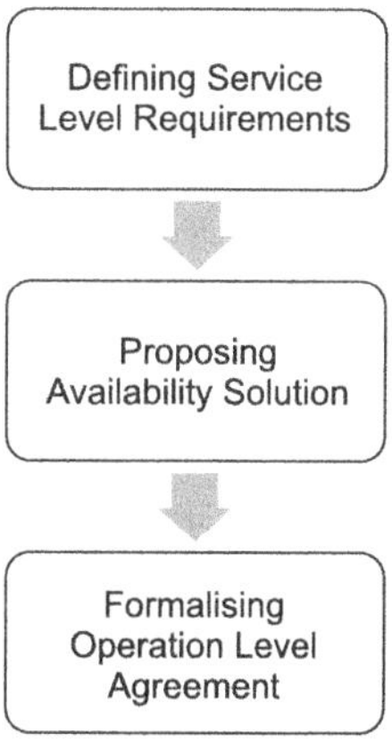

Fig. 3.13 *Availability management process flow*

To set up an adequate availability management procedure, a complete study of individual elements and negotiation on both sides is required. It is important because of the fact that the customer needs to understand the way to define and articulate availability requirements clearly. At the same time, IT organisation needs to understand the different customer functions that make up the overall IT service and which of these functions are the most critical.

The detailed description of the task of negotiating service level objects is the subject matter of service level management. A brief description is given below.

Determining Critical Customer Functions An IT service may contain multiple customer functions or transactions. These functions or transactions usually have varying availability requirements and impacts on the business if they fail. So business functions or transactions need to be studied carefully and ranked in an order. Based on the order, functions or transactions that are very important and critical for the business can be identified. Also, customers' requirements should be compared with what can be provided by the organisation. In case of any mismatch, the cost impact of this should be determined.

Determining the Availability Requirements Normally a customer puts his requirements in very simple terms without knowing and understanding its consequences. If inappropriate expectations are being set, it leads to many undesirable consequences such as misunderstandings between IT organisation and the customer, inappropriate levels of investment and at the end, customer dissatisfaction. For example, one availability requirement may refer to the availability of only the hardware platform while another may talk about the availability to mean the 'complete end-to-end service. Moreover, 'the definition of complete end-to-end service availability' can vary greatly.

To avoid such kind of problems and misunderstandings, it is very important to understand exactly how an availability requirement is to be measured. The availability manager should try to educate the customer and make sure that he or she fully understands the terminology and that the end results are realistic

Defining the availability requirement is the earliest possible stage of how the IT organisation can fulfil the customer requirements. This process must be carried out before a SLA is concluded and should address both new IT services and changes to existing services. This activity consists of the following:

- Define key business requirements
- Identifying and negotiating the periods of downtime for planned maintenance activity, technology upgrades and the introduction of new business functions
- Identifying quantifiable availability requirements
- Defining the business hours of the customer
- Setting up agreement about maintenance channels

Proposing Availability Solution Once the availability requirements for the business functions are identified and their relative importance and financial implications clearly defined, the process of designing IT Infrastructure that delivers the required levels of availability can be started. This process involves six major steps, namely identification of major IT service components, availability design, recoverability design, maintenance management, development of availability plan and measurement and reporting.

Identification of IT Service Components This is the first step of availability design process. In this step, the available IT services are divided into manageable components and these components are dealt with individually. For example, MOF breaks down the infrastructure that builds and supports IT service into following components:

- Service
- Application
- Middleware
- Operating system
- Hardware
- Network
- Facilities
- Egress

Design for Availability For each component identified above, the life cycle for each component is studied in detail. This helps in obtaining the maximum IT services that a component can provide. Study of each component can be done in two aspects:

- **Availability risk and countermeasures:** Risk associated with each IT component should be considered and appropriate countermeasure should be defined to overcome them.
- **Lifecycle management needs:** The full lifecycle management to achieve maximum availability of each component should be determined. The main goal of defining this step is to determine any operational task that can be undertaken to maximise the availability of the IT component, for example, startup and shutdown times. Common management needs for each IT component includes efficient handling of:
  a. Monitoring of IT components
  b. End-to-end health checks
  c. Startup and shutdown of components
  d. Proper password maintenance
  e. Housekeeping administration
  f. Backup and restore methodologies
  g. Upgrade and change methodology
  h. Emergency upgrade methodology
  i. Configuration documentation requirement
  j. Failover and feedback requirements.

Also, the problems which affect the availability standards should be determined at the earliest. This can prevent excessive development costs, unplanned expenditure at later stages, Single Points of Failure, additional costs charged by suppliers and delayed releases.

Design for Recoverability In spite of taking all the measures in designing and managing an IT service, problems in its delivery of service may still occur. So there is a need of a recovery plan which can be used in case of an incident such as an unexpected event or even in the failure of a countermeasure to protect a service. Efficient incident discovery and recovery mechanisms are also needed during less complicated situations, as even small problems may need to be handled properly to prevent errors from escalating further down the chain. For example, in the case of dual redundant power supplies, any failure in primary component needs to be identified and corrected before the secondary unit also fails and results in total loss of service. The lifecycle of a component includes elements shown in Fig. 3.14. Figure 3.15 shows the various periods that can be measured.

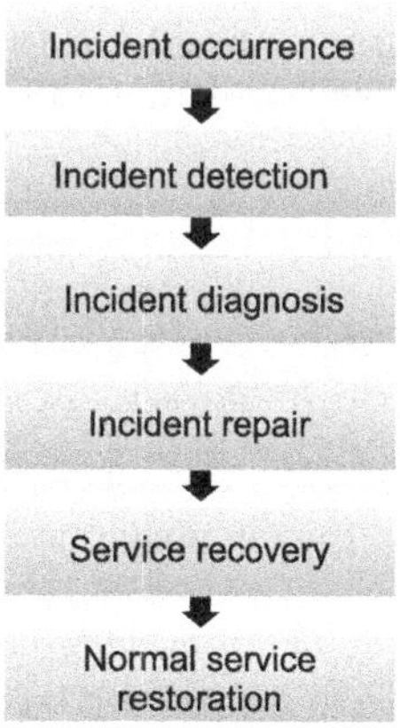

Fig. 3.14 *Incident life cycle stages*

- **Occurrence of the incident:** This is the time when the fault is identified by a user through other means (e.g., technically or physically).
- **Detection:** After the occurrence of the fault, service provider is informed about the fault. The time required for this is known as the detection time.
- **Diagnosis:** Service provider needs some time to respond. This is known as the response time. This time is used for diagnosis of the fault. The incident Management handles the fault following these steps: acceptance and registration of fault, classification of fault, matching, analysis and diagnosis.
- **Repair:** Diagnosis is followed by repair. At this stage, service provider restores the service or the components that caused the fault.
- **Service Recovery:** This is the stage when service is restored to the user. This includes activities such as configuration and initialisation.
- **Normal Service Restoration:** After the service recovery, normal services are restored.

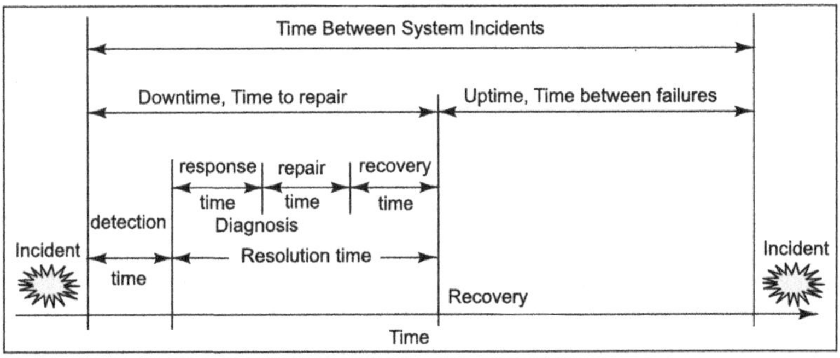

Fig. 3.15 *Availability measurement (source: OGC)*

Maintenance Management Maintenance refers to all technical, administrative and managerial actions during the lifecycle of a component intended to retain it in, or restore it to, a state in which it can perform the required function. Maintenance management characterises the process of leading and directing the maintenance.

Normally, when an organisation provides IT services, it keeps a scheduled time for windows unavailability, when normal services are not available to customers. This period is utilised in preventive actions, such as software and hardware upgrades. If any change is needed in any component, it can also be implemented during this period. The maintenance must be carried out when the impact on services can be minimised. So, it should be known in advance what the maintenance objectives are, when maintenance should be undertaken and what types of maintenance activities are involved. This information is useful for change management and other activities too.

Developing the Availability Plan Availability plan is a long-term plan concerning the availability of the IT services in next few years. The availability plan is the one of the important outcome of availability management.

At the initial stage, availability plan describes the existing state and at a later stage, it can be enlarged to include the activities for improving the existing service and guidelines. It can also be enlarged to include plans for new services and guidelines for maintenance. Development of an accurate and detailed plan requires communication with areas such as service level management, IT service continuity management, capacity management and financial management.

Measuring and Reporting These are important activities of availability management as they provide the foundation for verifying service agreements, resolving problems and defining proposals for further improvements. The following metrics are commonly used in availability management.

- **Mean Time to Repair (MTTR)**: It is defined as the average time between the occurrence of a fault and service recovery. It is also known as the downtime. It is the sum of the detection time and the resolution time (which is the sum of response, repair and recovery time). This metric is concerned with the recoverability and serviceability of the service.
- **Mean Time between Failures (MTBF):** It is the average time required between the recovery from one incident and the occurrence of the next incident. It is also known as uptime. This metric is concerned with the reliability of the service.
- **Mean Time Between System Incidents (MTBSI)**: It is defined as the mean time between the occurrence if two consecutive incidents. Thus,

$$\text{MTBSI} = \text{MTTR} + \text{MTBF}$$

Formalising Operating Level Agreements When an IT organisation and the customer agree on a cost-effective level of availability, the agreement needs to be formalised. This agreement document is called Operating Level Agreement (OLA). The OLA helps in defining the SLA. SLA is a two-way written agreement between an IT service provider and the IT customers while OLA is an agreement between internal IT service providers. To define an effective OLA, the mechanism for reporting availability back to the customer, the degree of granularity required, the format of presentation and the frequency of reporting need to be formally agreed upon.

3.5.2 Advantages of Availability Management

The IT services which implement availability management fulfil the agreed availability requirements. It aims to maximise the availability of IT services and customer satisfaction within the defined constraints. Other benefits of availability management include:

- Availability management ensures that new products and services fulfil the availability requirements and availability standards that are agreed with the customer.
- The associated cost is acceptable.
- It makes sure that the availability standards are monitored continuously and improved.
- In case of the unavailability of the service, it ensures that corrective action is taken when the service is unavailable and tries to minimise unavailability duration.
- It is easy to prove its added values for an organisation which follows availability management in providing its services.

3.5.3 Cost of Availability Management

In general, cost and availability are proportional to each other. That is, the cost increases as the availability increases. Therefore, finding the optimum solution is an important job of availability management. Experience shows that, in most of the situations, it is possible to reach an optimum with limited resources, rather than with significant investment. The availability management process can contribute to the objectives of the IT organisation in these areas by providing the required services at an acceptable and justifiable cost. The costs of availability management includes following major components:

Cost of Implementation It includes cost of implementation of availability management in the organisation.

Personnel Costs This is the cost incurred in providing training to personnel.

Facilities Costs This is the cost which is required to provide various facilities to customers.

Measuring and Reporting Tools It relates to the cost incurred in measurement and reporting tools.

In order to improve the availability, availability management should identify the areas where investment is needed. It is important that a cost-benefit analysis is carried out in all cases wherever investment is needed.

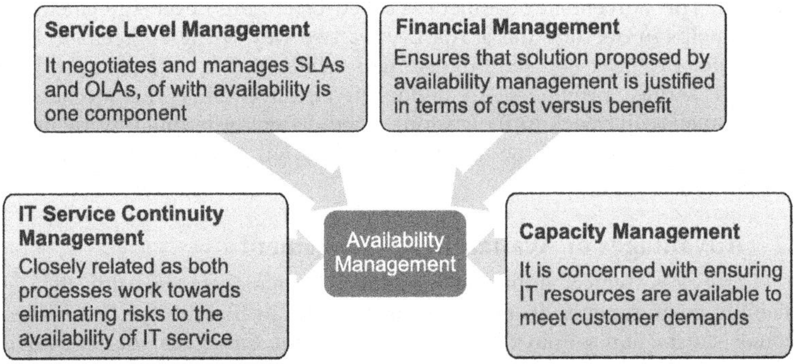

Fig. 3.16 *Relationship of availability management with other service delivery processes*

3.5.4 Relationship with Other Processes

Availability management is closely related to other service delivery processes. Figure 3.16 shows the diagram depicting the relationship of availability management with other service delivery processes.

Service Level Management Service level management is responsible for managing the service level agreements. It negotiates and manages SLAs and OLAs, of which availability is one of the most important components.

Financial Management The responsibility of financial management is to monitor, control, and if necessary, recover costs incurred by the IT organisation. Financial management is closely associated with other service delivery processes such as availability management, capacity management, and IT service continuity management. It acts as a filter and ensures that solutions proposed by availability management, capacity management or service continuity management are justified in terms of their cost to implement against the benefits that they offer to the customer.

IT Service Continuity Management Availability management and IT service continuity management are related because both processes work towards eliminating risks to the availability of IT service. In practice, many measures taken to enhance availability also enhance IT service continuity and vice versa.

While IT service continuity management is responsible for restoring the business processes after a disaster and deals with the more extreme and relatively rare availability risks such as fire or flood, availability management focuses on handling the routine risks to availability that can be expected on a day-to-day basis, such as the failure of a hardware component. The situations where no straightforward countermeasures are available or where the countermeasure is relatively expensive, availability risks are passed on to IT service continuity management to handle.

Capacity Management Changes in the capacity affect the availability of the service and vice versa. These two elements often exchange information about scenarios for upgrading or phasing out IT components and about availability trends that could change the capacity requirements. Availability management has a very close links with capacity management process since optimal use of IT resources to meet performance levels at a justifiable cost relates to the result of effective availability management. Capacity management is concerned with ensuring that IT resources are available to meet customer requirements by planning for additional resources when the use of the resources of the existing system begins to approach the point of full capacity.

Review Questions

1. What are the objectives of the service level management?
2. What is service level agreement? How does it help service level management process?
3. Define level-of-service in context to service level management.
4. Define the following terms:
   (a) Service in context of service level management
   (b) Service catalogue
   (c) Service level management
   (d) Service level objectives
   (e) Service level agreement review (SLA review)

5. Discuss the difference between service level and operational level agreements.
6. What are the important steps involved in implementation of service level management?
7. Discuss the following approaches of service level management process:
   (a) linear approach
   (b) cyclic approach.
8. List various advantages of service level management process.
9. What are the important cost factors involved in the implementation of service level management in an organisation?
10. Discuss the relationship of service level management with service desk, financial management and capacity management.
11. What is financial management? What are the various activities of financial management process?
12. What is cost-benefit analysis? Discuss following terms used in cost-benefit analysis.
    (a) Net present value
    (b) Payback period
    (c) Return on investment.
13. Define time value of money. What is its role in project investment appraisal activity?
14. List and explain various factors which a financial manager must consider while developing budget of an organisation.
15. Discuss two popular methods used for budget preparation.
16. What are advantages that zero-based budgeting of budget preparation has over the previous year budgeting method?
17. How does financial management benefit an organisation? What are the cost factors included in its implementation?
18. Discuss the relationship of financial management with configuration and availability management processes.
19. What is IT service continuity management? What are the advantages it offers to an organisation implementating it?
20. Discuss briefly the four important processes involved in the implementation of IT service continuity management.
21. What is a contingency plan? When is its used?
22. Explain failover and restoration processes of IT service continuity management with suitable examples.
23. What is capacity management? What are the advantages of capacity management?
24. Discuss various tasks involved in capacity management process.
25. Explain following sub-processes of capacity management.
    (a) Business capacity management
    (b) Service capacity management
    (c) Resource capacity management.

26. What are the various cost factors involved in the implementation of capacity management?
27. Define the term 'availability management'. What are the advantages of availability management?
28. What is availability plan? What are the management processes that need to be considered while designing availability plan?
29. Explain the difference between availability management and IT service continuity management.
30. What are the important metrics used to define the quality of service availability?
31. What is lifecycle of an IT component? Discuss the various elements involved in the lifecycle of a component.
32. Discuss the relationship of availability management with the capacity and IT service continuity management.

Service Support Process

Chapter 4

Service delivery focuses on the management aspect of the IT services while service support defines a framework that enables effective IT services. Service support describes the day-to-day operation and support of the IT services. Service delivery and service support processes are linked together through the Service Desk. Service desk is a function that provides a single point of contact between users and IT service department of an IT organisation and focuses on a activities such as rapid restoration of normal service operations to users, handling incidents and requests, providing an interface for other IT Service Management processes, etc. Figure 4.1 shows the interconnection between service delivery and service support processes. A service support consists of five sub-processes which are discussed in following sections.

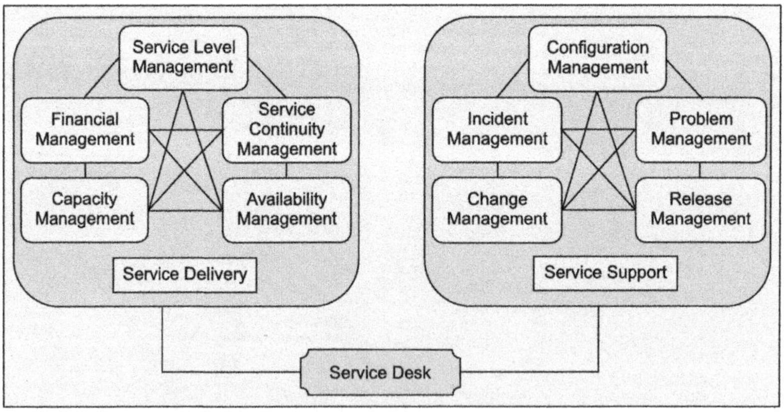

Fig. 4.1 *Interconnection between two service processes*

4.1 CONFIGURATION MANAGEMENT

Configuration management is a process which identifies and defines configuration items in a system. It involves monitoring the status of these items, processing requests for change and verifying the completeness and correctness of configuration items. It provides a logical model of the IT infrastructure (hardware, software and associated documentation) by identifying, maintaining and verifying the version of all configuration items. It controls the IT infrastructure and ensures that only authorised hardware and software are in use. Figure 4.2 shows process flow of configuration management. Some basic terminologies used in configuration management are defined below:

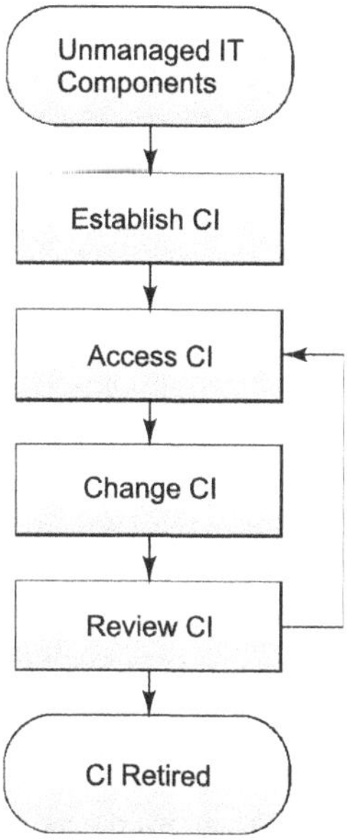

Fig. 4.2 *Process flow diagram of configuration management (Source: MOF)*

Configuration Item (CI) It is a fundamental component of IT infrastructure. It refers to the basic structural unit of a configuration management system. Size, type and complexity of one CI may vary from another and ranges from an entire system to a single software or a minor hardware component. Also, a CI can be composed of other CIs. Examples of CIs include individual requirements documents, software, plans, models and people.

Configuration Item's Attributes The information of a CI is stored in the database in the form of various attributes such as name of the item, location and description of detailed configuration settings and associated options.

Configuration Management Database (CMDB) It contains the details of all CIs together with important relationship among them. The database may include category, copy and serial number, version, model, location, responsibility or historical information about the item. It also contains information about the relationships between system components such as incidents, problems, known errors, changes and software releases. In addition to this, CMDB contains corporate data about employees, suppliers, locations and business locations. The level of details available in this database depends on either the objectives or the degree to which information is required to be available.

Configuration Manager It is responsible for managing the activities of the configuration management process of an IT organisation. Various roles of configuration manager include selection of staff, assignment of responsibilities to staff and their training.

4.1.1 Functions of Configuration Management

Configuration management does detailed recording and updating of information to describe an organisation's IT infrastructure. In addition to several other functions, it is responsible for following main tasks:

1. Identifying configuration items for entry into CMDB.
2. Finding relationship among configuration items.
3. Planning, designing and managing a Configuration Management Database (CMDB).
4. Verification of CMDB accuracy.

Configuration management is becoming an essential process but often it is difficult to introduce and keep it up to date mainly because of the following reasons:

- Configuration management is an overhead and requires resources which are costly and not easy to manage.
- Technical staff performing configuration management have other priorities. They have work to do which is in the "firing line".
- Technical staff also look down on administrative work and would rather correct a program than update a database.

4.1.2 Advantages of Configuration Management

Configuration management helps in providing cost-effective, high quality IT services. Following are the major advantages of implementing configuration management:

Managing IT Components and Services Configuration management monitors each component of the IT services which includes one or more configuration items. It also assists in processing changes, identifying and solving problems, and supporting users. This reduces the number of errors and therefore, also reduces costs by preventing duplication of effort.

Efficient Problem Solving Configuration management helps in identifying affected CIs and manages the modification and replacement of these CIs. It also provides information about trends, as an input to problem management.

Improved Security It helps in managing and monitoring the licensing of the software products. It manages the versions used and provides information about the authorised changes to CIs and the use of different software versions.

More Rapid Processing of Changes It can do quick and accurate impact analysis which enables changes to be processed more accurately and effectively.

Better Support for Other Processes Availability management and capacity management depend on correct configuration details for analysing and planning services. Configuration management provides the same to these processes. It also provides support to IT service continuity management by keeping properly and maintaining the backup copy of the CMDB. CMDB plays an important role in restoring services after any type of disaster. It also helps in identifying the desired CIs for disaster recovery.

Compliance with Legal Requirements Configuration management can help in preventing the use of illegal software in the organisation which may contain the viruses and lead to damage of the entire system. Illegal copies can be identified when audit results are compared with the CMDB entries.

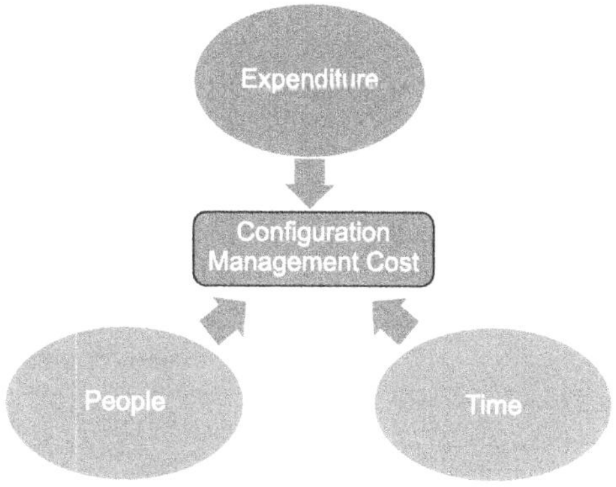

Fig. 4.3 *Implementation cost of configuration management*

4.1.3 Cost of Configuration Management

Implementation cost of configuration management largely depends on its scope and level of details. The cost has three main aspects—expenditure, people and time, which can be depicted as shown in Fig. 4.3.

Expenditure It includes the cost required to purchase software and hardware to create a CMDB. The cost of software and hardware depend on additional hardware and software required and their configuration, license fees of the software based on number of users, application and database design, database development and maintenance.

People The personnel cost depends primarily on the size of the organisation and level of detail of the CMDB. Configuration management requires full-time staff only if there is a large volume of continuous changes. These type of changes usually happens only in large organisations. In a small organisation, roles and responsibilities can be allocated to existing staff members.

Time The amount of time taken up by the configuration management process is difficult to quantify once it is operational, since this depends on the volume of changes in an organisation. Spending time proactively on a configuration management database and keeping it up to date can save time and effort spent later trying to track down equipment or trying to understand the infrastructure. System also takes some time for the implementation and integration of the process into normal day-to-day activities.

4.1.4 Relationship with Other Processes

Configuration management is heavily dependent on availability, capacity, change, release and IT service continuity management. It also supports a number of the other disciplines. Specifically, there is a close relationship among the three service management functions—change management, configuration management and release management. Following discussion gives more insights about the relationship of configuration management with other management processes. Figure 4.4 presents an overview of these relationships.

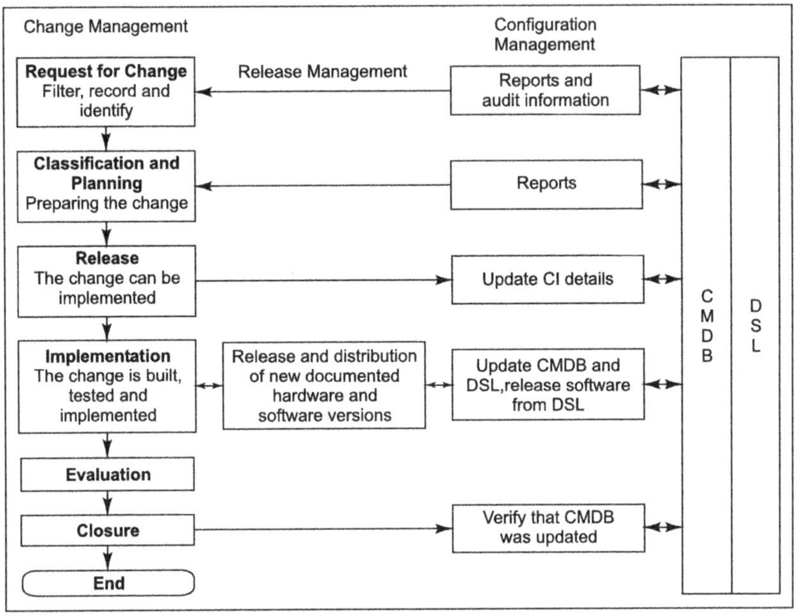

Fig. 4.4 *Relationship of configuration management with CMDB and other processes (Source: OGC)*

Service Level Management It requires information about services along with the relationship between services and the underlying infrastructure of CIs. Service level management data can also be stored on the CMDB and related to the appropriate CIs. The service level can be recorded against the service CI or the component hardware or software CI.

Financial Management It requires information about the use of services and CIs. For example, the required information could be the name of the department which uses a processing service and the name of the staff having a PC. It combines with information from the service level agreements to estimate the prices to be charged.

IT Service Continuity Management It uses standard configuration data from the CMDB to describe the requirements of disaster recovery and checks that these configurations are available at the disaster recovery site.

Capacity Management It uses data from the CMDB to plan and to optimise the IT infrastructure, to allocate the workload evenly and to develop a capacity plan.

Availability Management It has a strong relationship with configuration management. It uses the CMDB to identify the CIs which contributes to a service and for Component Failure Impact Analysis (CFIA), a way of evaluating (and predicting) the impact of failures and locating Single Points of Failure (SPOF).

It draws up plans for changes to address identified weaknesses. Configuration management provides information about the composition of the chain as well as about each of the elements.

Incident Management It requires information across the whole infrastructure. While registering incidents, incident management needs to access CI information. For example, it helps to determine the CIs location and its owner, to determine if there is a problem or a known error with a workaround associated with the CI, to know the customers and the services that are impacted and the relevant SLA.

Problem Management It needs to know the complexity of the infrastructure. It should be capable of linking problems and known errors to CIs and use CMDB data to analyse incidents and problems. Deviations or defects in the infrastructure can be identified by verifying the actual configuration of the infrastructure against the authorised configuration in CMDB.

Change Management It uses the CMDB to find out the impact of changes to be implemented in the system. It authorises changes and associates changes with the relevant CIs. Change management is responsible for recording Request For Changes (RFCs). Therefore, change management provides the major input for updating the CMDB. Change management is very much essential for the successful implementation of configuration management. It provides authorisation and tracking processes to ensure that only approved changes are deployed.

Release Management It provides a packaged release for all changes deployed into production. It provides information about release plans with versions and status of CIs including major and minor releases. Release management also provides information about implemented changes.

4.2 INCIDENT MANAGEMENT

An incident is an event or problem which causes or may cause interruption or reduction in quality of service to the customer of an organisation. The goal of incident management is to restore normal service operations (as defined in SLA) as quickly as possible with the least possible impact on either the business or the user and minimum disruption of services, at a cost-effective price. It also maintains continuity of the service levels and underlying service desk function. Inputs to incident management usually come from users but can also originate from other sources like management information or detection systems. The outputs of the process are typically RFC's, resolved and closed incidents, management information and communication to the customer.

Incident management handles all detected incidents and all service requests that can be raised through the Service Desk. Overall flow chart of incident management activities is shown in Fig. 4.5. Major activities of the incident management are summarised below:

1. Detection of incident and recording.

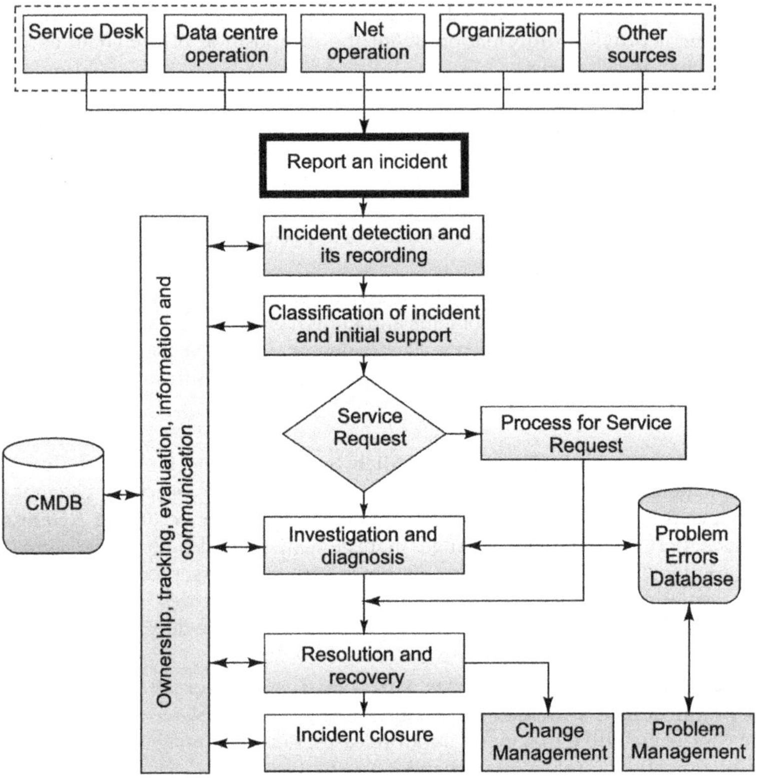

Fig. 4.5 *Flow diagram of incident management activities*

2. **Classification of incidents and initial support:** Incidents should be recorded and classified. Few examples of classifications are as follows:
   a. Application
      i. application error
      ii. disk usage full
      iii. service not available
   b. Hardware
      i. System down
      ii. automatic alert
      iii. printer not working
3. Investigation and diagnosis of incidents.
4. **Resolution and Recovery:** Resolve incidents and recover services as per agreed service levels.
5. Incident closure.
6. Incident ownership, monitoring, tracking and communication.
7. Prioritisation of incidents based upon impact and urgency.

Incident management is associated with service desk. Whenever an incident is reported, information related to the incident is recorded by the service desk. Common information which is recorded includes reporter details, incident details, systems affected due to incident, actions performed to resolve the problem. Figure 4.6 gives the details of the data associated with an incident.

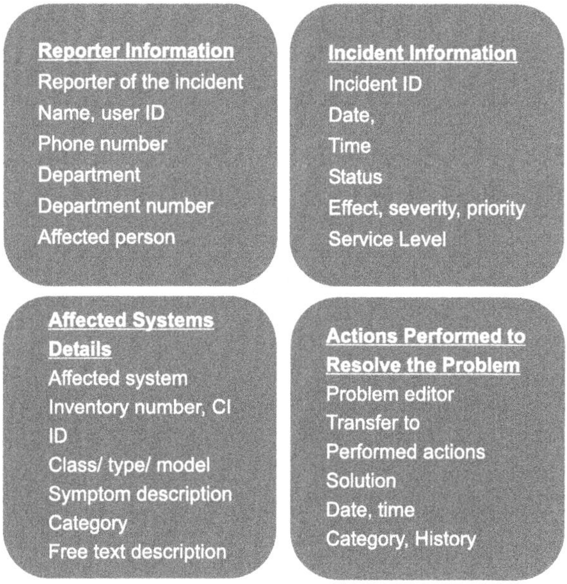

Fig. 4.6 *Normal data associated with an incident*

4.2.1 Advantages of Incident Management

Main task of incident management is to restore normal service operation as quickly as possible and to minimise impact of any service discontinuity on business operations. It ensures that service user gets best possible levels of service quality and availability. The implementation of incident management provides following benefits:

1. The use of incident management results into a decrease in down time of a user (where down time is defined as the amount of time that a user is on the phone to the service desk or cannot work because of a failure).
2. Using incident management for timely resolution of incidents results in reduced business impact and increases faith in the IT organisation.
3. Reduction of incidents provided by incident management improves quality of the IT service.
4. Incident management does pro-active problem resolution. It makes an IT organisation more effective as it decreases the incidents.
5. Incident management provides improved user and customer satisfaction with better utilisation of support resources.

6. Incident management provides better understanding of the impact of incidents on SLA targets and, as a result, it allows improved prioritisation.
7. It provides accurate information on the incidents that are occurring and eliminates "lost" incidents and service requests.
8. It supplies increased availability of management information.

An organisation which does not implement incident management may have to face the following problems:

Lack of Responsibility Due to the lack of incident management, responsibilities of the people may not be decided properly, resulting in an incident becoming unnecessarily severe and reducing the level of service. In such scenarios, users are repeatedly referred to other authorities without the incident being resolved.

Improper Use of Specialised Personnel Lack of proper incident management may cause interruption to specialists for answering the users' queries. This means that specialists cannot do their work properly and this may result in several people working on the same incident and unnecessarily wasting time and possibly coming up with conflicting solutions.

More Cost Because of the above-mentioned problems, the costs incurred by the customer and the IT organisation may be higher than needed.

4.2.2 Cost of Incident Management

Cost associated with the incident management can be divided into two parts: initial implementation cost and running cost.

Initial Implementation Cost Initial implementation cost includes the cost incurred in

1. Defining and communicating the processes and the procedures.
2. Training and instructing personnel. This includes customers as well as staff.
3. Selection and purchase of tools to support the process.

Running Costs It is the cost associated with the personnel and use of the tools. These costs depend greatly on the incident management structure, its scale of activities, its responsibilities and the number of sites involved. Cost of the incident management system can be significantly reduced by reusing the existing resources.

4.2.3 Relationship with Other Processes

Incident management is responsible for restoring normal service operation as fast as possible and minimising the impact on business operations. It is related to most of the service delivery and service support processes.

Service Desk It acts as the initial entry point to many of the IT processes including the incident management process. The job of service desk is to simply pass the received service requests to other IT processes. However, the connection between the service desk and the incident management process is much closer. The main tasks of service desk include recording, classification and initial support phases of incident management. When incidents are assigned to resolver groups, the service desk keeps responsibility for ownership by monitoring and tracking all the incidents. If the service desk works effectively, many service requests and incidents may be resolved efficiently without ever going outside of the service desk process.

Service Level Management It provides incident management with the essential information required to correctly classify new incidents. At the same time, incident management supplies the information of service target violations to service level management.

IT Service Continuity Management It aims to prevent or reduce the impact of future incidents by designing continuity plans and by implementing continuity measures. The plans supplied by IT service continuity management are used to recover failed services during major incidents.

Capacity Management It helps incident management in ensuring the availability of sufficient capacity for service desk tools, incident diagnosis tools and self service facilities. Also capacity management planning aims at preventing incidents occurring due to lack of resources such as CPU power, network bandwidth, etc.

Availability Management It deals with determination of the impact of incidents on service availability. Incident management gives information on the number and duration of service breaks, including their cause and the actions taken to resolve them. Availability management tries to reduce both the impact and the likelihood of future service breaks through the implementation of prevention and relaxation measures.

Configuration Management It provides important information which is used during the whole incident management process. The Configuration Management Data Base (CMDB) contains information that can be used to:

- Provide and check caller details
- Provide information on Configuration Items (CIs)
- Help to classify incidents by pointing out services and SLAs impacted by the failure of particular CIs
- Identify the relationship and mutual dependencies between CIs
- Recognise identical or similar CIs for comparison purposes
- Find out alternative routes and effective workarounds
- Record changes to configuration items caused by RFCs.

Problem Management Incident and problem management are very much related to each other but their focuses are entirely different. While Incident Management aims at restoring normal services as quickly as possible during an incident, problem management focuses on the identification of root causes and resolution of underlying problems from their roots.

Incident Management provides to problem management much of the information that is required to identify the existence of underlying problems. Problem management performs the analysis of incident statistics to identify the occurrence of multiple incidents or increasing trends for specific types of incidents. To prevent the recurrence of the incidents, problem management works towards resolving the underlying causes of these incidents.

Problem management also keeps information regarding existing problems and known errors alongwith known workarounds and solutions. This information is used by incident management to provide a quicker resolution of incidents.

Change Management Changes on any configuration item are carried out under the supervision of change management. Hence, in the case when incident management identifies resolution actions that need changes to configuration items, these changes are carried out under the control of the change management process. Change management process helps in decreasing the amount of changes that have to be backed out and ensures that the backed out plans are properly documented, in case they are required at a later date.

The coordinated testing of changes reduces the chance of succeeding incidents caused by the deployment of changes. Change management also provides to incident management important information on new changes, the configuration items affected due to these changes and the reasons for those changes.

Release Management Sometimes, resolution actions identified by incident management need to be incorporated and produced as new releases. Release management process plays an important role in coordinating and managing these releases. As in case of change management, release management also provides the effective planning, testing and coordination mechanism to ensure that releases can be rolled out with minimal incident.

4.3 PROBLEM MANAGEMENT

Problem management is responsible for ensuring that all possible problems and known errors affecting the IT infrastructure are identified and recorded properly. It assists in investigating and resolving the underlying root causes of incidents and preventing incidents of similar nature from occurring again. By removing errors—which often require a structural change to the IT Infrastructure—the number of incidents can be reduced over a period of time. There are three major types of causes for a problem to occur:

Presumptive Cause It is a cause that may be apparent at the beginning of the investigation or that may emerge in the data collection process. This type of cause needs validation.

Contributing Cause It is a cause that alone would not have created the problem but is important enough to be recognised as requiring corrective action.

Root Cause It is the most basic reason for a problem and, if it is corrected, recurrence of that problem can be prevented.

Overview of problem management is given in Fig. 4.7. The terminology used in further discussion can be defined as follows:

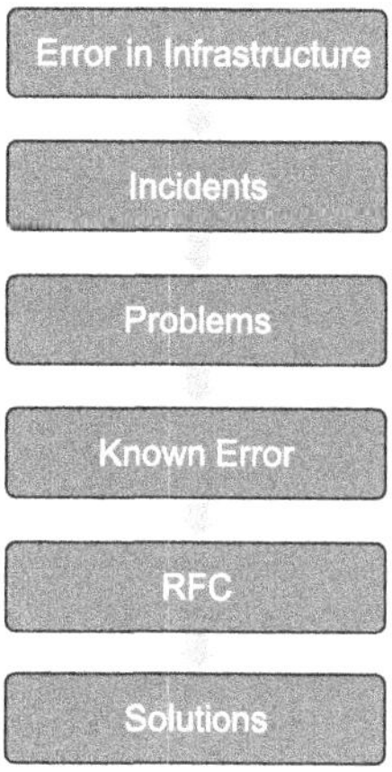

Fig. 4.7 *Overview of problem management*

Incident A fault or disruption that affects the normal operation of an IT service.

Problem A state that is identified from the incidents and indicates an error in the IT infrastructure. It is important to note that a problem remains in this state until its root cause is identified.

Known Error A problem for which the cause is known and is usually related to a fault with one or many configuration items within the IT infrastructure.

Problem management consists of both proactive and reactive activity measures. Proactive problem management aims to prevent repetition of incidents by identifying weaknesses in the infrastructure and making proposals to remove them. Reactive problem management works to identify the root cause of the past incidents and presents proposals for their improvement or rectification. Problem management gives valuable information (such as recording problems and known errors) for other service management functions like incident management, change management and service desk. The major activities of problem management are as follows:

Problem Control It includes defining, investigating and examining the problems. It is the process of transforming problems into known errors.

Error Control It includes the process such as monitoring and controlling all known errors and raising request for change.

Report Generation It is responsible for generating reports on problems and their solutions. Since reports maintain the solution for the problem, they help in resolving a problem of same nature, if it occurs again.

4.3.1 Processes Involved in Problem Management

Problem management includes two important activities—problem control and error control. These activities are explained below:

Problem Control It is responsible for identifying problems and examining their root cause. Figure 4.8 shows various problem control activities, which are summarised below:

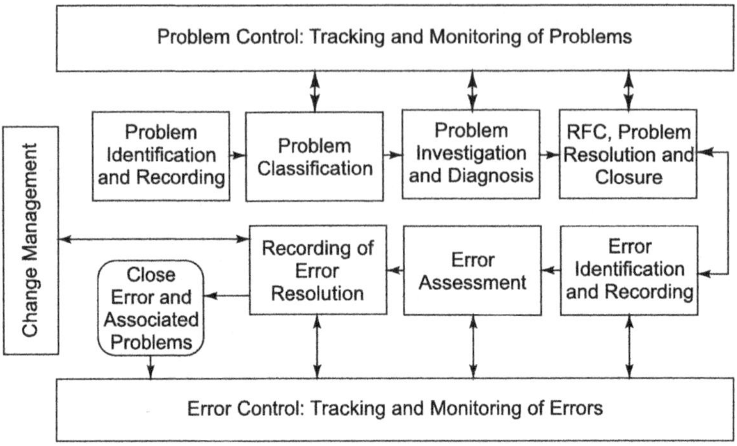

Fig. 4.8 *Problem and Error Control in Problem Management*

Problem Identification and Recording Any incident which has an unknown cause should be linked with a problem. A problem can result from a variety of situations, sources and mediums and this process deals with the initial detection and recording of the problem. The activities of this process are normally worthwhile if the incident occurs repeatedly or is expected to recur or even if there is a single significant incident.

The activity of 'identifying problems' is usually done by problem analysts. However, other personnel, such as personnel involved in capacity management, can also assist to identify problems. One example of identification of problems is the analysis of the infrastructure—it identifies weak areas where new incidents may arise.

Problem Classification and Allocation Classification is made by an impact analysis. It determines the seriousness of the problem and its effects on the services (urgency and impact). Usually, classification includes the following:

- **Category:** It is related to identifying the domain of the problem, e.g., whether it is a hardware problem or software problem.
- **Impact:** Impact of the problem on business processes.
- **Urgency:** It indicates the extent up to which postponement of the solution is acceptable.
- **Priority:** It is decided based on the urgency, impact, risk and resources required for the problem.
- **Status:** It refers to status, such as problem, known error, resolved errors, etc.

Personnel and resources are allocated on the basis of the problem classification and then time is made available to resolve the problem.

Problem Investigation and Diagnosis This process deals with the investigation of the problem and diagnosis of its root causes. Problems are not only caused by hardware and software, but also can be caused by a documentation error, human or procedural error, such as releasing the wrong software version. Therefore, it is very essential to include procedures in the CMDB and subject them to version control. Normally, most errors can be traced to infrastructure components. This data can then be used to help problem management team to assess the resources and skills required to resolve the causes of the problem.

Problem Closure Problem resolution details need to be fully recorded in the problem management system. Also, it is very crucial to save the data on the Configuration Items (CIs). Sometimes, it may be necessary to approve a temporary fix or emergency fix in case of the problem causing serious incidents. If a temporary fix requires modification of the infrastructure, then an RFC is required to be submitted first (before the root cause has been determined). If the matter is very serious and delay is unacceptable, the urgent RFC procedure may have to be followed.

Error Control Error control also follows similar type of steps as problem control. Its first job is to identify and record the errors, followed by assessing, monitoring, and controlling of known errors until they are successfully and appropriately resolved. Error control performs its functions by raising a RFC to change management and by evaluating the changes in a Post Implementation Review (PIR). Error control monitors all known Errors from their identification through resolution. Error control may involve many departments and covers both the production and development environments.

4.3.2 Advantages of Problem Management

Problem management can improve the Quality of Service (QoS) by significantly reducing the number of incidents and reducing the workload on the IT organisation. Some of the apparent advantages are listed here:

Improved IT Service Quality and Management Since problem management helps in documenting and/or eliminating the failures, it improves IT service quality as well as management.

Increased User Productivity Service quality and user productivity are related to each other. Hence, improvement in service quality increases the users' productivity.

Increased Support Personnel Productivity Because of the proper documentation of the solutions of earlier identified problems, incident management agents can resolve incidents more quickly and efficiently.

Improved IT Service Reputation As a result of improvement in the stability of the services, customers are more likely to trust the IT organisation with new business activities.

Improved Incident Recording Problem management introduces standards for incident recording and classification to identify problems and their symptoms effectively. This also improves incident reporting.

4.3.3 Cost of Problem Management

It includes two major costs—the cost of support and cost of personnel.

Cost of Support It includes the cost of support and diagnostic tools used in the process of problem management.

Cost of Personnel Personnel costs must be considered while estimating the total cost of problem management. Apart from internal IT personnel involved in problem management, there is also the cost of hiring additional expertise from external suppliers and support organisations.

4.3.4 Incident Management vs. Problem Management

It is important to differentiate incident management from problem management. The difference between them arises mainly due to the different focus areas of these processes. Some of the prominent differences are discussed below:

Restoration vs. Root Cause Incident management is solely concerned with returning the service to an operational state. It is not concerned with the analysis of root cause which would essentially slowdown the process. Problem management is concerned with the analysis of the root causes behind an incident.

Combat vs. Remedy The main difference between incident management and problem management is that the former deals with fighting symptoms of incidents while the latter attempts to permanently remove the causes of incidents from the IT infrastructure.

Reactive vs. Pro-active In incident management, interaction with the customers is generally reactive, where the main objective is always to find a workaround solution to restore normal services for the customer as early as possible. In problem management, IT support staff is more proactive, since they deploy resources to identify the underlying causes of incidents.

Customer Interaction Incident management process has direct interaction with the customer. In problem management, there is usually very little or no interaction with the customers, as this is left to the responsibility of the Service Desk.

4.3.5 Relationship with Other Processes

Problem management is closely related to many of the service delivery and service support processes. Overview of these relationships is given in Fig. 4.9. Some of the important relationships of problem management are discussed below:

Service Level Management It assists problem management by providing information that is used to define problems. The problem management procedures should support the agreed service quality levels to financial management and IT service continuity management.

Financial Management It assists problem management in assessing the costs associated with resolving known errors. Financial management is a major source of information for error control. If an error control fixes some error, financial management will be able to make informed decisions.

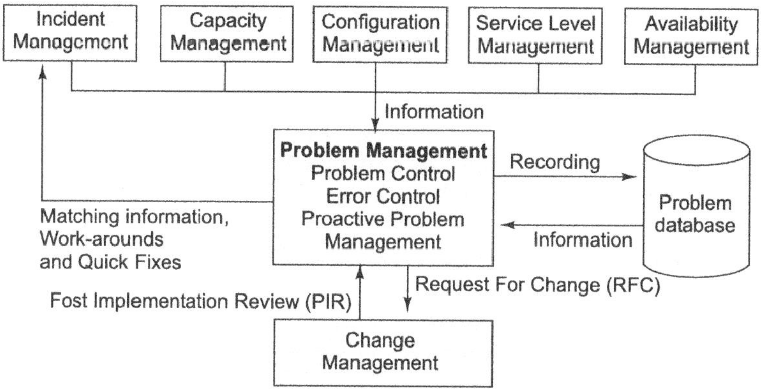

Fig. 4.9 *Relationship of problem management with other processes (Source: ITSMF)*

IT Service Continuity Management It helps to propose solutions for the resolution of continuity-related problems. Problem management assists IT service continuity management with the justification and prioritisation of resolution actions. It may also report continuity-related problems to problem management.

Capacity Management It helps in finding the way to utilise the IT resources optimally. Capacity management provides essential information to problem management which can be used to define problems. Problem management supports capacity management by identifying the causes of capacity related problems and rectifying them.

Availability Management It addresses the design and architecture of the infrastructure and aims to prevent problems and incidents by optimising availability design, planning and monitoring. Problem management often works with availability management in the analysis of service failure activity.

Configuration Management It provides essential information about components of the infrastructure, blueprints, hardware and software configurations and services. Configuration management defines the interrelationship among the IT infrastructure components.

Incident Management It plays an important role in problem management. Effective incident records are essential for successful problem management since this information is used to identify problems. Problem management supports the incident management process and analyses the problem until a solution for the problem has been found.

Change Management It assists problem management in such a way that it provides controlled implementation of changes to RFC that has been proposed by problem management to eliminate the problems. Change management is responsible for assessing the impact of and resources required for the planning, coordination and evaluation of requested changes. It also assists problem management by providing the information about the progress and completion of corrective changes.

Release Management It provides confirmation to problem management as to whether the expected resolution has been reached. Problem management assesses the release in the production environment to validate that the known errors have been permanently fixed. In a similar way to change management, release management provides the planning, testing and coordination to roll out these releases without any changes resulting in further incidents.

4.4 CHANGE MANAGEMENT

From an ITIL perspective, "Change" is defined as the addition, removal or modification of hardware, network, software, environment, people and/or associated documentation. The goal of change management is to ensure standardised methods and procedures, such that it minimises the impact of the change on service quality. Change management attempts to introduce the required changes into the IT environment with minimal disruption to ongoing operations. It formally initiates a change through the submission of a Request for Change (RFC) and then passes RFC to a change manager and the Change Advisory Board (CAB) for approval or rejection of the change.

4.4.1 Processes Involved in Change Management

Change management implements the requested changes to eliminate known problems and errors in the system. A change process formally goes through the steps shown in Fig. 4.10. These steps are explained below:

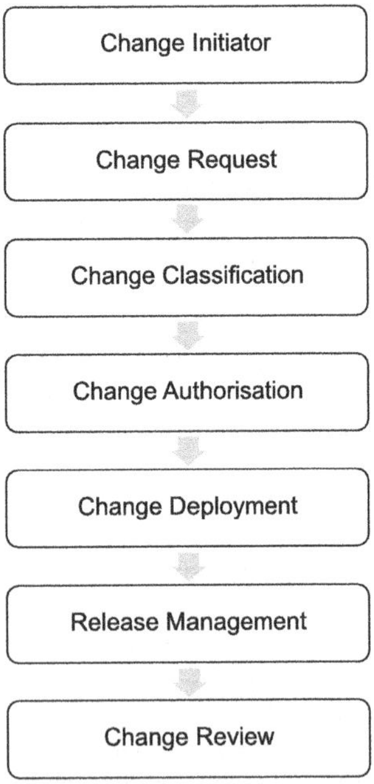

Fig. 4.10 *Change management process flow (Source: MOF)*

Change Request Typically, any person within a business environment can request a change and, by doing so, he becomes a change initiator. Change management is responsible for ensuring that all sources of changes submit RFCs and that they are adequately recorded. Each RFC is a standard document in which all relevant information about the proposed change is recorded. The RFC must answer questions such as what, why, who, when, where and how of the proposed changes. It must describe the change, the effort that is expected for implementing the change, the method of implementation and the configuration items involved.

Change Classification The next requirement is to classify the priority and the category of the change. Even though the classification and the priority would have been entered by the change initiator, the change manager also reviews them and makes any necessary changes, if required. The **priority** indicates the importance of such a change with respect to other RFCs and it is derived from the urgency time scale and the business need for the change. Change Management determines the **category** on the basis of the impact of the change on the risk to services and the availability of resources.

Low Priority It shows that a change is desirable but it can wait until a convenient time.

Normal Priority It signifies that there is no great urgency or major impact but that the change should not be deferred. In the CAB meeting, it is given a normal priority when allocating resources.

High Priority It refers to a serious error affecting a number of users or an inconvenient error affecting a large group of users or related to other urgent matters. This change is given the highest priority in the next meeting of the CAB.

Highest Priority The RFC concerns a problem that seriously affects the use of essential services by users or it concerns an urgent IT change. Changes with this priority are classified as 'urgent changes'. Urgent changes do not follow the normal procedures and, if required, resources are immediately made available. An emergency meeting of the CAB or the IT steering committee may be required for this purpose. A CAB/EC (Emergency Committee) should be installed in this regard, with the authority to make emergency decisions. All earlier plans may be delayed or interrupted.

Determining the Category Change management which indicates the impact of the change and the demand that it makes on the IT organisation, determines various categories. Some examples of categories are as follows:

Minor This category shows the requirements of a small change involving low risk. The change manager can approve these changes without submitting them to the CAB.

Substantial For changes falling in this category, a significant effort is needed and it may have a substantial impact on the services. These changes are discussed at a CAB meeting to determine the required efforts and potential impact. Before the meeting, the relevant documentation should be circulated among the CAB members and, possibly, to specialists and developers for their valuable comments.

Major In this type of change, a very large amount of effort is needed and could impact a major part of the organisation. The change manager requires prior authorisation from the IT management or IT steering committee, after which the change must be submitted to the CAB.

Most of the changes fall into the first two categories. In addition to the classification, the groups working on the solution and the services affected by the change must also be specified.

Change Authorisation After a change has been correctly prioritised and categorised by the change manager, the change must be authorised. The process of authorising a change request depends upon the category and priority of the change:

- **Emergency** priority changes are raised to the CAB or EC for fast-track approval.
- **Standard** changes are approved automatically and progress directly to the change development and release phase.
- **Minor** changes can be approved by the change manager without reference to the CAB.
- All other changes must be approved by the CAB.

If the RFC is rejected and the change is not approved, the RFC is closed and the change initiator is informed of the decision. The reasons for the rejection are added to the change log. Once an RFC has been closed, it cannot be reopened. If the change initiator wishes to resubmit the request, he or she must open a new RFC, make reference to the original RFC and add any additional information that is necessary to get approval of the request.

Change Development After an RFC has been approved using the appropriate path—based on its priority and category—it moves onto the change development phase. This phase is concerned with the steps necessary to plan the change and develop the deliverables of the change. Major tasks of change development phase are listed here:

- Scheduling the change according to business priorities, change pipeline, category and priority.
- Appointing a suitable change owner, according to the requirements of the change in terms of technology, size, priority and category.
- Ensuring that the change development process follows a recognised development life cycle.
- Conducting milestone reviews with the participation of CAB members to ensure that each phase has been completed successfully.
- Ensuring that the change developed and passed to the release process has met acceptance criteria.

Change Review Following a successful release and deployment into the production environment, a review process must be conducted to establish whether the change has had the desired effect and has met the requirements of the original request for change.

Major activities of the change review process are listed below:

- Monitors and reviews performance of the change after implementation into production in line with the objectives of the original RFC and the objectives of the MOF Team Model role clusters.
- Analyses lessons learned from the deployment and documents them for future benefit.

- Deals with unsuccessful change implementations by backing out, considering further remedial changes or using the "accept issues and continue" policy.
- Closes successful RFCs and informs the initiator.

4.4.2 Advantages of Change Management

To be able to provide IT services effectively, the organisation should be able to deal with a large number of changes smoothly and responsibly. Specific benefits of change management includes following:

Reduced Impact Change management reduces the impact of changes in the quality of IT services.

Better Cost Estimation Change management helps to estimate better the cost of the proposed changes.

Better Management Information Implementation of change management provides better information to management about the changes in the IT infrastructure which enables a better diagnosis of problem areas.

Improved Personnel Productivity Productivity of IT personnel is increased since they are not distracted from their planned work by urgent changes or back-out procedures. It also increases user productivity.

Increased Ability to Accommodate Changes Change management increases the ability to accommodate frequent changes without creating an unstable IT environment.

4.4.3 Cost of Change Management

There are two major components involved in the cost of change management—personnel cost and tool cost.

Personnel Cost It includes the cost for coordinating the changes. An additional personnel cost may be incurred in fulfilling the change manager task and setting up the change advisory Board.

Tool Cost It includes cost for hardware and software required to implement change management. Often, when introducing several processes, an integrated tool is purchased for change management, problem management, configuration management and incident management. When dealing with complex IT environments, it becomes almost impossible to control these management processes without such tools.

4.4.4 Relationship with Other Processes

Though change management is related to most of the IT service management processes, it has a close connection with incident and problem management. This relationship has been shown pictorially in Fig. 4.11 and Fig. 4.12. Detailed description of the relationship of change management with other processes is given below:

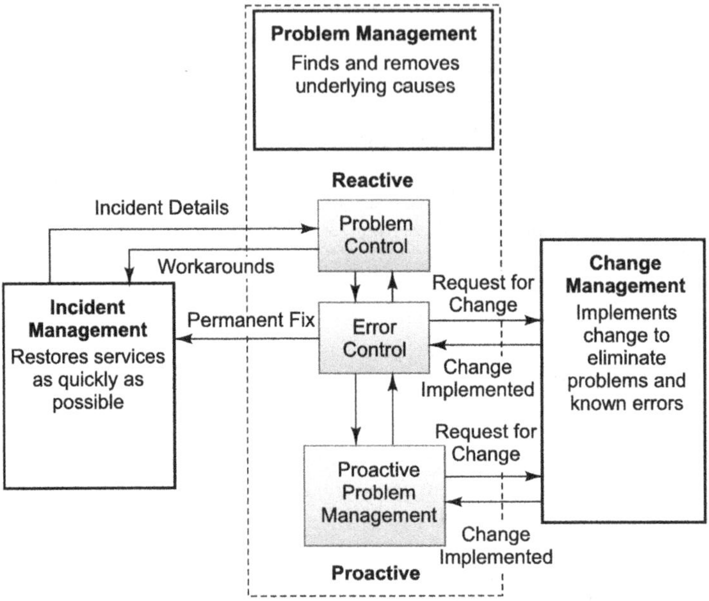

Fig. 4.11 *Relationships among problem, change and incident managements*

Service Level Management Service level management is involved in determining the impact of the changes on services and business processes. Depending on the situation, service level management may be represented on the CAB. If a change has a major impact or high risk, its implementation and the time frame must always be discussed with the customer.

IT Service Continuity Management Prevention measures and recovery plans that ensure continuity of the services have to be monitored clearly since changes in infrastructure could make a plan unworkable. Change management works closely together with IT service continuity management to ensure that IT service continuity management is aware of all changes that could affect recovery plans and can take steps to ensure the complete recovery.

Capacity Management It assists change management. On the basis of the capacity plan, capacity management regularly proposes enhancements and changes in the form of RFCs to improve use of existing capacity as well as to extend it.

Availability Management It initiates changes to improve service availability. It also verifies if the intended improvement has been actually obtained. Availability management is often involved in estimating the potential impact of changes since such an impact could affect the availability of the service.

Configuration Management Change management and configuration management are so tightly coupled processes that the two processes can effectively be integrated. This is a step which is recommended in the ITIL service support guidance. Changes are recorded under the control of configuration management. Impact analysis of changes is also done through this type of management. The relationships between the CI (in the change being addressed) and other CIs have been identified by configuration management in order to show the effects of the changes.

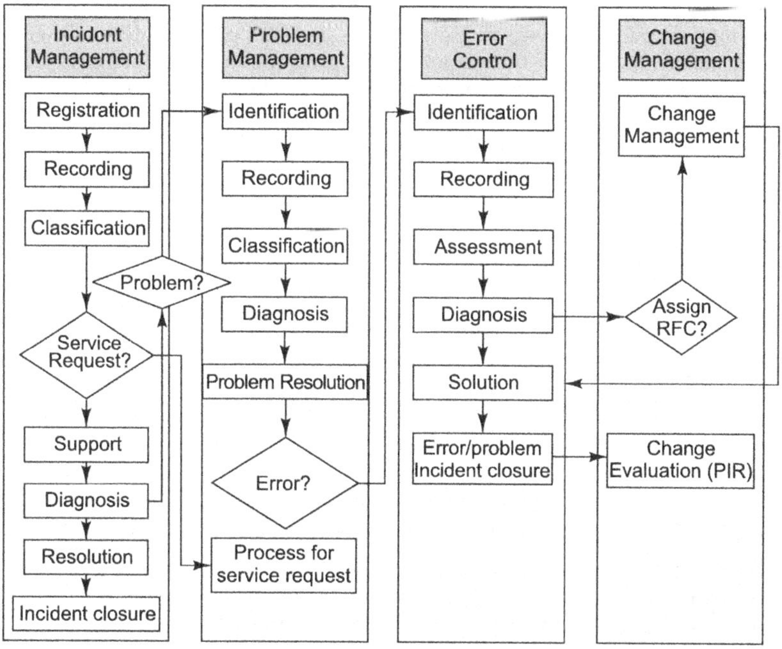

Fig. 4.12 *Relationships among problem, change, incident managements*

Incident Management It has a two-sided relationship with change management. On the one hand, change management puts through the changes requested by incident management to counteract the effect of an incident while on the other hand, the implementation of the changes could still lead to errors and incidents even though enough precautions have been taken.

Problem Management The relationship between change management and problem management is similar to that between change management and incident management. On the one hand, changes are often requested to correct errors and thereby solve problems while on the other hand, if the implementation of changes is not adequately controlled, the changes can introduce new errors and problems.

Release Management Changes often result in the development and distribution of a new set of applications or technical infrastructure which are subject to release management disciplines. Also, many changes affecting the same area of IT applications or infrastructure are packaged together into a release that is subject to release management.

4.5 RELEASE MANAGEMENT

It deals with the mechanisms of building and releasing a new software version, and is an integral part of service support process. It offers proactive technical support which mainly focuses on the planning and preparation of new services. Release management aims to ensure the quality of the production environment by using formal procedures and checks while implementing new version. Unlike change management which is concerned with the complete change process and focuses on risk, it is concerned with the implementation. Release management manages and distributes software and hardware version used for production, which are supported by the IT department to provide the required service level. Release management is responsible for the following activities:

- It performs planning, coordination and implementation (or arranging for implementation) of software and hardware.
- It is accountable for designing and implementing efficient procedures for the distribution and installation of changes to IT systems.
- It manages the release of software into the live environment and its distribution to remote locations.
- It is responsible for communication with the users and for considering their expectations during the planning and rollout of new releases.
- It ensures that the original copies of software are securely stored in the Definitive Software Library (DSL). It also observes that the CMDB is updated. The same applies with respect to the hardware in the Definitive Hardware Store (DHS).

The need for release management is to oversee the integration and flow of development, testing, deployment and support of these systems. Where project managers are looking after development of a project, they are generally more concerned with high-level, grand design aspects of a project or application. But release managers oversee the more technical or day-to-day aspects of the development. Hence, they must have knowledge of every aspect of the Software Development Lifecycle (SDLC), various applicable operating systems and software application or platforms as well as various business functions and perspectives.

4.5.1 Processes Involved in Release Management

The objective of release management is to control the release of new configuration items into live environment and protect them in that environment. This applies to both software as well as hardware. The function of release management process is more than just creating a new version or updating of a program. Whenever a new release is needed, there are various steps to be followed. Figure 4.13 provides overview of these steps and following discussion elaborates them:

Release Planning The first step in the release management process is the preparation of a plan, identifying the activities and the resources required to successfully deploy a release into the production environment. During any project planning activity, it is required to determine the tasks that are to be carried out, time needed to complete (i.e., timescale) and their priorities in relation to other tasks. It is often seen that programs consist of many modules which are dependent on each other. Changing one module affects the other. Hence, in order to develop an efficient system, these dependencies should also be known in advance. Once these issues are fully understood and dependencies are known, Release manager can draw a detailed plan of activities and assign appropriate resources to the project.

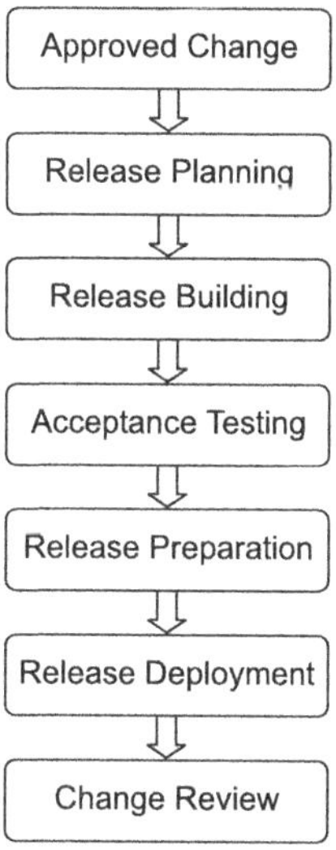

Fig. 4.13 *Release management process flow (Source: MOF)*

Release Building After obtaining the requirements, dependencies and planning, the building process of the new release can begin. The first step of release building process is to design the new release. Design can be carried out with the help of various software development techniques such as UML, etc. Once the design is ready, it can be converted into a program using a suitable programming language such as C, C#, C++, Java etc. The pieces of developed code, classes, etc. are combined together, compiled into working subsections and finally put together in the form of a working program.

It is always advisable to develop standard procedures for designing, building and configuring releases. A release may be based on sets of components developed in-house or purchased from third parties and then configured. Instructions for installation and configuration releases should also be treated as a part of the release under the control of change management and configuration management. It is also advisable to set up and test all hardware and software in a 'laboratory' before installing it on site.

Back-out Plan A back-out plan at the level of the entire release defines the activities required to recover the service if something goes wrong with the release. Change management is responsible for ensuring that back-out plans are created whereas release management should help in ensuring that the back-out plans are practical.

Acceptance Testing The most common cause of unsatisfactory changes and releases is inadequate testing. To prevent this kind of situation, before actual implementation, a release should go through a functional test by representatives of the users and an operational test by IT Management personnel who consider the technical operation, functions, performance and integration with the rest of the infrastructure. The release should be reviewed to verify whether it works correctly and lives up to the requirements and dependencies. The tests should also include the detailed installation scripts, proper back-out procedures and any change in the management procedures. During the time of the test, the entire process is documented to serve as a future knowledge base. The purpose of acceptance testing is the following:

- It is responsible for performing the key functionality user acceptance tests aligned to the requirements of the change and release to ensure confidence in the release.

- It evaluates testing results of acceptance to make a confident decision to move toward release preparation.

Release Preparation After getting a correct and verified release, it is prepared for release to the production environment. For this, the release is packaged as a final product to be sent to customers. Packaging is supported by procedures, records, and accompanying documents (such as packing slips) so that it can provide reliable information to configuration management. Software release can be made internet downloadable or packaged in a CD. It is advisable to use automated tools for software distribution and installation where ever it is possible. This can reduce the time required for distribution and improve the quality while requiring fewer resources. These tools often help in verification of a successful installation.

Before undertaking any installation, it is advisable to check the environment to ensure the release can fulfill the conditions such as sufficient disk space, security, environmental controls or limitations such as air conditioning, floor space, power backup, etc. After installation, the information in the CMDB should be updated to facilitate verification of any license agreements. A final step is to verify the package against the requirements, resulting in audit reports. This is a last verification before the entire package is released.

Release Deployment The deployment of a release consists of two aspects—getting the release version to the customer and then implementing it. In a production environment, the process of deployment depends on the type and the nature of the release. The selected release mechanism also affects the deployment. However, in all the cases, in order to facilitate the deployment, release manager should be provided with the status reports and also the tools and technologies that can enable tracking and monitoring the progress of deployment, wherever it is appropriate.

As changes are made to IT components during deployment, corresponding changes must reflect in the configuration items and their interrelationship in the CMDB. After the deployment of the release, the release manager should confirm that it is working perfectly before proceeding for further deployments.

4.5.2 Advantages of Release Management

Together with effective configuration management and change management, release management helps to ensure the following:

Minimised Errors and Risks The risk of errors in software and hardware combination or release of an incorrect version is minimised. The risk of incidents and the occurrence of known errors can be reduced by testing and controlling implementation. Testing before rollout minimises incidents affecting users and requires less reactive support.

Involvement of Users in Testing Release management ensures the involvement of users during the testing of a release. This helps in providing a better release to users since it assists the developers in testing the release as per users' requirement.

Ensures High Quality of Releases Software and hardware in live use are of high quality because they are developed and tested under quality control before being released. Release management also provides a structured approach for rolling out all new software or hardware which is efficient and effective.

Puts Checks on Illegal Software Usage The risk of illegal software is reduced as well as the risk of incidents and problems due to introduction of the wrong or infected software or hardware versions into the live environment. Unauthorised copies and incorrect versions are more easily detected.

Helps in Better Planning Release management provides an opportunity to plan expenditure and resource requirements in advance.

Helps in Tracking Changes Changes in software are bundled together for one release. This minimises the impact of changes on users.

4.5.3 Cost of Release Management

Release management is an important part of service support process. Its implementation costs includes following main components:

Personnel Costs This is the cost incurred for the staff used in the implementation of release management.

Storage Cost Storage cost includes cost for the DSL (Definitive Software Library) and DHS (Definitive Hardware Store), building and testing and distribution environments.

Tools Cost It includes the cost of software tools and required hardware.

4.5.4 Relationship with Other Processes

Release management is closely related to service level, change- and configuration-management. Figure 4.14 provides an overview of these relationships. More details are as follows:

Service Level Management It provides the infrastructure hardware together with standard software developed in-house. Release management is responsible for making hardware and software available and for managing it.

Configuration Management It is responsible for recording the available software and hardware version in the CMDB as basic configuration. The software added to the DSL and hardware for the DHS is recorded in the CMDB at an agreed level of detail.

Change Management It is responsible for ensuring that there is adequate testing of the release. It decides about version changes in a release. Change management describes the procedures to ensure that changes are authorised, including the impact analysis and analysis of the required resources.

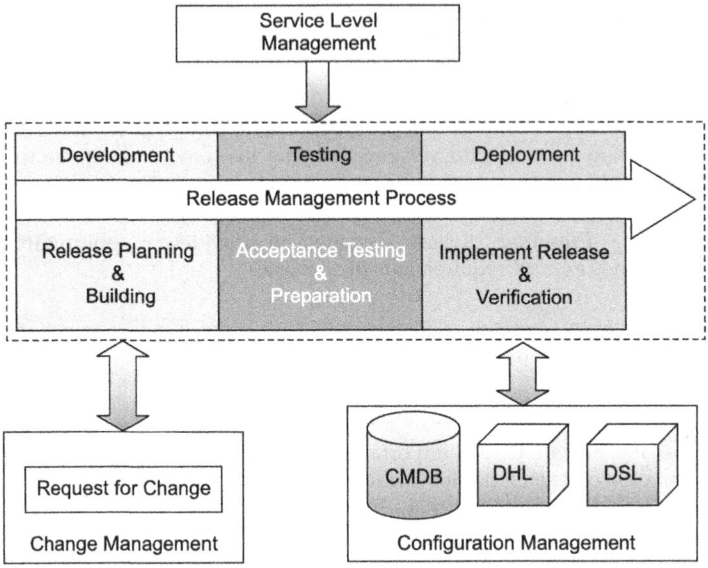

Fig. 4.14 *Relationship of release management with service level, change and configuration managements*

Review Questions

1. What is configuration management? Discuss various steps involved in configuration management process implementation.
2. Define following terms:
   (a) configuration item
   (b) attributes of configuration item
   (c) configuration manager
   (d) Configuration Management Database (CMDB)
   (e) Compact Failure Impact Analysis (CFIA).
3. What are the main functions of configuration management? How does it help in providing better services to customers?
4. What are the main problems that occur while implementing configuration management function?
5. Discuss the three important cost components which are incurred while implementing configuration management.
6. What does incident management do? Discuss various steps involved in the implementation of incident management process.
7. What is an incident? What are the various attributes associated to an incident?
8. What is the difference between incident management and problem management?

9. Enumerate and discuss the advantages of incident management.
10. What is the implementation cost of incident management?
11. Discuss the relationship of incident management with availability management, configuration management and release management
12. Discuss the differences between the following:
    (a) IT service continuity management
    (b) availability management
    (c) incident management
    (d) problem management.
13. Discuss problem management. What are the various steps involved in problem management process? Discuss them in detail.
14. Explain proactive and reactive problem management.
15. What are the advantages of problem management? How does it improve the service delivery process of an IT service management?
16. What is the difference between problem management and incident management?
17. What is the reason for separating incident management and problem management? Why can't one investigate the root causes of incidents in incident management?
18. Discuss the relationship of problem management with other service delivery and service support processes.
19. Discuss change management and various steps involved in its implementation.
20. What are the advantages of implementation of change management process in an IT organisation?
21. Explain in detail the relationship among problem management, change management and incident management.
22. Why is release management important? What are the benefits it offers to an IT organisation in providing services to its customers?
23. Discuss various processes involved in release management.
24. What are the main cost components incurred in implementation of release management?
25. Differentiate between release management and change management processes.
26. Describe the relationship of release management with service level management, change management and configuration management.
27. What are the differences in the job responsibilities of project manager and release manager?
28. There is a close relationship among change management, configuration management and release management. Justify.

Storage Management

Chapter 5

5.1 INTRODUCTION TO STORAGE

Storage or memory often refers to computer data storage. In a computer, storage is an electronic holding place for instructions and data which the computer's microprocessor can access quickly. It also refers to a computer component, computer device and recording media that retain digital data used for processing the data. Storage provides one of the major functions of the modern computer, that of information retention. There are two major types of storage, known as *primary storage* and *secondary storage*. In modern usage, primary storage (*memory*) is a form of semiconductor storage, also known as Random Access Memory (RAM). Similarly, secondary storage (*storage*) which holds data on other media like hard disk and tapes drives. It is a form of magnetic storage, also known as Read Only Memory (ROM). The major limitation of primary storage is that it is volatile, meaning that, when the power is turned off, the data in primary memory is lost forever. Hence, to store the data for longer duration, a computer requires a non-volatile storage medium. Secondary storage also refers to mass storage which is slower than primary memory but of a more permanent nature.

The basic unit of memory is *bits*. All digital computers work only on two states which is ON (1) and OFF (0). These two values are represented by two different voltages within the circuit. For example, 0 volt represents an OFF state and +5 volt represents an ON state. One such value (either 0 or 1) is called *binary digit* or *bit* and each bit can be considered a symbol for a piece of information. A digital computer represents data using the binary form. Text, numbers, pictures, audio and nearly any other form of information can be stored in the form of bits, or binary digits, each of which has a value of 1 or 0. Computers generally deal with a group of eight bits which is referred as a byte. A byte has 256 different bit patterns and represents 256 different symbols. The various units used to measure computer memory, are as follows.

Bit It is an abbreviation for binary digit and is the basic unit of memory. It is the smallest unit of information on a machine and a single bit can hold only one of two values (0 or 1).

Byte A unit of eight bits is known as a byte. Hence a byte is able to contain any binary number between 00000000 and 11111111.

Kilobyte In the decimal system, kilo stands for 1000. But in a binary system, kilo stands refers to 2^{10}. Therefore, a kilobyte is equal to 1024 bytes. It is usually represented as KB.

Megabyte It comprises 1024 kilobytes, or 1,048,576 bytes. Megabyte is the standard unit of measurement for RAM and is abbreviated as MB.

Gigabyte A gigabyte consists of 1024 megabytes (1,073,741,824 bytes). Gigabyte is the standard unit of measurement for a hard disk and is abbreviated as GB.

Terabyte Terabyte refers to 1024 gigabytes of memory. Often abbreviated as TB, terabyte memory is usually associated with super computers only.

The earlier stage of digital computers is based on the von-Neumann architecture. It is based on the stored program concept and defines a computing model having a processing unit and a memory unit. Processing unit is used to carry out execution of instructions while memory unit is used to store the data and its operating instructions. The instruction consists of a sequence of operation that is to be performed on the data. This is termed 'multipurpose computers'. They do not have to reconfigure their hardware for each new program. The design architecture of this machine looks very simple. In that case, a relatively simple processor may keep state between successive computations to build up complex procedural results. In a modern digital computer, central processing unit (CPU or simply, a processor) is a major functional unit because it takes the data as input. It performs operations on it and produces the appropriate results.

5.1.1 Storage Hierarchy

In general, almost all computers use a variety of memory types, organised in a storage hierarchy around the CPU as a trade-off between performance and cost. Generally, the lower of storage is in the hierarchy, the lesser is its bandwidth and the greater is its access latency from the CPU. Figure 5.1 shows the storage hierarchy. This traditional division of storage to primary, secondary, tertiary and off-line storage is also guided by the cost per bit.

Primary Storage It is also known as main storage or memory in which data is stored for quick access by the computer's processor. Primary storage is the only one directly accessible to the CPU. The CPU continuously reads instructions stored in the primary storage and executes them as and when required. Any data actively operated on is also stored in the primary storage in uniform manner. The term *main storage* has originated in the days of the mainframe computer to distinguish the more immediately accessible data storage from storage that required input/output operations.

On today's modern computers, especially personal computers (desktop computers) and workstations, instead of primary or main storage the term random access memory (RAM) or just memory is used. The other storage devices such as DVD, hard disk, CD and diskette are collectively called as secondary storage or auxiliary storage. There are two main components of the primary storage known as *registers* and *cache* memory. In addition there is a large capacity memory known as Random Access Memory (RAM). Registers are located inside the processor. Each register is capable of storing a word of data (often 32 or 64 bits). CPU instructs the arithmetic and logic unit to perform operations on this data (or with the help of it).

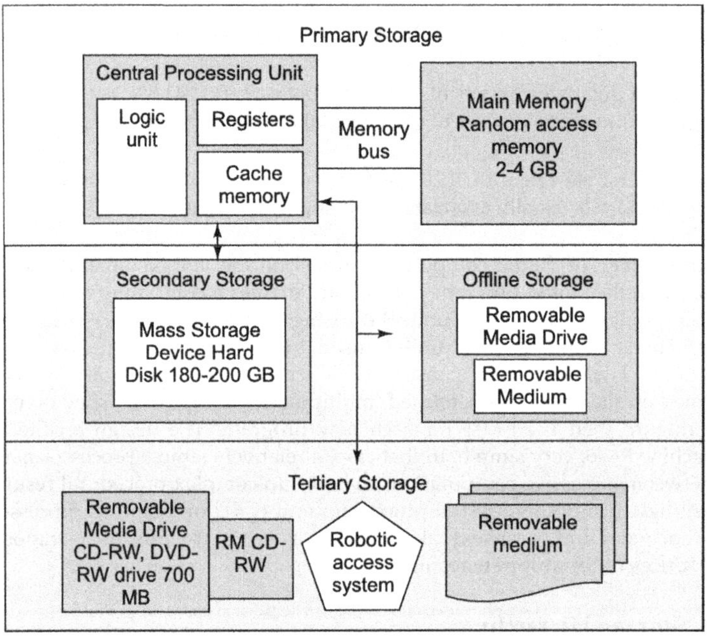

Fig. 5.1 *Memory Hierarchy*

In general, register is one of the fast components in computer data storage. The next important component is the cache memory. The cache is an intermediate stage between ultra-fast registers and slower main memory. It is introduced mainly to increase the performance of the computer. It stores the duplicate copy of the most actively used information in the main memory which is faster but is of much lesser capacity. Primary storage is sometime used to mean storage for data that is in active use in contrast to storage used for backup purposes. Multi-level hierarchical cache setup is also commonly used where *primary cache* is the smallest, fastest and located inside the processor while *secondary cache* is somewhat larger and slower. In order to boot a computer, the program has to be stored somewhere; so whenever the computer is on, it executes program to start. As RAM are volatile (cleared at start up), in nature we cannot make use of this memory. Hence, non-volatile primary storage containing a small start-up program (BIOS) is used to bootstrap the computer. A non-volatile technology used for this purpose is called ROM which is referred as read-only memory.

Secondary Storage It, sometimes called *auxiliary storage*, is all data storage that is not currently in a computer's primary storage or memory. Secondary storage is not directly accessible by the CPU. The data from the secondary storage is transferred to main memory through input/output channels. Secondary storage is non-volatile memory. It does not loose the data when the device is powered down. It is less expensive than primary storage and is usually formatted according to a file system format which explains the abstraction necessary to organise data into files and directories. It also provides additional information about the owner of a certain file, the access time, the access permissions and other information.

In a personal computer, secondary storage typically consists of storage on the hard disk and on any removable media, if present, such as a CD or DVD. Hard disks provide larger and faster secondary storage capabilities than diskettes. The time taken to access a given byte of information stored on a hard disk is typically a few seconds or milliseconds. But the time taken to access a given byte of information stored in random access memory (primary memory) is measured in microsecond or nanoseconds. This shows the significant access-time difference between solid-state memories from rotating magnetic storage devices. Hard disks are typically about a million times slower than primary memory. The optical storage devices such as DVD and CD dives have billion times slower than primary memory. Some other examples of secondary storage technologies are: paper tape, floppy disk, flash memory (e.g., USB sticks or keys), standalone RAM disks, magnetic tape, Zip drives and punch cards. Consequently modern computer systems typically have an order of magnitude more secondary storage than primary storage and data can be kept for a longer time there.

Off-line Storage Data can be stored on media separated from the server. It is also known as **removable storage** and is storage on a medium or a device that is not under the control of a processing unit. The medium is recorded, usually in a secondary storage device and then physically removed or disconnected. This storage medium must be inserted into a storage drive by a person before it can be accessed by the computer system. It is considered to be a type of off-line storage. The most common forms of offline storage are tape media and optical media. Although optical media is becoming more prevalent, tape media is the most common media. Another option is virtual optical media. Virtual optical media is to save to a virtual image which is stored on your disk units. Since the detached medium can easily be physically transported, off-line storage is used to transfer the data. Additionally, in case of a disaster, for example fire; it may destroy the original data. However, a medium which is located remotely can be probably unaffected, enabling disaster recovery. Hence the use of off-line storage may increases the data security. The reason for this may be physically inaccessibility of medium from a personal computer. Also it ensure data confidentiality or integrity cannot be affected by computer-based attack techniques.

Tertiary Storage It, also known as tertiary memory, consists of anywhere from one to several storage drives. Figure 5.2 shows the tertiary storage. It involves a robotic mechanism which can *mount* (insert) and *dismount* the removable storage according to the demand of the system. This data has been copied to secondary storage before it use. When a computer needs to fetch information from the tertiary storage, it consults a catalogue database to determine which tape or disc contains the information. Next, the computer instructs a robotic arm to fetch the medium and place it in a drive. When the computer has finished reading the information, the robotic arm returns the medium to its place in the library. A computer can access tertiary storage without being told to do so, which is not the case of off-line storage. Tertiary storages are slower access times, larger capacity, and lower cost than main storage or secondary storage. Typical examples include tape libraries and optical jukeboxes.

Fig. 5.2 *Tertiary Storage*[1]

5.1.2 Introduction to Storage Management

The goal of storage management is to define, maintain and track data and data resources in an organisational environment. The important activity of storage management is to take care of the operation and maintenance aspects of storage media. Also, it takes care the data stored on such media. It is more than just performing data backups and restoration processes in the case of a data-related incident. It also covers other important activities such as selecting and maintaining storage media, archiving and tracking the important data of the organisation.

Storage management has become a vital element of today's IT business needs. The goal of storage management is to manage the operations and maintenance of the storage media. It deals with both onsite and offsite data storage for the purpose of data restoration and historical archiving. It also maintains the physical security of archives and backups. Storage management helps in increasing business continuity and reducing the risks of data loss. It reduces the managing cost, complexity and helping to meet the strict compliance requirements.

Storage management faces a variety of ongoing challenges. Backup, recovery and constant changes that threaten application availability are some of the challenging tasks of storage management. In addition to this, maintaining interconnected networks around the clock and ensuring efficient storage management and infrastructure has become more difficult than ever before. Hence, the cost of maintaining the storage infrastructure increases continuously whereas there is not much increase in the IT budgets. Storage management consists of two main processes—(i) data backup, Restore, and recovery operations, and (ii) storage resource management. First process involves planning and implementing a backup strategy while the second process deals with storage event monitoring and media management. Figure 5.3 shows the storage management process and activities.

[1] Source: http://en.wikipedia.org/wiki/Computer_data_storage

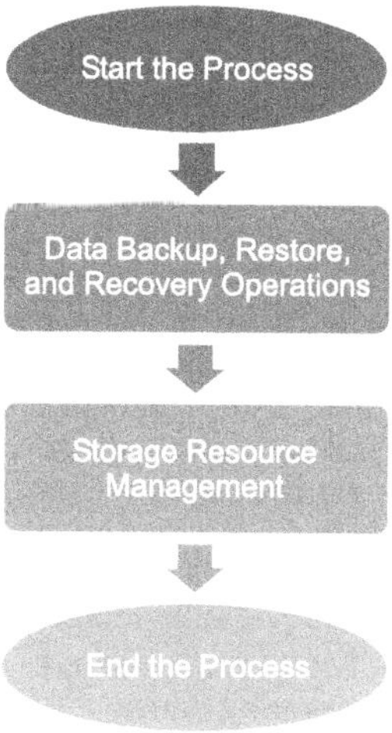

Fig. 5.3 *Storage management process and activities*

5.1.3 The Need of Storage Management

The objective of storage management is to protect the information system. In any organisations, the task of information systems is to process data into information that helps the organisation to achieve its goals. This information has been stored in the database and it becomes available in the form of files. Information has become an increasingly important asset in any organisation and it is therefore necessary to protect the information system. Storage management can mitigate risks to an organisation arising out of non-availability of data.

5.2 BACKUP AND STORAGE

Storage, backup and service recovery management cover all aspects of information storage and data restoration such as storage management, storage allocation, system back-ups and restoration, information management, database management and administration. By information management, we mean the management of information with respect to the type of information, the type of media and the location of information storage. Operational process of storage management involves the following major areas: data backup, restore, recovery operations and storage resource management. Each one of these areas contains various activities and associated tasks.

A backup is the process of periodically saving data in some other device which is different from its own hard disk. There are a number of ways to do this. One simple method is to move data from the hard disk to a secondary storage medium for potential retrieval at a later stage. Periodicity of a backup may be between a few days to a couple of months. The secondary storage medium may be hard disk, CD-ROM, magnetic tape or optical disk. There are some policies defined for backup based on the type of data. For example, in order to take back up of any personal data, the individual user is solely responsible to store and restore the same. If it is company data, then everyone is responsible for it. It is often stored on servers that are subject to scheduled backup, thereby ensuring data restore and recovery capabilities. Specific policies can be informed to users regarding their responsibilities regarding backup.

The key operations of storage management include data storing, backup, and restoring and recovering data. The backup procedures ensure that data is stored properly and are available for recovery. It also supports restoration of the backup data according to business needs. It has to define the proper backup strategy to ensure that restore, recovery and backup operations can be performed to fulfill the objectives of business requirements. Storage resource management is focused on managing the data resources. Its important activity is to check whether disks are formatted properly and installed with the appropriate file systems. It also checks for the removable storage media (for example, tapes, CDs and so on), the way that they are used, recycled, organised and eventually retired, according to business needs.

Data recovery is the process of restoring data to the state as it was earlier. In general, data recovery is performed when there is loss of data. For example, in case of some kind of disaster that has caused serious corruption or loss of data or both. Disasters may happen due to various reasons such as natural (an earthquake) or man-made (like a computer virus). A disaster can also be defined as an event that can stop the business process. For example, a hard disk crash on a production system can stop the operation of an e-Commerce system. Proper planning and execution can mitigate these circumstances.

5.2.1 Planning a Backup Strategy

As already pointed out, in any organisation, the most important task includes activities such as data recovery, backup, and restores. Businesses organisations are not ready to compromise the data, even for a minute. Therefore, the organisation should have a well-developed plan to follow—this is called a backup strategy.

It may be difficult to follow the backup strategy consistently. The reason behind this is that the backup strategy policies and technologies used may differ from one business unit to other. Hence, it is always good to develop individual strategies for various business units or user groups, depending on application usage.

The process steps of backup strategies are iterative. Each step can be performed with variations whenever there is any change in customer's Service Level Agreement (SLA). There might be other reasons such as change in business needs, restore and data recovery requirements, etc.

5.2.2 Definition of Backup Requirements

Once the classification of the data types is done, the degree of importance of each data is known. Based on this, requirements and specifications for each data can be defined in terms of the following:

What Data You Need to Backup? It defines the important data items that need to be backed-up.

How Often to Backup? Frequency and timing of the back-up can be defined. Business organisations decide the frequency of backup for each type of data needs. For example, we may want to backup users' working files daily, system data weekly and critical database transactions twice or thrice a day.

When to Schedule the Backups? Backups should be taken regularly, the schedule should be followed strictly and a determination of the allowable timeframe for backups is required. For instance, one can take backup of user files at any time when users are not working on them. But this is not the case with some databases (such as email systems and management information systems), where one can get only a few hours for backup.

How Long to Keep the Backup Data? Storing data for long times needs a lot of physical storage and it may be difficult to keep the data for forever. Hence, depending upon the importance and the requirement, a proper planning should be done for duration of retaining backup of each type of data. There should be some evaluation procedure that analyses the time and the amount of data that one has to take backup. For this purpose, some existing technologies and infrastructure could be used. In the case of offline backups, all these factors can affect users' access to data. For this reason, the proper estimation for backup time requirements should be compared to specific requirements.

5.2.3 Backup and Restore Policies

Prior to implementation of storage management, there is a need to define and agree various policies and procedures. There is an important aspect of storage management called 'storage resource management'. The key aspect of storage resource management is managing of the resources. As already stated, its important activity is to check whether disks are formatted properly and installed with the appropriate file systems. In addition, it also considers the management issues. It includes monitoring storage resources so that they meet availability, capacity and performance requirements. In a network environment, monitoring and managing the storage resource are extremely important tasks. Therefore, it is necessary that the tools and technologies used by technical staff should provide facilities like tuning, monitoring and configuring, etc. The other major tasks of storage resource management are the following:

1. It should ensure that data is stored properly so that it is available for restore and recovery operations when needed.
2. It also enables to check, for instance, whether enough storage space is available and whether it is ready and fast enough when a user needs to use it.

5.3 ARCHIVE AND RETRIEVE

Archiving refers to maintaining all the various versions of a file in a manner that is they are accessible at all times, so that it is possible to go back and retrieve the file in the state that it was on any particular date and time. Archiving is a completely separate concept to that of backup. The difference between the backup and the archiving is described below. Archiving makes it easier to deal with more complex operations and multiple files. In archiving, the individual file has to be selected to go into an archive which it is not the case with a backup. An easy way to select files for archival is the manual method. Additionally, by its very nature, archive suggests an inherent value in the data to be secured. Some areas to consider before archiving the project data are:

Multiple User Accounts The account (username) used to do the archiving is also important. On a UNIX system, only the user who archives a file is allowed to see it within the archive and he is only allowed to retrieve it. It simplifies the system operation.

Archive File Deletion This allows deletion of files archived on the server. Clearly, enough care should be taken for this task because, once a file is deleted from the server; the file cannot be retrieved later.

Local File Deletion This allows deletion of local files immediately on successful archival to the server. This is recommended for the reason of memory space management. Deletion should stop until the day following the archival process for any particular file. Moreover, it should be carried through commands of the local operating system.

Archive File Identification Whenever there is backup at the client side, the location of a file has to be identified, i.e., its directory/folder path. This is because of the fact that the archive client permits *unlimited* versions of the same file to be kept. The path structure—local directory/folder—may help in identifying the location but does not give information about the changes in versions of the same file. One of the possible solutions to this problem is to add a README or INDEX file. Each directory folder shows dates, times and listing descriptions of each file archived in that location. In addition, the description field may be used. More descriptive entries would be helpful to group and distinguish archived files.

Symbolic File Links (Unix) When we use symbolic file links in an archive operation in the UNIX, the object pointed to by the link is archived not the link data. This behavior differs from that of backup where the link data is backed up.

5.4 DISASTER RECOVERY

It is a major area of concern for most of the IT organisations and should not be equated with backups, archiving and data recovery. It refers to the process, policy and procedure related to recovery or continuation of technology infrastructure critical to an organisation after a natural or human-induced disaster. Hence, it requires extensive planning efforts in case of terrible events like fire, earthquake and destruction of a facility and/or mission-critical systems. For this reason, the plan must enclose the recovery procedure not only for data but also for all aspects of recovering IT infrastructure components. However, if the data is of less importance and not enough data, recovering all the infrastructure components may not be a good solution. This is the reason why data recovery, restore and backup procedures must be defined and followed as a part of disaster recovery plan.

The main difference between traditional backups and archival storage is the duration of storage retention. For example, traditional backups are short-term which archival storage is long-term. The other difference is that the physical location of the data in traditional backups is onsite but archival storage is offsite. Thus, the archival storage improves the recovery process at the time of disaster because the IT organisation can get its data from an offsite location. Some companies even build and maintain redundant IT sites with complete data duplication. Sometimes, an organisation takes help from third parties to provide such services in order to address their disaster recovery needs.

5.4.1 Classification of Disasters

Disaster can be classified in two categories known as **natural** disasters and **manmade** disasters. Preventing a natural disaster completely is very difficult but precautions can possibly minimise losses. It includes smog, flood, hurricane, fire and earthquake. Manmade disasters are due to human error—intentional or unintentional—which can cause loss of communication and utility. These disasters include virus, walkouts, accidents, intrusion and burglary.

5.4.2 Disaster Recovery Planning

A Disaster Recovery Plan (DRP) is sometimes referred to as a Business Process Contingency Plan (BPCP). It describes strategies of an organisation to fight against potential disasters. It is a subset of Business Continuity Planning (BCP). It has to include planning for recommencement of data, hardware, applications, communications and any other computer infrastructure. A BCP may also include planning for non-IT related aspects such as facilities, key personnel and crisis communication and reputation protection. It should refer to the Disaster Recovery Plan (DRP) for IT-related infrastructure recovery and continuity.

Since a disaster is an unexpected event or an accident that collapses the whole system, the execution of DRP minimises the effects of a disaster. A proper plan and training certainly help the organisation to either maintain or quickly resume mission-critical functions. Typically, DRP deals with an analysis of business processes and continuity needs; it also focuses on prevention of disasters.

5.4.3 Testing Disaster Recovery Plan

The Certified Information Systems Security Professional (CISSP) recognises five methods of testing the DRP. They are:

Walk-through Members of the key business units meet to trace through the steps of the plan, to find all or some omissions and inaccuracies.

Simulations The simulation session should include mimicking the response to a true emergency as closely as possible. It also includes meeting of some critical personnel to perform a 'dry run' of the emergency.

Checklist Members of the key departments check critically the tasks for which they are responsible and estimate the accuracy of the checklist. This is typically the first step toward a comprehensive test.

Parallel Testing The backup processing occurs in parallel with production services which never stop. This is a familiar process for those who have installed complex computer systems that run in parallel with the existing production system until the new system proves to be stable. An example could be the installation of a new payroll system by a company. Until the new system is ready for full cut-over, both the existing system and the new system are operated in parallel.

Full Interruption Production systems are stopped to see the performance of the backup services. They either work or they fail; in the latter case, the lesson learned can be as painful as a true disaster.

5·5 SPACE MANAGEMENT

Space management identifies and moves low-activity and inactive files to the hierarchy of storage. Storage manager for space management uses Hierarchical Storage Management (HSM) techniques to migrate—automatically and transparently—unused or infrequently accessed data files from a computer's local online storage to the offline storage managed by a server. Through this migration storage manager can help administrators and users from time-consuming manual file-pruning tasks, stretch the usability of a given amount of online storage space for a longer period and reduce the overall cost of retaining large numbers of (easily retrievable) data files for long periods.

5.5.1 Use of Hierarchical Storage Management (HSM)

HSM automates space management to achieve lifecycle management. Some other uses of Hierarchical Storage Management are listed below:

Supports Unlimited Online Data Storage Storage manager can automatically send the data files that meet user definable, policy-based migration criteria to a designated server for offline storage. After the file is migrated, a stub file replaces the original file on the client computer's online storage. The stub file retains the original file attribute information, indicating that the original file still resides on that online storage. This facilitates the automatic recall of the file from offline storage when a user or application tries to read or write the file. These space-managed files held on offline storage are an integral part of the storage manager server's functionality. Centralised lifetime management of the data files held on offline storage is a primary task of the storage manager. These files are retained and managed along with files that have been backed up or archived from other client computers. Like other backup client computers, if a space management client computer suffers a disk crash or accidental file deletion, storage manager can restore just the stub files or the entire files, to the client computer.

Data Backup Data backup and file migrations coordinate in two ways with the help of the storage manager. First, an option setting allows a migration to occur only if a data backup of that file has already been performed. Second, if a file has been previously migrated, the storage manager server can clone the migrated file and move it to the data backup storage pool as a backup copy. This technique avoids the need to first recall and then to re-send files from the client to the server.

Maintains Total File System Sizes Storage manager for space management triggers on maximum and minimum sizes of total file systems. Space management works only with file systems specified by administrator. The administrator specifies the amount of local online storage that must be filled with data before any migration occurs and the amount that should remain before they stop. When a file system crosses this maximum space-utilization threshold, the storage manager selects the files to migrate to the server, based on the include/exclude list and the priorities assigned to file size and its age.

Maintains the Stub File Sizes The administrator can also specify various stub file sizes. A larger size of stub file means the existence of more data locally on the client's storage. Generally, a portion of the complete data file remains in the stub file. Hence when some application wants to read the file, the stub file may be adequate and there is no need to recall the entire file from offline storage.

Improves Scalability Storage manager increases the scalability and processing performance over the previous version. These enhancements allow the system to handle large numbers of files and can separate the candidate search from the optimised reconciliation process that synchronises the hierarchical storage management client and the storage manager server. This can provide better scalability for large numbers of files in a Hierarchical Storage Management managed file system. This is because of the fact that the candidate search can be performed continuously in the background while the synchronisation process can be independently run or scheduled.

Pre-migration It helps in increasing the network efficiency by allowing the administrator to schedule pre-migration during the period when either the network or the client is less active. It moves a copy of the selected file to the offline storage of the server of the storage manager, leaving the entire original file on the client's online storage. The client software of space manager can then quickly and easily convert the original client copy of the file into a stub file, freeing its space when needed with no further requirement of data transfers. Storage manager supports the client/ server data backup and is managed by the same server policies and storage classes.

Benefits Storage manager can help to provide benefits such as:

- It releases administrators and users from manual file-pruning tasks which are time consuming.
- It stretches the usability of a given amount of online storage space for longer periods
- It helps to reduce the need to purchase increasing amount of online storage, as data grows
- It automatically integrates and coordinates with the storage manager for comprehensive data protection
- It helps to reduce the overall cost of retaining large number of easily retrievable data files for a longer period.

5.6 DATABASE AND APPLICATION PROTECTION

The Symantec of database and application protection has a clear goal in mind, i.e., **Simplicity** and **Availability**. It is responsible for performing online backup of databases and applications. When it comes to database and application recovery, the goal is defined well, in such a way that it simplifies the complexity of database backup while increasing availability and flexibility. It is also responsible for high-performance online backup and recovery of databases and applications. It allows consistent data protection policies to be established across the enterprise. Backup of the database includes the process of taking the backup of table space and data file level. Backup and recovery operations may be performed either locally or remotely. Organisations can centrally manage all aspects of backup and recovery for database. Database protection should provide the following facilities:

Flexible Data Protection It includes backup and recovery of databases, database related files, file groups and transaction logs.

Archiving Integrated capability enables the archiving data in XML format for long term storage.

Faster Recovery It should support faster recovery in damaged pages.

Point-in-Time Recovery It should recover the databases to the exact point in time.

Continuous Logical Log Backup The database has to configure the automated logical log backup to prevent logical logs from filling up and locking up the database server.

Parallel Backup and Restore It enables the database administrator to run more than one tape device at a time while taking backup or during restore procedure. Hence, it reduces the time required to complete the operation.

Centralised Backup Operations Centralised management dramatically reduces the cost of backing up large environments.

Parallel Backup and Recovery This permits the user to run more than one tape device at a time for backup or restore, so that the time necessary to complete the operation is reduced.

Track Backup History Detailed views of backup history simplify restore activity since backup of databases and transactions logs are easier to track.

5.6.1 Application Protection

It includes the non-disruptive mechanisms to protect exchange data along with the data in the enterprise. Every new application which is brought to online adds another degree of difficulty for data storage operation. It includes critical applications such as ERP, mail and application servers and database that must be available all the time. It helps to provide the performance and flexibility required for effective backup and recovery operations within the large exchange environments. Direct attacks against web applications through manipulation have become common place due to the relative ease. Rigorous security on the client side and an understanding of manipulation techniques are essential to identity the potential failure points of web applications. Other application attacks include exploitation of privileges, buffer overflow attack and client side manipulation. There exist several sub-categories of applications on the top of web server's operating system in which vulnerabilities may be exploited, including the following:

Web and Application Server It includes vulnerabilities for CGI, Java, Perl, default files and other resources called by applications and web servers IIS, Apache and development environments.

Website and application It includes HTML and XML applications.

Flexible Restore It works on granular recovery of databases and mailboxes, including individual message restores.

Database Application vulnerabilities for database include bugs, mis-configurations and default/blank passwords. Considering all the above mentioned applications and taking vulnerabilities into account, the application protection provides the following facilities:

Alternate Restoration Techniques It must support an alternate system or an alternate directory for backups and restoration.

Online Backup It provides non-disruptive protection of exchange database and mailbox components including incremental mailbox backup.

Centralised Backup Operations Centralised management dramatically reduces the cost of backup for large environments.

Robust Data Integrity Data protection includes all portal content including web store data, the application folder and any content sources that refer the local file system.

5·7 BARE MACHINE RECOVERY (BMR)

Bare Machine Recovery is "the ability to recover the operating system of a machine to the identical state that it was in at a given point in time". It returns the system to the state of the last backup. It also covers customising, streamlining and recovering all the changes in the operating system. Hence it eliminates the need for a skilled professional to manually reinstall hardware, network configurations and patches. BMR has become a high profile issue, being a key element of business continuity planning. The method by which servers can be recovered simply cannot be ignored. It has to document the steps that can be taken if it is necessary to recover a server or a number of servers in the event of a disaster in a data centre. Rebuilding a single server from scratch may be an option but to simultaneously rebuild such a large number of servers from scratch may not be a good idea. Either way, we should look for Bare Machine Recovery to automate this process.

5.7.1 Automated Recovery

It schedules regular backup of the operating system, so that a recovery brings back the latest information which includes operating system, service packs, patches and hardware drivers. Support is also offered for dissimilar hardware recovery with the Windows product. If a disk or RAID system fails or an irrecoverable corruption of the operating system occurs, booting can be done from the installation CD of CBMR. The previously-saved configuration data can be supplied on either floppy disk, memory stick, network share or part of the system backup. This data is used to repartition and reformat the machine's hard disks, RAID system or SAN volumes. A post-recovery command then allows the recovery of data files from the storage manager backup to proceed automatically. Bare Machine Recovery simplifies the backup process and minimises the storage and network usage. The restoration process only takes a few minutes of human intervention per client. Recovery of systems can thus be performed with confidence and minimal time and effort.

5.7.2 Other Benefits with BMR

For some reason, if the storage manager is not available or the bandwidth is too small to do large restores, then Bare Machine Recovery can still take backup to a local network share such as Network Attached Storage—either Common Internet File System (CIFS) or Network File System (NFS). This network share can then be used to do a simple, fast and reliable restore locally from the centralised backup environment. Following factors need to be considered while building the BMR software:

Speed of Recovery The ability to recover in minutes rather than in hours or days can be vital.

Complexity Difficulty in software installation and its administration should be taken into account. Complexity of the recovery process is also an important factor and it is desired that it should be fully automated.

Storage Requirements This may also be a consideration if the BMR software requires large amount of additional storage for its backup. This is particularly the case if one uses image backup which requires the copy of the whole of the boot partition.

5.8 DATA RETENTION

It defines the policies of persistent data and records management for meeting legal and business data archival requirements. Most countries are planning for compulsory data retention on the grounds that it helps in fighting against terrorism, organised crime and the maintenance of national security. Data retention policies weigh legal and privacy concerns against economics. It has to determine the archival rules, retention time, data formats and encryption. Data retention is often used to describe the forced archiving of customer's e-mail details and web browsing history by ISPs for future investigation by government organisations, based on the need. It retains important business communication and data such as the following:

Capture and Archive It helps to capture and to archive important e-mails, system event logs and databases. With rule-based solutions, it automatically categorises and captures just the data that are needed and stores the same to meet regulatory and internal retention policies. Moreover, it compresses archived data, thereby reducing the storage space required to retain large number of emails or event logs.

Search and Discovery It enables to quickly discover and retrieve evidences related to a lawsuit or internal investigation. With its extensive reporting and ad hoc search capabilities, the system can quickly identify and retrieve relevant documents in their original form.

Archive Security It provides access controls to ensure that archived data remains unaltered and is accessible by authorised personnel only. Moreover, it make a complete audit trail of all searches and administrative events.

Review Questions

1. Define the terms 'kilobyte' and 'megabyte'.
2. What is meant by memory hierarchy?
3. Define storage management.
4. What is tertiary storage? How it is different from other types of storage?
5. What is the need of storage management? Explain the process activities of storage management.
6. Define backup Mention some of the requirements for backups.
7. What are the process activities involved in backup storage?
8. Explain about backup and restore policies
9. Define the term 'archive'. Explain in detail about archive and restore.
10. Define disaster recovery. What are the different classifications of disasters?
11. Explain the activities involved in DRP (Disaster Recovery Plan). Give five different methods of testing the DRP.
12. Define space management.
13. Explain the uses of hierarchical storage management.
14. Mention the benefits of storage management.
15. What are the facilities database protection provides?
16. Explain in detail about application protection. Give some examples of application protection that you see around you.
17. Explain in detail about BMR (Bare Machine Recovery). Give some benefits of BMR.
18. Explain in detail about data retention.

Security Management

Chapter 6

6.1 INTRODUCTION

Security management prevents unauthorised access to information. It is a significant activity that controls the provision of information. For many years, security management was given less importance. However, it is being given more importance nowadays. In forthcoming years, security will be considered to be one of the important activities. Because of growing use of the internet and e-Commerce technologies day by day, internet security has been increased. The growth of the internet has introduced tremendous changes in the business activities. More and more companies are dependent on their information system which provides all the information to their partners and suppliers. Therefore, it is important to know the type of access control and user rights to be provided. Access control is essential in order to securely access the information system. In addition to this, it is also an important factor to know the components of the company that need to be protected. The modern infrastructure facility allows the virtual connection to access the information system which means all the employees can access the information source from anywhere and anytime. Also, it allows carrying outside a part of the information system from company's secure infrastructure. This introduces the risk of intrusion and raises some important questions for business, such as different types of risk, the means to cover them and measures to be taken in the next budgeting round. The higher authorities have to undertake a thorough risk analysis in order to take the decisions. The output of this analysis should serve as an input to the system, in order to determine the security requirements.

Security can be defined as preventing unauthorised access, use or modification of the information system. It also means protection of information and system. A threat is a type of action that is of harm and vulnerability refers to the level of exposure. And, in particular context, the countermeasure is the action taken to prevent the threat. Risk in terms of security can generally be characterised by the following equation:

$$\text{Risk} = \frac{\text{Threat} \times \text{Vulnerability}}{\text{Countermeasure}}$$

The countermeasure includes technical solutions, user training and awareness. It also explains clearly the defined rules. Safety means avoiding unknown risks as well as vulnerability to the known risks.

6.1.1 Goals of Security

Security generally tries to ensure that, in an organisation the usage of material and software is only for their intended purposes. It generally is comprised of following five major goals. Figure 6.1 shows an overview of these goals.

Fig. 6.1 *Goals of security*

Integrity It ensures that the information cannot be modified in unexpected ways.

Confidentiality It ensures that the system protects the information from unauthorised users.

Availability It ensures the continuity in providing the information and accessibility at any agreed time.

Non-repudiation It ensures that all the operations and activities cannot be denied.

Authentication It ensures that only authorised individuals have access to the resources.

Following discussion provides detailed insight about the above–mentioned five security goals:

Integrity Data integration helps us to determine whether data has been changed during transmission (accidentally or intentionally). It ensures that the data cannot be modified without authorisation. When an employee accidently or intentionally deletes data or any important files, it violates the rule.

For example, a violation occurs if the employee is able to modify his own salary in a payroll system, when an unauthorised person purposefully destroys a web page or web site, in an online poll when someone is able to poll for a very large number of votes, etc. Integrity could be violated in many ways without intent. In a simple case, a data entry operator, while entering the details, could mistype the data. If any process in an automated system is not correctly written and tested, during bulk updates on a larger scale, it may happen that the incorrect alteration of data may compromise the integrity of the data. Security professionals are engaged in the task of finding ways to-prevent the errors of integrity.

Confidentiality It protects the information from unauthorised users. In case of credit card transaction through internet, there is a need to provide the credit card number. The buyer has to send the credit card number to the merchant through the internet. Then, the credit card number is transmitted to a network for further processing. During transmission, the system encrypts the card number in order to ensure confidentiality. It also restricts access to the location where it is stored in the database, such as log files, backup and so on. A violation of confidentiality has occurred if any unauthorised party attempts to obtain the card number in any way. There could be a number of ways in which confidentiality can be violated. If someone looks at your computer screen displaying confidential data, it violates the confidentiality. Again, if any caller, who is not an authorised person, has some confidential information, then sending out this information by him through a media such as telephone, is a violation of confidentiality. Confidentiality is an important factor to be considered for maintaining the privacy of the people whose personal information is kept in the system.

Availability The information system must be available at any time in order to serve its purpose. This means, it guarantees the proper operation of the information system. The security system is used to protect the computing systems such as storage, processing system and communication system, from various attacks. The system should provide high-availability, meaning that the services should always be available and that service disruption due to hardware failure, any upgradation in the system and power failure should be prevented. It is also prevents the denial-of-service attacks.

Non-repudiation It gives guarantee that the operations and activities involved in the transaction processing cannot be denied. This means that none of the parties involved in the transaction processing can deny an operation performed by him, at a later date. One cannot deny having received any transaction nor can the other deny making any transaction, in the entire transaction processing. To establish non-repudiation, electronic commerce system uses digital signature and encryption technology during transaction processing.

Authentication and Authorisation Authentication is an act to verify a claim of identity, to ensure that only an authorised individual has the access to the system resources. There are three ways to use the information for authentication—something you are, something you have and something you know. Examples of 'something you are' consist of a person's fingerprint and palm print (also referred to as biometrics characteristics). Examples of 'something you have' include an identity card or a magnetic swipe card. Examples of 'something you know' include items such as password and Personal Identification Number (PIN). After the success of person identification and authentication through program or computer, the user's access control needs to be determined. Access control means up to what extent the user is permitted to access and what actions are allowed to be performed (create, delete, modify or view). This process is called authorisation.

6.2 COMPUTER SECURITY

It refers to protection of a computer and the information stored in it, from the unauthorised users. It also includes the policies, procedures, hardware and software tools that are necessary to protect the computers and the information processed, stored and transmitted by the systems. It refers to the measurement of confidentiality, integrity and availability of the information, by a computer. These aspects are responsible for effective computer security.

6.2.1 Security Threats

Computer systems are vulnerable to many kinds of threats that can cause various types of damages which may result in significant data loss. This can range from errors that can cause integrity violation of the database to a natural calamity which can completely destroy entire computer centres. Some threats affect the confidentiality or integrity of the data, while the others affect the availability of the system itself. A threat can occur from many ways—it can arise from intentional modification of sensitive information or an accidental error or an act of natural disaster (flood, storm, fire). Some of the commonly occurring threats are discussed below. Figure 6.2 shows their overview.

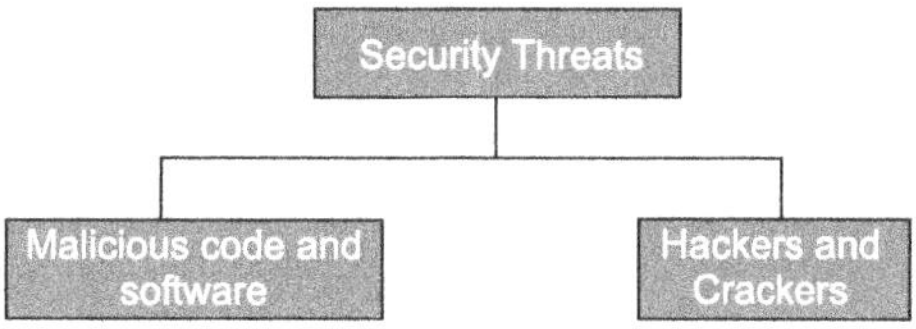

Fig. 6.2 *Security threats*

Malicious Code and Software Malicious code is a software program that generates threats to the computers and data stored on it. This code can be in the form of worms, logic bombs, viruses, Trojan horses and other types of software. Virus is a small segment code which replicates by attaching copies of itself to the exiting executables files. When a user executes the new host program, a new copy of the virus is executed. Worm is a self-replicating program which is self-contained and does not require a host program. In order to propagate to other host systems, worms commonly utilise network services. Trojan horse is a program that performs a desired talk but also includes unexpected tasks. Most organisations and institutes use antivirus software and other protective measures, to limit the risk of virus infection.

Hacker and Cracker A hacker is a person who breaks into computers without authorisation. Hackers are actively involved in computer security and are non-professionals or programmers without formal training. The threat generated from a hacker should be considered in terms of the past and potential future damage. Another class of people, called a cracker, also poses security threat. Cracker is an individual who attempts to access computer systems without authorisation.

Cracking refers to modification of software to remove protection methods including serial number, copy protection, trial/demo version, hardware key, date checks, etc.

6.2.2 Malicious Program

Any computer program or code that is designed to do harm, can be termed a malicious program. It does this by destroying, consuming valuable resources, exposing, creating or installing vulnerabilities in a computer system. These malicious programs are often called virus, worms, Trojan horse, logic bomb, spyware and so on (Fig. 6.3).

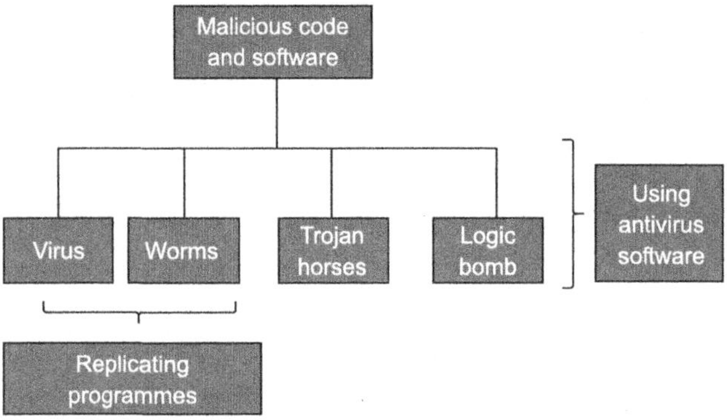

Fig. 6.3 *Various malicious code and software*

Virus It is a computer program that can copy itself and infect a computer without the permission or knowledge of the owner. It executes when an infected program is executed. On MS-DOS system, these files usually have the extensions .EXE, .COM or .BAT. Virus attaches into the program from an external software source and easily hides in healthy software. They become destructive as soon as they enter a system or they wait until activated by a trigger. Virus has the ability to infect different parts of the computer system. There are different types of viruses and some of them are mentioned here. **Boot sector virus** infects the Master Boot Record (MBR), boot sector on hard disks, floppy disks as well as other bootable media, such as CD's and DVD's, on a computer system. This type of virus first moves or overwrites the original boot code with the infected one and then moves the original boot sector information to another sector on the disk. It then marks that sector as a bad spot on the disk. Once the infected boot code successfully boots, this type of virus stays in the memory. It infects floppies and other media, when they are written to by any infected computer. This type of virus is very difficult to detect since the boot sector is the first program that is loaded when a computer starts. In effect, the virus takes full control of the infected computer. Another type of computer virus is **File infecting virus** which infects executable files on a system. This type of virus usually resides inside the memory and infects most of the executable files on a system. The virus replicates by attaching a copy of itself to an uninfected executable program. It then modifies the host program and subsequently, when the program is executed, it executes simultaneously. This type of virus targets a large range of operating systems such as UNIX, DOS, Macintosh and Windows. **Polymorphic virus** is a virus that changes its signature whenever it infects a new file. Unlike other virus, it consists of a static virus program that gets copied from file to file as it propagates. Such virus is difficult to detect because each copy, whenever it generates, appears different from the other one. It uses encryption algorithm to multiply new copies of the program. For an encrypted virus to execute, it must decrypt the encrypted portion of itself.

Worms A computer worm is a self-replicating computer program designed to destroy data. Worm programs often use network connections to spread from one computer system to another system. Thus, worms attack systems that are linked through communication lines. Viruses almost always corrupt or devour files on a targeted computer while worms always cause at least some harm to the network like consuming bandwidth. To reproduce themselves, worms make use of the network medium, depending on the type of network and systems. These are:

- Remote log in capability, whereby a worm can log into a remote system as a user and then use commands to copy itself from one system to another.
- Network mail facility, in which a worm can mail a copy of itself to other systems.
- Remote execution capability, in which a worm can execute a copy of itself on another system.

Trojan Horse The term 'Trojan Horse' is from ancient Greek mythology. In the war between Greeks and Troy, the Greek army blocked the city of Troy but were unable to penetrate inside the city. Therefore, they decided to cheat their enemies by building a large wooden horse with soldiers hidden secretly inside it and by presenting it as a gift to the citizen of Troy. At night, the warriors came out from the horse and overran the city. In the context of computer terminology, Trojan describes a class of computer threats. Trojan appears to perform a desirable function but, in fact, performs undisclosed, malicious functions. These programs enter into a computer through an e-mail or free programs that are downloaded from the internet. Once they safely pass into the computer, they may lie inactive for months before they are activated or complete control of the computer is given to a hacker. It allows unauthorised access to the host machine, giving them the ability to save their files on the user's computer or even to watch the user's screen and to control the computer. It can also includes software which is downloaded free. Based on the way Trojan horses violate systems and make damages, they can be classified into seven major groups:

- Remote access Trojans
- Data sending Trojans
- Destructive Trojans
- Proxy Trojans
- FTP Trojans
- Security software disabler Trojans
- Denial-of-Service (DoS) attack Trojans

Logic Bomb This is one of the oldest types of programs and it embeds its code into legitimate programs. Like a bomb it explodes all the data when certain conditions are met. This could be either destroying or deletion of certain files on a particular day and at a particular time, and so on. The time bomb is the logic bomb that reacts based on time and date.

6.2.3 Antivirus

It is a software utility which mainly prevents and removes computer viruses, including worms and Trojan horses. It scans the hard disk for viruses and tries to remove them, if found. Such a program may also detect and remove spyware, adware and other forms of malware. There exist many varieties of strategies.

'Signatures' refer to searching for known malicious patterns in executable code. However, signatures can only be updated as new viruses are created; user can be infected during the time taken to create and distribute a signature. In order to counteract such zero-day-viruses, heuristics may be used to guess if the file is truly malicious. Generic signature is the one that searches for known malicious code and uses wild cards to identify variants of a single virus. An antivirus may also take after a program in a sandbox, monitoring for malicious behaviour. Success depends on striking a balance between false accept rate and false rejection rate. False accept rate can be as destructive as false rejection rate. One faulty virus signature, generated mistakenly, may remove essential operating system files, leaving a number of personal computers unable to boot. Most antivirus software includes an auto-update feature that enables the program to download profiles of new viruses, so that it can check for the new viruses as soon as they are discovered. The most popular antivirus software available are Norton antivirus and McAfee antivirus programs.

Antivirus software has many drawbacks. If it is of the type that scans continuously, antivirus software may cause a significant delay in performance, or it may ask users to choose an option with a decision which the users may not understand. Antivirus software generally works at the highly trusted kernel level of the operating system, creating a possibility of attacks. The effectiveness of antivirus software is a controversial issue. It has been found that the success rate of detecting viruses by major antivirus software has dropped over a one-year period. A **Virus removal tool** is a software that can remove some specific viruses from infected computers. Unlike complete antivirus scanners, it is usually not intended to detect and remove an extensive list of viruses; rather it is designed to remove specific viruses, usually more effectively than normal antivirus software. Examples of this type of software include McAfee stringer and the Microsoft windows malicious software removal tool which runs automatically by windows update.

6.2.4 Security Techniques from Hackers and Crackers

There are some techniques which are used to secure data while transmitting over the internet, to save it from hackers and crackers. Following discussion provides some of these techniques in detail. Overview of these techniques is given in Fig. 6.4.

Cryptography When the data is transmitted over the network, it passes a number of intermediate servers before it reaches the destination. This data is stored on servers for months and at any stage, it is vulnerable to interception. Therefore, the best way is the use of cryptography technique. In simple terms, cryptography is the process of altering the original messages to hide their meaning from opponents who might intercept them. Cryptography can be referred to as encryption which is the process of converting plain text into cipher text. The reverse is decryption that converts cipher text to plain text. Cryptography relies upon two basic components: an algorithm and a key.

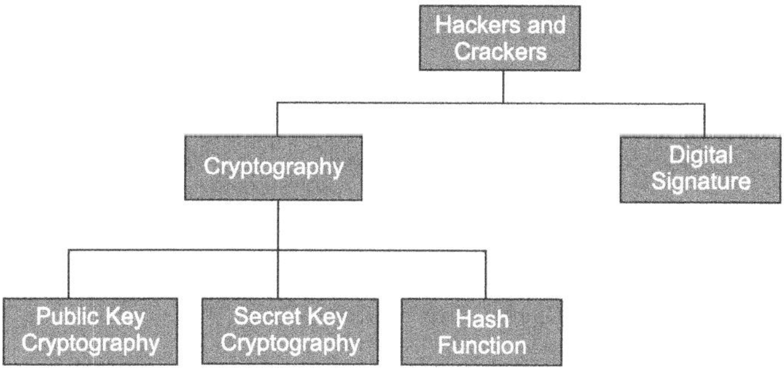

Fig. 6.4 *Different types of security from hackers and crackers*

Algorithms are complex mathematical structures and keys are strings of bits. In order to communicate over the internet, two parties must use the same algorithm and key. Communications through the internet, for example e-Commerce or e-mail may not be secure, if there is no encryption. Hackers may be able to read messages or even modify the messages, if cryptography technique is not used. There are several categories of cryptographic algorithms, all based on the number of keys that are used for encryption and decryption algorithm. Some of the algorithms are discussed here:

- Secret Key Cryptography (SKC)
- Public Key Cryptography (PKC)
- Hash Functions (HF)
- Digital Signature.

Secret Key Cryptography A single key is used in SKC for both encryption and decryption of data. In this form of cryptography the key must be known to both the sender and the receiver. If the key is compromised, the security offered by secret key cryptography is violated. SKC assumes that the two communicating parties rely upon each other and are not to disclose the key and to protect it against modification. SKC is categorised as stream ciphers and block ciphers. Stream ciphers operate on a single bit at a time with different key. On the other hand; a block cipher encrypts the data block wise. It encrypts one block at a time, using the same key. In general, a block cipher always generates the same cipher text when using the same key with the same plain text, whereas in a stream cipher, the same plain text encrypts to different cipher text when using the different keys.

Figure 6.5 shows that the sender uses the key to encrypt the plain text and sends the cipher text to the receiver. In order to decrypt the message, the receiver also applies the same key. As this scheme uses a single key for both encryption and decryption, secret key cryptography is also called symmetric cryptography. A significant disadvantage of symmetric cryptography is the key management necessary to use them securely. If the two parties are in different locations, they have to rely on a third party to provide the secret key. If anyone intercepts the key in transit, he can later read, modify and forge all messages encrypted, using the key.

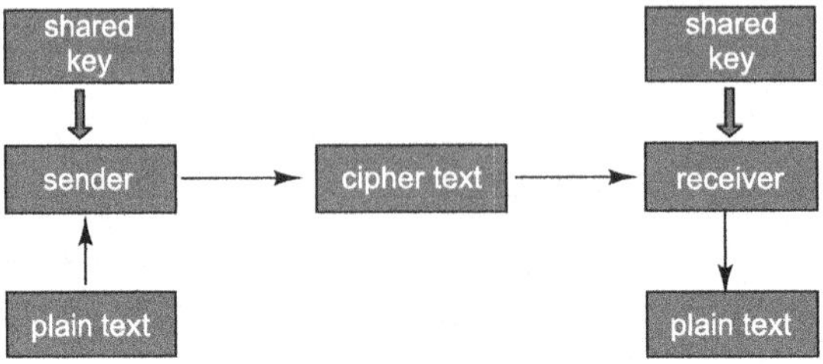

Fig. 6.5 *Secret key cryptosystem*

Public Key Cryptography This concept has been introduced to solve the problem found in secret key cryptography. Each person in this technique gets two keys known as the public and the private key. Each person's public key is publicly known and the private key is kept secret. Hence, the need for the both parties involved in communication to share secret information is eliminated. All communication takes place only with the public key and no communication uses the private key. It is therefore not necessary to trust some communication channels. Anyone can send confidential information by using the public key but the decryption can be done only with the private key which is the sole asset of the intended recipient. Public key cryptography can also be used for the authentication (digital signature) of data. The sender uses the receiver's public key to encrypt the message and, when the receiver receives the encrypted message, he uses his private key to decrypt the message. Figure 6.6 shows the process.

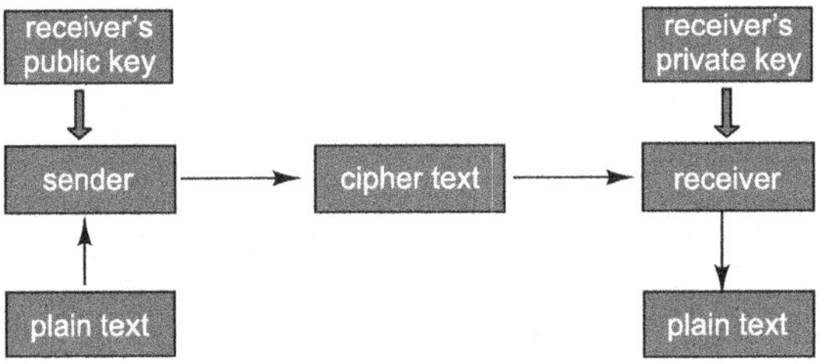

Fig. 6.6 *Public key cryptosystem*

Hash Function It is also called *message digests* and it is a one-way encryption algorithm that does not use any key to encrypt or decrypt the message. This technique generates a fixed length hash value based upon the plain text. The hash function makes it impossible to recover the contents of the plain text. It uses a digital fingerprint of a file's contents, in order to ensure that the file has not been changed by an intruder or any type of virus. It is also used by many operating systems to encrypt a password and preserve the integrity of a file. This process is shown in Fig. 6.7.

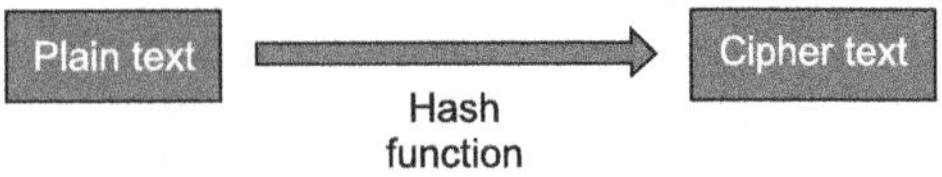

Fig. 6.7 *Hash function*

Digital Signature A digital signature is a type of asymmetric cryptography. It enables the receiver to believe that the one who has sent the message is the claimed person. In many respects, it is equivalent to traditional handwritten signature. But a digital signature is more difficult to forge than a handwritten signature since a digital signature is created and verified by cryptography, a branch of applied mathematics. It transforms the messages into cipher text and back to plain text. Digital signature uses the public key cryptography technique. It uses two different keys in an algorithm but these are mathematically related to each other. One is for digital signature creation and another key for verifying a digital signature. The owner of the digital signature cannot successfully claim that he has not signed a message. Hence, the digital signature may be used for non-repudiation.

The private key in asymmetric cryptosystem for digital signature is known only to the owner. It is used for creating a digital signature. The public key which is known to public is used for verifying the digital signature. If more than one person wants to verify the digital signature, the public key is distributed to all of them. Although the two keys are mathematically related, the asymmetric cryptosystem has been designed in such a way that it is computationally infeasible to derive the private key from the knowledge of the public key. Hence, it is impossible to discover the owner's private key and to use it to forge digital signatures. Digital signature uses hash function both for creating and verifying a digital signature. The use of digital signature involves two processes, one performed by the signer (i.e., digital signature creation) and the other by the receiver, to verify the signature (i.e., digital signature verification). Figures 6.8 and 6.9 shows the major process.

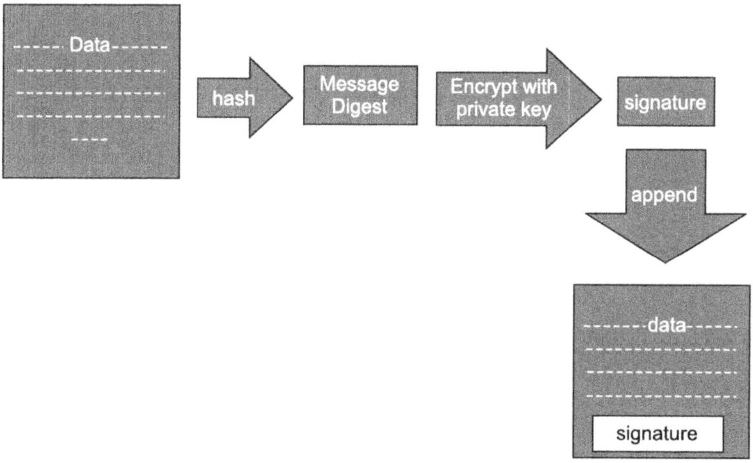

Fig. 6.8 *Block diagram of digital signature creation*

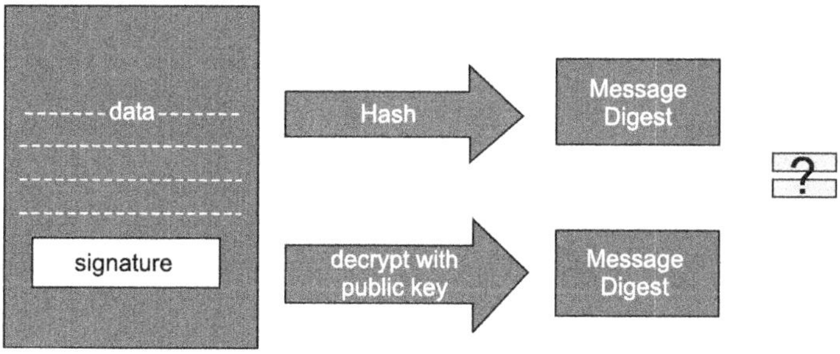

Fig. 6.9 *Block diagram of digital signature verification*

- **Digital signature creation:** It uses a hash function to both the given message and a private key to create a digital signature.
- **Digital signature verification:** A signature verifying algorithm authenticates a message with the help of the public key and the digital signature.

CAPTCHA It is a computer program that can tell whether its user is a human or a computer. It is acronym for "**C**ompletely **A**utomated **P**ublic **T**uring test to tell **C**omputers and **H**umans **A**part". In modern computers, a robot or an automated program generates undesired information in the web pages and websites. Automated programs are written to generate the spam. In order to prevent abuse generated from robot or any other programs, CAPTCHAs are used. It uses the simple concept that the computer programs are not intelligent. It cannot read distorted images or text as well as human can. Hence, a robot or any automated program cannot navigate websites protected by CAPTCHAs. Most of us have probably seen the CAPTCHAs at the time of filling web registration forms. It displays colourful images with distorted text at the bottom of web pages.

A **CAPTCHA** (or **Captcha**) is a type of test in computing to make sure that the response is not generated by a computer. A CAPTCHA is a program that generates images that human can understand but a program cannot. It uses these images as the test images and grades them to verify whether the user is a human or a computer. For example, a human can read distorted text as shown in Fig. 6.10 but current computer programs cannot.

Fig. 6.10 *An example of CAPTCHA*[1]

A common type of CAPTCHA requires that the user types the letters or digits from a distorted image that appear on the screen. This process involves one server which asks the user to complete a simple test which is able to take a decision. Any user entering a correct solution is assumed to be human. This looks like a reverse Turing test in contrast to the standard Turing test. Standard Turing test is typically administered by a human and targeted to a machine whereas the reverse Turing test is administered by a machine and targeted to a human. The following are the various applications of CAPTCHA:

Website Registration Protecting website registration is one of the most important applications of CAPTCHA. Most of the server machines which offer free email

[1] Image source: ReCAPTCHA.

services suffered from specific type of attacks. One of the most important attacks is the automatic sign up. These are the automated computer programs which would sign up for thousands of emails every minute. One of the solutions is the use of the CAPTCHA to make sure that only humans are the users and not computer programs.

Preventing Spam Comment spam is an automated program that submits bogus comments for the purpose of raising the search engine ranks of some website. The solution to avoid this type of problem is to make use of CAPTCHA. If we can avoid the user sign up methodology for entering comments, it may help in avoiding bogus comments. It also makes sure that only humans are the users.

E-mail Worms and Spam CAPTCHA can be used to prevent email worms and spam. CAPTCHA is used because it accepts the emails only if it knows that humans are the composers. Otherwise, it simply ignores those mails.

Dictionary Attacks In password system, use of CAPCHA prevents dictionary attacks. If the **CAPTCHA** is not successful after a certain number, then a computer is prevented from being able to sign up, by assuming that the user is not a human but some automated program attempting to login.

Search Engine Robots It can enter into a web page and perform abusive actions. We do not want to allow them to access the web pages. For this purpose, there is an HTML tag which prevents search engine robots from reading web pages. However, it does not guarantee that robots cannot read a web page. But the CAPCHA is more powerful than an HTML tag to guarantee that robots will not enter a website.

Online Polls In November 1999, *http://www.slashdot.org* released an online poll, asking for about best graduate school in computer science. In order to prevent single user from voting more than once, IP addresses of voters were recorded. However, a Carnegie Mellon student wrote a program that voted for their college rapidly. As a result, the score of CMU went high. In the next day, MIT students wrote their own program and the poll became a contest between two robots. Finally, MIT finished with 21,156 votes, Carnegie Mellon with 21,032 and the remaining schools with less than 1,000 votes. Hence, the result of any online poll cannot be trusted unless it is sure that the entries are made by the human. In this case, CAPCHA's use is more recommended to avoid abuse.

6.3 INTERNET SECURITY

The internet is growing faster than any telecommunication system including the telephone system. For the intruders, the internet and the internal networks are the target to attack the systems. New internet sites, in particular, are often prime targets for malicious activity including file tampering, service distribution and tampering. Information experts and security practitioners must be aware of the risk of computer security incidents from the internet and the steps that they can take to secure public and private sites. This section discusses management and the technical concerns related to telecommunication and network security.

6.3.1 The Open System Interconnection (OSI) Reference Model

OSI reference Model is a model for network communications. The International Standards Organisation (ISO) developed OSI in the early 1980s to promote interoperability of network devices. The basic structure is that it divides network architecture into seven layers, named as the Application, Presentation, Session, Transport, Network, Data-Link and Physical Layers. Therefore, it is also referred as the **OSI Seven Layer Model**. Figure 6.11 shows the seven layers and their functions.

	OSI model		
	Data unit	Layer	Function
Host Layer	Data	Application	Network process to application
		Presentation	Data representation and encryption
		Session	Inter host communication
	Segment	Transport	End-to-end connections and reliability
Media Layer	Packet	Network	Path determination and logical addressing
	Frame	Data link	Physical addressing
	Bit	Physical	Media, signal and binary transmission

Fig. 6.11 *The open system interconnection (OSI) reference model*

A layer is a collection of functions that provides services to the upper layer and receive's the services from the layer below. This is known as layered communications. Each of the layers is an instance providing service to the upper layer. Hence, it is also known as computer network protocol design. Each of the layers is briefly explained below:

Application Layer This layer is responsible for a specific application. It is also known as end-user processes. It is responsible for user authentication, identification of the partners and for providing the quality of service. This layer provides application services for file transfer, email and other network services. Telnet and FTP are applications that exist completely in the application level. It is also responsible to identify constraints in the data syntax.

Presentation Layer This layer is responsible for translating the application specific to network specific format and vice versa. Its function is to make the application layer to understand the data. Before sending the data into the network, it encrypts the data according to the standard format. Hence, it is also known as syntax layer.

Session Layer This layer is responsible for end-to-end connection. This protocol maintains this property and is known as three-way hand shaking. It is responsible for initiating, maintaining and terminating the connection. It properly maintains the session between two terminals. It is also responsible for setup, exchange of data and terminating the connection between two terminals.

Transport Layer This layer is responsible for transferring the data between two end systems or between two hosts and is also responsible for end-to-end error recovery and flow control. It ensures completion of data transfer.

Network Layer This layer takes care of the responsibilities of switching and routing technologies. In order to transfer the data, it establishes the path between two terminals. This logical path is known as a packet-switched network. The major functions of this layer are the routing and forwarding of packets between the nodes. It is also responsible for data fragmentation, congestion control and error handing.

Data Link Layer This layer receives the bits from the physical layer enclosed in the standard format known as data packets. The data link layer is divided into two sub layers: The Medium Access Control (MAC) layer and the Logical Link Control (LLC) layer. The MAC sub layer encodes the bits into a data packet and it provides permission to transmit it. The LLC controls error checking, frame synchronisation, flow control and error control.

Physical Layer This layer is responsible for converting an electrical impulse, light or radio signal into a bit stream. It converts any form of signal into a carrier signal and sends it via a physical medium such as cable, cards, etc. It provides the hardware means for sending and receiving the data. It operates at the low level of signals that only the machine can understand. It is known as binary digit (Bits).

6.3.2 Security for the OSI Model

ISO has in fact identified following security services to protect networks from attack:

Authentication Access to documents can be restricted in two ways. One of them is to use username and password. This is referred to as "user authentication" and requires creation of a file of user IDs and passwords and to define critical resources to the server.

Access Control This is referred to as restricting access based on something other than identity, called access control. It allows or denies accessing network services or resources, based on host name or address.

Logging and Monitoring These services enable the security specialist to observe system activity during and after the fact, by using monitoring and logging tools. This includes operating system logs, server records, application log errors, warning and network switch and router traffic between network segments.

Data Integrity The aim is to secure the data from accidental or malicious modification occurred during data transfer, data storage or from an operation performed on it and to preserve it for its intended use.

Non-repudiation This is to guarantee that both the sender and the receiver cannot deny their operations or activities at a later stage.

Data Confidentiality It protects data from unauthorised users. It consists of two components. The first one is content confidentiality and the second one is message flow confidentiality. The content confidentiality is the one protecting the plain text from unauthorised users. Encryption is the technique for content confidentiality. Message flow confidentiality is protecting the information from being observed or modified by some unauthorised users. Digital signature is the technique for message flow confidentiality.

6.3.3 TCP/IP Reference Model

TCP/IP is based on a four-layer reference model. As shown in the Fig. 6.12, each layer of the TCP/IP model corresponds to one or more layers of the seven-layer Open Systems Interconnection (OSI) reference model proposed by the International Standards Organisation (ISO). All protocols that belong to the TCP/IP protocol suite are located in the top three layers of this model.

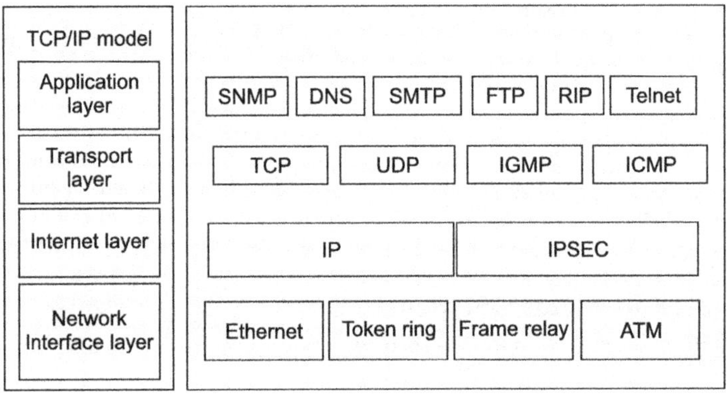

Fig. 6.12 *TCP/IP reference model*

Application Layer It defines the interface between application and transport layer. This layer is an application-specific layer. The remote login permits a user to log into a remote machine and work there. This enables the virtual connection between two terminals. In order to transfer the files from one machine to another, initially Electronic mail has been used. But later, a specialised protocol has been developed for it, known as File Transfer Protocol (FTP). The File Transfer Protocol transfers data efficiently between two terminals. Other well-known application protocols are HTTP, Telnet, TFTP, SNMP, DNS, SMTP and X Windows.

Transport Layer It is responsible to maintain the session between the host computers. The session has to be maintained completely until the two machines finish the operation. In order to create the session, this layer specifies two end-to-end protocols, known as TCP and UDP.

TCP (Transmission Control Protocol) It is also known as reliable connection-oriented protocol. It is reliable because it transmits the data without error. It maintains the connection permanently until it transmits all the data from one machine to another. It divides the data into small segments and passes them to the internet layer. The internet layer encloses the data in the form of data packets. TCP deals with flow control to make sure that a fast sender cannot overwhelm a slow receiver. At the destination, it collects the packets which are out of sequence and reassembles the data into its original form.

UDP (User Datagram Protocol) It is also known as unreliable, connection-less protocol. UDP is used in some applications where sequencing order of receiving the packet at the receiver is not required. So it may be used for client-server type request-reply queries. Also, it does not control the flow when the data is transmitting between the nodes.

Internet Layer Packet-switching network depends upon a connectionless internet work layer. The internet layer specifies an official packet format and protocol, known as internet protocol. The major goal of internet layer is to avoid congestion and to control the flow of data. Routing and switching are the essential tasks in order to avoid congestion. The function of internet layer is to insert the packets into a network in any order. The packets are known as IP datagram which contains source and destination address. This information is used to forward the datagram between hosts and across networks. At the destination, the packets are in different order from the order in which they have been sent. Based on its sequence number, it rearranges them at the destination. For this reason, it is said that TCP/IP internet layer performs the same function as that of OSI network layer. Other well-known internet protocols are IP, ICMP, ARP, and RARP.

Network Interface Layer This protocol varies from host to host and network to network. This layer is similar to the physical layer in the TCP/IP model. It transforms the signal into bits and transmits the bits through a physical medium such as coaxial cable, optical fiber or twisted-pair copper wire. The other well known network interfaces are Ethernet, Token Ring, FDDI, X.25, Frame Relay, RS-232 and v.35.

6.3.4 Security for the TCP/IP Model

The following are the security devices and the techniques used for protecting TCP/IP five layer architecture models:

Routers A router is a network traffic management device designed to forward the packets. It consists of hardware (hubs) and software (routing table) to implement the task of forwarding the packets. Different routing algorithms play a role in delivering the packets by the shortest path. The term "layer 3 switch" is frequently used interchangeably with router. For example, on the internet, information is directed to various paths by routers. Routers sit at the intermediate node in the network, called Local Area Networks (LANs) and forward the packet to its intended destination.

Firewall Firewall in a system has been designed to prevent unauthorised access to or from a private network. It is a part of a computer system or network to block unauthorised access while permitting authorised access. Firewalls can be implemented in both hardware and software or a combination of both. The goal of a firewall is to prevent access to the network by unauthorised users. Firewall is especially designed to protect the intranet. It is a device configured to permit, deny or proxy all computer traffic between different security domains, based upon a set of rules and other criteria. All messages entering or leaving the intranet pass through the firewall. It examines each message and permits only if it meets the security criteria and denies if it does not. There exist several types of firewall techniques and the following subsection explains the techniques in detail:

Packet Filtering It is also referred to as *static* packet filtering. Packet filtering is one of the techniques for implementing security firewalls. It controls access to a network by analysing the incoming and outgoing packets. Based on the IP address of source and destination, either it halts or passes the packets into the network. Packet filtering is fairly effective and transparent to users, but it is difficult to configure. In addition, it is also vulnerable to IP spoofing. Packet filtering is the selective passing or blocking of data packets as they pass through a network interface. Packet filtering is used when inspecting packets at the time of passing through on the Layer 3 (IPv4 and IPv6) and Layer 4 (ICMP, TCP, ICMPv6 and UDP) headers. The criteria used for inspecting the packets are source and destination port, protocol and source and destination address. In packet filtering firewall, only the protocol and the address information of each packet are examined. It ignores its contents and context. This packet filtering firewall does not care about application layer on the host or local network and it does not know anything about the sources of incoming data. Accepting or rejecting the packets based on some predefined rules is called policies. Packet filtering policies may be based upon any of the following:

(a) Accepting or rejecting the packets based on the IP address

(b) Accepting or rejecting the packets according to the protocol

(c) Accepting or rejecting the packets based on the destination port

Application-level Gateway It allows the network administrator to implement stricter security policies compared to a method adopted by packet filtering routers. It can provide proxy services for some application protocols. Such application protocols include FTP (File Transfer Protocol), SMTP (Simple Mail Transfer Protocol), HTTP (Hypertext Transfer Protocol) and Telnet. These types of firewalls perform traffic monitoring on the host system and notify an operator under some defined conditions. It may also be instructed to produce sound alarms based on some events. Note that a separate proxy must be installed for each application-level service. Application-level gateways are generally regarded as the most secure type of firewall. They certainly have the most sophisticated capabilities. It not only evaluates IP addresses of the server but also looks at the data in the packets for corruption and alteration. An application gateway is normally implemented on a separate computer on the network whose primary function is to provide proxy service. With proxies, security policies can be much more powerful and flexible since the administrator makes use of the packet information to define the rules. These rules determine the way of handling packets by the gateway.

Circuit Level Gateway It is another type of firewall. All internal computers establish a 'virtual circuit' with the proxy server. It applies some security mechanism when the connection is established between the two terminals. Once the connection has been made, packets can flow between the hosts. This type of proxy server provides a controlled network connection between internal and external systems. The proxy server performs all communications with the internet. External computers only see the IP address of the proxy server and never communicate directly with the internal clients.

Proxy Server It sits between a user's application (such as a web browser) and the server, providing the application services and resources. It intercepts all messages entering and leaving the network. The proxy server effectively hides the true network addresses. It takes all requests to the proxy server to see if it can fulfil the requests itself. If not, it forwards the request to the real server. Proxy servers have two main functions to be performed, namely:

i. **Filter Requests:** Proxy servers can be used to filter requests. For example, a company might use a proxy server to prevent its employees from accessing a specific set of web sites.

ii. **Performance:** Proxy servers can drastically improve the performance for groups of users. This is because it saves the results of all requests for a certain amount of time. Consider the case where both users Ram and Shyam access the World Wide Web (WWW) through a proxy server. First user Ram requests a certain web page which we will call Page 'X'. Sometime later, the user Shyam requests the same page. Instead of forwarding the request to the Web server where Page 'X' resides (which may be a time-consuming operation), the proxy server simply returns the Page 'X' that it has already fetched for user Ram. Since the proxy server is often on the same network as the user, this is a much faster operation. The proxy server can handle hundreds or thousands of users at the same time.

6.4 PHYSICAL SECURITY

The connection between physical systems (computer hardware) and logical systems (the software that runs on it) ensures that, in order to protect logical systems, the hardware which is alive at that time must be physically secured. Controlling physical security involves protecting sites from natural and man-made physical threats. Physical security involves determining and preventing attacks for accessing resource or any valuable information that is stored in physical medium. It also gives an idea of structural design to resist various hostile acts. It deals with who has access to building, computer rooms, and the devices within them. The physical devices can protect from unauthorised contact through proper guidance, and by developing and implementing the plans.

6.4.1 Physical Security Threats

The site selection depends heavily on a list of potential physical security threats for a given location. The goal of identifying these threats is to provide assured, uninterrupted business and service, reduce the risk of physical damage to a site from natural or man-made causes, and reduce the risk of both internal and external theft. The major categories of physical security threats are:

- Weather: hurricanes, floods, fire, snow, ice, heat, cold, humidity
- Earth movement: earthquakes, mudslides
- Structural failure: building collapse
- Fire/chemical: explosions, toxic waste/gases, smoke, fire
- Energy: loss of power, radiation, magnetic wave infrastructure
- Biological: virus, bacteria, infestations of animals or insects.

6.4.2 Providing Physical Security

The field of security engineering has identified five areas that address the aforementioned types of physical security threats. These areas are:

- Educating personnel
- Administrative controls, such as site selection
- Physical controls, such as keys and locks, alarm and guards
- Technical controls, such as smart cards, audit trails, intrusion detection and biometrics
- Environmental/life safety controls.

Educating Personnel An organisation can educate its staff members on the importance of their physical security through the use of self-paced or formal instruction, security education bulletins, posters, training films and tapes or awareness data that drive home the importance of constant vigilance. Each employee must be aware of the importance of security which helps to secure their surroundings including:

- Must know the security objectives of their organisation
- Realise their own responsibilities associated with their own security
- Adhere to emergency and disaster plans
- Make others—such as their co-workers—know the equipment they use and how to use them.

Administrative Access Controls This is an important category of physical access control. It addresses the procedural application of physical controls. There exist different types of physical control devices that make a site more secure. One of the most important administrative access controls is the site selection which involves the planning for the design of the site before it is constructed. Site engineers and planners must take following important factors into considerations when deciding on the location for a construction:

Visibility of the Location The site location should be such that it does not advertise itself and attract undue attention.

Locality Consideration It includes factors such as the local ordinances and variances. It specifies the existence of crime rate of the surrounding neighbourhood, if any.

Easy Transportation System This type of system is for the delivery of goods and services and for emergency evacuation procedures, in disaster recovery plan.

Weather Consideration Probability of minimising the risk, by examining local weather patterns and the history of natural disasters and determining their risk tolerance.

Physical Security Controls This is the next category of the physical access control which includes mechanical and electronic access controls such as gates, doors, keys and combination locks. By physical security, most people understand these types of access control because these devices are the least complicated and inexpensive. Controlling locks with key is a problem with large populations and any user can easily turnover. Keys are very easy to break and become unmanageable and, as a result, it forces the adoption of electronic access control. Electronic access control easily manages large user populations. For example, rights of a user's access could allow access from 0800 hrs to 1900 hrs, Monday through Friday and valid for 90 days. Current trend introduces a programmable type of lock and key instead of using a key to open the old type of mechanical door lock. It also controls the user lifecycles like times, dates and individual access points. These electronic access controls makes use of magnetic strip, swipe card or other magnetic mechanism.

Technical Controls The next category of physical security control is the use of computer hardware and software. Some of the technical security measures are discussed here. A **Smart card**, which is similar to a regular payment (credit) card, carries a semiconductor chip with logic and non-volatile memory. Unlike a security access card, the smart card has many purposes, such as medical identification, travel ticketing identification and building access control. The card can store software on the chip itself, which detects unauthorised access and intrusions. And if the card is misplaced somewhere, it can still be possible to lock or destroy the contents of the chip to prevent unauthorised usage. **Audit trails/access logs** help organisations involved in financial settings, such as banks. It allows to trace the last transaction. Bank auditors or examiners are able to determine details of the transactions during a specified time. For example, change or modification that has occurred is studied to understand the type of irregularity, if any, and if so, to determine the procedure to rectify it. The goal of this type of security control is to detect the problem in order to prevent similar problems in future. The audit trail should contain information such as user ID, where the transaction has been made, the time and date of the transaction and the type of the transaction.

Environmental/Life Safety Controls The infrastructure required to maintain the optimum operating environment for man and machine, are power and ventilation, air conditioning (HVAC). Computer systems depend on an uninterrupted and regulated **power** supply, to assure constant voltage and current. Threats to power systems include 'noise' (such as electrical radiation in the system), decrease in voltage (when there is prolonged drop in voltage), and humidity. Computers and its peripherals are sensitive to the smallest fluctuation in temperature and humidity. When the humidity goes above 60 percent, condensation on computer parts can occur, resulting in loss of efficiency. Reliable and uninterrupted **Heating, Ventilation and Air Conditioning (HVAC)** systems are always critical environmental controls. The person who is responsible for these systems should know exact course of action in case of any failure. Routine maintenance of critical infrastructure systems should prevent any significant failure of HVAC systems.

6.5 IDENTITY MANAGEMENT

Identity management is a discipline which encompasses all tasks required to create, manage and delete user identities in computing environment. It identifies the individuals in a system and restricts their access to the system. The driver licensing system is an example of identity management. Drivers are identified by their licence numbers and the user specification is linked to the identifying number. Identity management is used in the computer system to automatise the administrative process, such as adding or removing access to specific systems, password reset for lost password followed by change of password and enforcing periodic changes of password to increase network security. Enabling the users to reset their own passwords can save significant money and resources because of the fact that large percentage of help desk calls are password related issues. Another way of thinking about identity management is to imagine an enormous blueprint of an office building. It clearly defines the rooms into which each person working in the building can enter. It also explains what kind of key each person would need to open the door to get into that room. A computer system is similar to the building and each room represents a file, database or application on that network. The employees working in the system are the users. The keys are the privileges given by the administrator to each person working on the system, such as providing access to a file, database or application. The key distribution also determines what they can do while accessing a specific file or application. Like physical security, identity management is the most essential component of information protection that an organisation uses. In the context of online access systems, identity management can be viewed as the following model:

The Pure Identity Model It deals with the creation, management and deletion of identities

The User Access (log-on) Model It allows users to register, log in and log out. For example, a smart card and its associated data are used by a customer to log on to a service.

The Service Model It deals with the system that delivers online, personalised, on-demand and role-based services to users and their devices.

Following discussion provides more insights about these models:

The Pure Identity Model A general identity model is based on some set of axiomatic principles. For example, each identity in the world is unique and distinctive. Such identities follow a specific relationship to corresponding entities in the world. This type of axiomatic model is considered as a pure identity model. This specifically means that the model is not constrained by the context in which it is applied. In general, in the world, an entity can have any number of identities and each identity may have more than one (multiple) attributes.

The User Access Model The user access model in identity management involves the user "log-on" perspective. It protects personal and business information from unauthorised access and is an integrated technology of business policies and processes that allows companies to promote themselves and to control access to the information system. It is a type of access control provided to the user when they are accessing the system resources such as online application, requesting for password or change of password, etc. In the past, organisations have given less importance to user identity control. Later, after many incidents of system attacks such as cracking and phishing, email emphasises the importance of user access control.

The Service Model With respect to the organisation, the service model deals with development of their systems to provide information services to the world. The application of service model is critical and quite important. One of the most important applications is to provide online services by each organisation. Online service includes all resources such as forms, products, equipment, address books, telephone services, internet services, desktop terminals and servers.

6.6 ACCESS CONTROL SYSTEM

Access management is a collection of mechanisms that works together to create a security architecture to protect the assets of an information system. The main goal of access management is personal accountability, to prove that someone has performed a computer activity at a specific point of time. Every business model has the need to protect the systems from any unauthorised disclosure. In order to protect the information, companies define policies that can allow an access to specific type of business or personal information. Access management is the heart of an Information Technology-based security system and is needed to meet the major goals of information security—confidentiality and integrity.

There are few terminologies that are required to understand the principle of access management. Some of these terminologies are discussed below:

Mandatory Access Control (MAC) The system which uses MAC has to decide who gains access to information, based on the concepts of subjects, objects and labels. MAC is primarily used by the military and the government. Under MAC, all the resource accessibility is controlled by the system administrator. Actually, MAC deals with the hierarchical approach in providing access to the system resources. As such, all access to resource objects is strictly controlled by the configuration set by the system administrator and the users cannot change the access control under the MAC.

- **Subjects:** The people who are granted a clearance to access an object within the information system.
- **Objects:** The elements that are being protected from the use or access within the information system.
- **Labels:** This is the mechanism that binds objects with the subjects. A subject's clearance permits access to an object based on the labelled security protection assigned to that object.

MAC assigns security labels to all the resource objects on the information system. This contains two components, known as classification and category. Under MAC control, when a user requests for a resource, the operating system checks the user's classification and categories. It then tries to compare with the properties of the object's security label. If the reference of the user matches with the MAC security label, it is then assumed that he is a valid user and the system allows him to access the resource. It is important to note that both the classification and categories must be matched.

Discretionary Access Control (DAC) The principle of discretionary access control states that the owner is the one who decides who can get an access to the system. Unlike MAC, where access to system resources is under the control of operating system and the administrator, DAC allows each user to control access to their own data. This is how the most corporate systems operate. DAC authority may be delegated to others, who then are responsible for setup of user, revocation, and changes. Most of the common operating systems such as Windows, Unix, Novell's Netware, etc. rely on DAC principles for access and operation. DAC provides a much more flexible environment than MAC but also increases the risk by providing access to restricted data. DAC is typically the default access control mechanism for most desktop operating systems.

Access Control Lists (ACL) It refers to a list or a file of users who are given the privilege of access to a system or any other resources in a network, such as database, devices and so on. The file contains information such as user ID and an associated privilege for a particular user. The privileges are typically *read, write, update, execute, delete or rename*. A system uses ACL to reduce the amount of administrative effort.

Rule-Based Access Control (RBAC) It provides access based on a set of rules defined by a system administrator. In DAC, access properties are stored in ACL associated with each resource object. Similarly in RBAC, the rule has been defined corresponding to the user. It includes details such as who has been given the permission to access the system, for how many hours and what are the privileges given to that user, etc. When a single user or a group of users tries to access a resource, the operating system checks the rules contained in the ACL for that object. One such example of rule-based access control includes assigning a certain number of hours to use the system for a particular account type. Another option may be to give permission to access the system based on user designation. Like MAC, this type of access control cannot be changed by users. All rules and access permissions are defined only by the system administrator.

Role-Based Access Control (ROBAC) Computer based access management can prescribe not only who or what process may have access to a specific system resource, but also the type of access that is permitted. The traditional form of access control systems assigns privileges based on the individual user names (like Ram and Shyam). The addition of user groups has improved the access control methods. The system administrator can now assign privileges to groups (such as development or testing group) and can add users into each of these groups. ROBAC is the next evolutionary step in the access control methods. It enables privileges to be assigned to arbitrary roles which can then be assigned to users.

In ROBAC, the access permission is defined based on the roles of the user with respect to the organisation. In general, it defines the role based on the process flow, policies and functions of the organisation. It should include input from a wide spectrum of users in an organisation. Users take the assigned roles (like manger, teller, doctor and nurse). Access rights are grouped by role name and the use of resources is strictly restricted to an individual's role. For example, within information technology solutions, the role of an administrator can include creation, insertion, deletion and modification of the privileges of all users or the role of a researcher can be limited to gathering anonymous technical information for studies to improve the whole system. The use of role based access control provides some enhancement in the system security. It also reduces the amount of administrative effort required to add or delete system users.

6.6.1 User Possessions

Some techniques developed for access control are solely based on user's requirement, based on what the user possesses, generally known as *tokens*. Such *tokens* are divided into two categories—memory tokens and smart tokens.

Memory Tokens It is meant for storing information. For data writing and reading, it requires a special reader and writer to and from the tokens. A magnetic strip card is the most common type of memory token. The surface of the magnetic strip card consists of thin stripes of magnetic material. One of the applications of memory tokens is Automatic Teller Machine (ATM) for authentication to the computer systems. However, this method also has certain limitations. The major drawbacks of the memory tokens are token loss, their manufacturing cost, user dissatisfaction, administration and the loss of PINs itself. Much efforts have been made to increase the security of memory token systems related to the protection of PINs.

Smart Tokens They are more powerful than the memory tokens because authentication usually takes place on the card. A smart card is an extension of the memory token, since it includes one or more integrated circuits into the token itself. It varies depending on the type of usage. In general, type provides stronger security than memory cards. It is another example of authentication based on user possession category. It also requires the user to provide something that only the user knows (PIN or password) for use. It can solve the problem of electronic monitoring. However, like the memory token, it also has the same problem of manufacturing cost, user dissatisfaction and administration of the system. Moreover, smart tokens are costlier than memory tokens and are more complex to handle.

6.6.2 Biometric Techniques

Traditionally, authentication is mainly performed using two kinds of techniques—possession-based and knowledge-based. These techniques are briefly described below:

Possession-based It is based on some token which the user possesses. Some common examples of possession-based tokens are keys, smart cards, etc. In this type of authentication, security is compromised if the token is lost.

Knowledge-based It is based on a token which user knows. Password and PIN are very common examples of knowledge-based tokens. In this case, user has to remember the token to confirm his or her identity. Even though it appears a better solution than the possession-based method, yet it has some limitations. In order to protect the token, some encryption algorithms have been used. Even if the best possible encrypting algorithm is used, the whole concept is based on a key[2]. If the

[2] It is used in hashing technique to convert plain text to cipher text

key is too short, it may be possible to crack it by number of attempts. But if the key is too complicated, it is difficult to remember and the common user may have to keep it written somewhere which is prone to loss or theft.

These limitations of traditional authentication systems are generally overcome by biometric-based authentication, where our own body becomes the token or key and can be used for access control. This makes the access control system more difficult to forge, due to the fact that human characteristics and habits vary significantly much from one person to another. It is evident that use of biometrics helps to improve the complexity of the access control system. Because of the reliability and robustness, biometrics has been identified as an important technique for a persons' authentication.

Biometric-based authentication system measures and analyses a person's unique characteristics (which may be physical or behavioural) and uses it for authentication. The particular characteristic which is used for authentication is called *biometric trait*. Some of the common physiological-based biometric traits include fingerprint, face, hand, iris or retina, while some common behavioural-based biometric traits are speech, signature, gait, key strokes, etc. The main advantages of biometrics over a traditional access system are:

- Biometric traits cannot be forgotten or misplaced and cannot be lost, whereas a traditional access control system which uses passwords can be forgotten and tokens are easily lost or misplaced.
- Biometric traits are relatively more difficult to forge whereas the password-based systems are easier to crack.
- The use of biometric traits in the authentication system requires only the person to be present at the time. The users need not carry any token or remember the password or PINs.

Moreover, if any access control system uses both biometric as well as passwords or tokens, it improves the security of existing systems without replacing them.

Physiological Biometrics This kind of biometric uses physical traits such as fingerprint, iris, hand, face, etc for authentication. The physical traits are measured, analysed and digitally stored. For example, a fingerprint technique uses numeric encryption of its ridges, splits, dots, valleys and minutiae points. The iris is digitally stored using an algorithm in a similar way using its visual features such as the connective tissue, cilia, contraction furrows, crypts, rings and corona. Similar steps are followed for other traits also. Some of the physiological traits are discussed here:

Face Recognition Face recognition uses facial features of a human being for authentication. Though the concept of authenticating a person using facial features looks intuitive, facial recognition—as a biometric—converts human recognition process into a computerised and automated process. Common examples of face recognition are access control, surveillance, etc. For example, if public safety authorities want to locate particular individuals such as wanted criminals, suspected terrorists and missing children, facial recognition may have the potential to help them.

Fingerprint Recognition Fingerprints are considered reliable biometric characteristics which can be used for authentication purpose. A fingerprint image consists of ridges and valleys, where ridges exhibit various kinds of discontinuities (minutiae), making a fingerprint capable of capturing the invariant and discriminatory information about an individual. Most common discontinuities which are used in fingerprint recognition are ridge bifurcation and ridge ending. Fingerprint matching process involves determining the similarity value between two fingerprint impression by comparing their ridge structure and/or the spatial distribution of the minutiae points. Fingerprint recognition is based on two basic premises, namely *Persistence* and *Individuality*. *Persistence* tells that the basic characteristics of fingerprints do not change with time while *Individuality* tells that a fingerprint is unique to an individual.

Iris Recognition Iris is a textural colored part of the eyeball surrounding the pupil. This textural pattern is considered to be unique for every individual. Iris recognition is a method of biometric authentication which uses high resolution images of the eye and exploits the uniqueness characteristic of the iris pattern for personal authentication. In iris recognition, unique iris patterns are converted into digital templates using mathematical representations. These templates are subsequently used for authentication. Performance of iris recognition is unaffected by glasses or contact lenses. Key advantages of iris recognition are its stability and small number of outliers.

Vein Recognition Like iris and fingerprint patterns, a person's vein patterns are also found to be unique. It is observed that even twins do not have identical veins and a person's vein differs between their left and right limbs. To develop a vein recognition system, an infrared camera is usually used to capture the data. To use the system, a person has to put his/her finger, palm or the back of her/his hand on or near the camera. When infrared light passes through the body part, haemoglobin present in the blood absorbs the light, leaving veins to appear black in the picture. As done in other biometric recognition systems, a reference template of the vein image is constructed, based on the shape and location of the vein structure and is used for authentication. Since veins are generally invisible through the skin, vein recognition systems are difficult to forge or tamper with. Also, a vein's shape does not change much as a person grows old. Vein recognition systems can therefore handle aging problem efficiently.

Ear Recognition Among the various physiological traits, ear has gained much attention in recent years, as it has been found to be a good and reliable biometrics for human verification and identification. Reason behind the ear biometrics gaining popularity is that ears are found to be remarkably consistent. Unlike faces, they do not change shape with different expressions or age and remain fixed at the middle of the side of the head against a predictable background. Also, ear is smaller in size and more uniform in color. As a result, it is suitable for biometric recognition. Other characteristics are that it is less invasive than iris or fingerprint recognition and is more reliable than voice recognition.

ECG (Electrocardiogram) ECG is a test which is performed to capture the electrical activity of the heart. The heart is a muscular organ which beats in rhythm to pump the blood through the body. The signals, which are responsible for heart's muscle fibres to contract, come from the sinoatrial node. It is the natural pacemaker of the heart.

ECG records the electrical impulses made while the heart is beating and is usually shown on a piece of paper. ECG trace expresses cardiac features that are unique to an individual. Figure 6.13 shows an example of ECG trace. To compute the unique features from the ECG trace, data filters are designed based upon the observed noise sources. Fiducial points are identified on the filtered data and are extracted digitally for each heartbeat. Stable features that characterize the uniqueness of an individual and used for authentication are computed from the fiducial points.

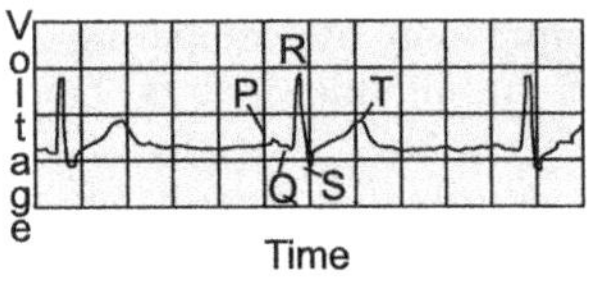

Fig. 6.13 *ECG signal*

Behavioural Biometrics It is based on behaviour of an individual. Common examples of behavioural biometrics include speech patterns, signatures, gait and keystrokes. Some of important behavioural traits are discussed below.

Signature Recognition Signature has been used for authentication for many years and all of us are familiar with the importance of signing a document. Signature recognition automates the traditional signature-based authentication process. Digital images are captured either by scanning the signature provided on a paper or by directly capturing them using a digital pad. The signature recognition system based on the first type of data acquisition is known as offline system while the system based on latter type of signature acquisition is known as online system. The unique characteristics are extracted from the signature image and are used for authentication. The advantage of online system is that they not only capture the pixel coordinates of the points but also records the signature characteristics such as amount of pressure applied in the pen stroke, time for making stroke, etc. This reduces the risks of forgery that are found in two-dimensional signatures.

Gait Recognition Gait refers to the walking style of a person, which is unique for every individual. Gait recognition exploits this information for authentication. Gait recognition is particularly very useful when no other biometric technique—such as fingerprint or face—can be used. For example, when the face is covered with a mask, face recognition fails. Gait has recently been explored as a biometric trait for variety of applications such as security, access control, gender and age discrimination, etc.

Keystroke Dynamics The way in which we type on computer keyboard vary from one person to another and is unique enough to define the identity of a person. In keystroke recognition, a person is asked to type a specific word or group of words for enrolment purpose. It is important that the same phrase should be used in both enrolment and verification phases, else the behavioural characteristics of typing may be significantly changed. The unique behavioural features measured in keystroke recognition include cumulative typing speed, time that elapses between consecutive keystrokes, time that each key is held down, the sequence utilized by the person when attempting to type an uppercase letter.

In comparison to the other biometric technologies, keystroke recognition is considered the easiest since it is easy to implement and administer. This is because of the fact that keystroke recognition only uses an existing computer and keyboard, and can be made completely a software-based solution. There is no need to install any new hardware for it.

Multi-biometrics In recent years, biometric-based authentication techniques have seen important improvements in reliability and accuracy, with some of the traits offering good performance. However, even the best biometric traits existing today face numerous problems, some of which are inherent to the technology being used. Particularly, biometric authentication systems generally face problems in enrolment due to various reasons such as non-universal biometric traits, susceptibility to spoofing, insufficient accuracy caused by noisy data acquisition, etc.

One way to solve these problems is the use of multi-biometrics which makes use of more than one biometric trait for authentication. Multi-biometric system uses multiple sensors for data acquisition, allowing the capture of multiple samples of a single biometric trait (known as multi-sample biometrics) and/or samples of multiple biometric traits (known as multi-source or multimodal biometrics). Multi-biometric approach eliminates enrolment problem and makes the system universally usable by enabling a user—who does not possess a particular biometric trait—to enrol and authenticate using other available traits.

Multi-biometric systems address the problem of non-universality by providing the facility to use the system by an alternative trait(s) in case when some biometric characteristic is not available with the user or is of poor quality. Multi-biometric systems also provide anti-spoofing measures by making it difficult for an intruder to simultaneously spoof multiple biometric traits.

6.6.3 Biometrics Applications

The primary applications of a biometric systems include governmental applications in the areas of national security, e-governance, national level cards such as voter ID, PAN, National ID, driving license, social security benefits, etc. Some of the major biometric applications are discussed here:

Authentication Systems Biometrics is integrated with large-scale systems used for various purposes such as driver licensing, surveillance, identity cards, health and benefits issuance. There are many applications where there is a requirement of unique identification, and biometric serves this go purpose well. Transactional verification has also emerged in various public and private sector environments where biometrics-based solutions are helpful.

Network Security As increasingly valuable information is made available to people via network, the danger associated with unauthorised access to sensitive data is growing larger. Protecting this information over network using a password is problematic since the password can be easily compromised. In this kind of application, biometric-based security might be a good option.

Combating Cybercrimes Though information technology's positive impacts on individuals and businesses are considerable, cybercrime continues to represent one of the greatest threats in the digital world. It is emerging as an international problem and a major concern for anyone who manages or accesses computer systems connected to the World Wide Web (WWW). Advances in biometric technology hold promise for solving this problem by offering users greater protection. Use of biometrics and smart cards has curbed the threat of cyber crime up to some extent.

Biometrics Enabled Smart Cards Biometrics offers a way for authentication while smart cards can be used for storage, processing, and/or authentication. In certain kinds of applications, these two technologies compete with each other. For example, an organisation may use smart cards based security instead of biometrics for access control or vice versa. In the current scenario, these two technologies are very often used in conjunction to strengthen each other's capabilities.

E-Commerce and Internet Biometrics has been proposed as a viable solution for e-Commerce and internet security. It ensures that only authorised persons can get access to sensitive data or are able to execute transactions. In many cases, effective e-Commerce and internet solutions can be simplified by replacing a password dialog with a biometric interface.

6.7 INTRUSION DETECTION

Intrusion Detection (ID) system tries to detect an intruder breaking into the system or an unauthorised user misusing the system resources. The IDs operate continuously on the system, working in the background and notify only when something considered suspicious or illegal is detected. An ID system collects and analyses information from various areas within a computer or a network to detect a possible security violation which includes both intrusions (outside intruders) and misuse (inside intruders). ID uses sensitivity assessment (sometimes referred to as scanning) which is a based on the technology to assess the security of a computer system or network. The goal of an ID system is to identify any malicious programs that can violate the security of a computer system. That means, it identifies malicious behaviour of the system, like unauthorised logins and access to system, resources, host-based attacks such as modifying the user privilege, application attacks and all types of malicious programs. The functions of intrusion detection are as follows:

- Monitoring and analysing both user and system activities
- Analysing system configurations and vulnerabilities
- Assessing system and file integrity
- Recognising patterns typical of attacks
- Analysing abnormal activity patterns
- Tracking user policy violations.

An ID is composed of several parts; the most important being—(i) **Sensors** to generate security alerts, (ii) a **Console** to control the sensor and to monitor events and triggers and (iii) a central **Engine** to use a system of rules to generate alerts from security events received and to list out the records events logged by the sensors in a database. The ID system follows a two-step process:

Active Component This type of mechanism is set in place to reenact known methods of attack and to record system responses.

Passive Component This type of component includes activities such as inspection of the system's configuration files and password files, to detect inadvisable settings and passwords. It also inspects the other system files to detect policy violation.

6.7.1 Types of Intrusion Detection Systems

There exist following types of intrusion detection systems. Each has a distinct approach to monitor and secure data, and has distinct advantages and disadvantages.

Host-based Intrusion Detection System It identifies intrusions by analysing system calls, application logs, file system modifications and other host activities.

Protocol-based Intrusion Detection System It monitors and analyses the communication protocol which is used in between connected devices. It sits at the front end of a server.

Hybrid Intrusion Detection System It is a combination of two or more approaches. The network information has to combine with the host agent information to form a comprehensive view of the network.

Network Intrusion Detection System It gains access to network traffic by connecting to a hub or network tap. By examining network traffic and monitoring multiple hosts, it detects the existence of any intrusions.

Application Protocol-based Intrusion Detection System It deals with the application-specific intrusions. It includes functions such as monitoring and analysing the application specific protocols. For example, in a web server, this could monitor the SQL-specific protocols which is specifically designed for the middleware/business-login, as it transacts with the database.

There are many ways to categorise intrusion detection systems, depending on the type and location of the sensors and the methodology used by the engine to generate alerts. The following are the some examples of such type of an intrusion detection system:

Misuse Detection vs. Anomaly Detection Misuse detection is a two step process. It first gathers the intrusion information. Then it analyses the information by comparing it to large databases of attacked signatures. Misuse detection system performs well in database of attacked signatures, since it uses the packet information. Essentially, the intrusion detection system looks for a specific attack that has already been documented. **In anomaly detection**, the system administrator defines the types of anomalies, such as the normal or baseline, typical packet size, state of the network's traffic load, protocol and breakdown. The anomaly detector monitors network segments to compare their current states to the normal baseline to identify the anomalies.

Network-based vs. Host-based Systems In a **network-based system**, the packet that passes through a network is analysed. Firewall is used to detect the malicious packets by defining filtering rules. In a **host-based system**, the intrusion detection system examines the activity on each individual computer or host.

Passive System vs. Reactive System In a **passive system**, the IDs identify a potential security breach and give an alert signal. It also logs the information into a log file. The reactive detection system responds to the suspicious activity by logging off a user or by reprogramming the firewall to block network traffic from the suspected malicious source.

In many simple intrusion detection systems, the implementation of all three components is combined in a single device or appliance.

Review Questions

1. Define the terms 'risk and security'. What are the major goals of security?
2. Define non-repudiation and authentication. Also mention the different types of authentication.
3. Give the difference between authorisation and authentication.
4. Discuss two important threats to computer security.
5. What do you mean by malicious code, hacker and cracker? What is the difference between hacker and cracker?
6. Describe different types of malicious codes. Are they really harmful to the computer?
7. What is a virus? How do you identify whether your system or some files are affected with the virus? How do you characterise the type of virus?
8. What is the difference between boot sector virus and file infected virus? If the system is affected with the boot sector virus, how do you recover it?
9. How are worms generated in computers? In which way does it affect the computers?
10. Explain different types of Trojan horse.
11. Describe the similarities between worms and virus. Which is more powerful in affecting the computer?
12. What do you mean by antivirus tools? Mention some of the applications of these tools.
13. Define the terms 'cryptology and cryptography'.
14. What are the two basic components of the cryptography? Discuss.
15. Explain the three different types of cryptographic algorithms.
16. Define the terms 'encryption' and 'decryption'.
17. What is cipher text? How is the cipher text represented?
18. What is the difference between secret key cryptography and public key cryptography?
19. Define 'digital signature'. Discuss two main tasks of digital signature.
20. How is digital signature related to asymmetric cryptography? Explain.

21. Explain digital signature creation and verification procedures. What is the role of hash function in digital signature?
22. How is digital signature used to verify the non-repudiation?
23. Define CAPTCHA. How are CAPTCHAs generated?
24. What is the role of CAPTCHAs in preventing in email worms and spam? Also mention some of the applications of CAPTCHAs.
25. Discuss ISO/OSI reference model. What are the main goals of ISO/OSI seven layer reference models?
26. What is the relation between OSI and TCP/IP layer architecture? Discuss.
27. What is a protocol? Mention some application layer protocols.
28. What is the difference between connection-oriented and connection-less protocols? Give some examples of these protocols.
29. What is the IP segment in internet protocol layer?
30. Explain firewall and routers. What are their usages?
31. Explain different types of firewall. Also give their advantages and disadvantages.
32. Give the difference between packet-switched and circuit-switched network.
33. Define following terms:
    (a) terms audit trial
    (b) logs
    (c) ACL
34. What are different access control systems? Explain electronic access control.
35. What is pure identity model? How is this model important in identity management?
36. Give the difference between smart token and memory token.
37. What is biometric security? How is it different from other security techniques which are based on key, password and PIN?
38. What is the difference between identification and verification biometric systems?
39. What are the limitations of knowledge-based and possession-based identification system?
40. What is the difference between physiological and behavioural biometric systems?
41. What is multimodal biometrics? What is the drawback of single model biometric system?
42. How is biometric technology used in e-Commerce and internet technologies to identify the users? Explain.
43. What is intrusion detection system? Discuss.

IT Ethics

Chapter 7

7.1 INTRODUCTION

When we are talking about Information Technology (IT), its infrastructure and management, it becomes very important to discuss the ethical aspects of IT. This chapter deals with the legal issues related to security and privacy in IT with special emphasis on intellectual property rights and privacy. This is an exciting period where the popularity of computers and availability of internet connections provides unparalleled opportunities to people to communicate and interact with each other. Although majority of the users utilise the internet as a greatly-beneficial tool for communication and education purposes, some individuals misuse the power of the internet for felonious and unlawful activities.

The harm caused due to these activities by such individuals can be reduced if we train and make ourselves aware of ethical aspect of IT and know how to use the internet securely and responsibly. Ethics defines a set of moral principles and values to provide guidelines for certain activities and acts. It is distinct from law. Laws are formal written directives that apply to everyone, interpreted by the judicial system and enforced by the police. Ethics is a broad philosophical concept that goes beyond simple right and wrong and looks towards making life better.

In the present time, our society has become an information society and we are living in the era of information. There are many ethical challenges that one faces in this age of information. There are many ethical issues which are critical in nature. Richard Mason[1] has pointed out four ethical issues in the information age. These are summarised by means of an acronym—**PAPA**:

Privacy As the technology around us increases, it creates more threat to our privacy. In this information age, people, in fact, do not clearly know what information they should reveal to others about themselves and under what

---

[1] "Four Ethical Issues of the Information Age", Management Information Systems Quarterly, Vol. 10, No. 1, March, 1986.

conditions and with what protection measures. Also, sometimes they do not have any idea about the things that they can keep to themselves and should not be forced to reveal to others.

Accuracy Internet contains plenty of information but it does not have any check on the accuracy of the information. In most of the cases, it is not known who is responsible for the authenticity, fidelity and accuracy of information. Also, sometimes it is very difficult to determine as to who should be held accountable/responsible for incorrect information.

Property It is required to know the true owner of the information and whether he has the right of intellectual property. It is unethical to copy some information without taking the permission. For example, it is not correct to download and use an image from a webpage without permission and/or acknowledging the source.

Accessibility Ethical issues of access to information are very important. It is important to know what information a person or an organisation has privilege to see or obtain and what are the conditions for which he has been allowed to see or obtain such information.

The term 'cyber ethics' refers to a code of safe, secure and responsible behaviour for the internet community and is concerned with the safe use of the internet. Acceptable behaviour on the internet is similar to that in day-to-day life. Some common examples of violation of cyber ethics are given below:

1. **Plagiarism:** It refers to copying of information from the internet and using it without proper acknowledgement or permission.
2. Sharing of the copyrighted material over internet without proper authorisation.
3. Pretending to be someone else while communicating with others over the internet.
4. Using rude or bad language in e-mails and during chatting.
5. Sharing of inflammatory material over the internet, which may lead to an unhealthy atmosphere in the society.

Practicing good cyber ethics includes knowing the risks of harmful and illegal online behaviours and getting prepared to protect ourselves and other internet users from such threats. Cyber ethics also has the role to teach young and new internet users, the various methods to be followed to use the internet safely, securely and responsibly.

7.2 INTELLECTUAL PROPERTY

The term 'intellectual property' refers to the idea that its content is the creation of the mind or the intellect. It is the legal property rights over creations of the mind. It should be noted that the term 'intellectual property' not only describes the intellectual work but also provides specific legal rights of the intellectual work. There could be many forms of intellectual properties such as patents, trademarks, trade secrets, industrial designs, plant variety protection and copyrights.

Like any other form of property, intellectual properties are also protected through laws. These laws govern the issues related to intellectual property. Under intellectual property laws, owners of an intellectual property are granted certain exclusive rights to a variety of intangible assets. The majority of intellectual property rights provide creators of original works, some economic incentive to develop and share ideas through a form of temporary monopoly. Intellectual property can be a matter of trade which means that they can be owned, endowed, sold or purchased. The major features that distinguish it from other forms are their intangibility and non-exhaustion by consumption.

Intellectual property can be divided into two categories: industrial property and copyright. Industrial property includes inventions (in the form of patents), trademarks, trade secrets, industrial designs, etc. Copyright includes artistic and literary works such as books, novels, poems, musical works, artistic works such as drawings, paintings, photographs and sculptures and architectural designs.

7.2.1 Patent

A patent is an exclusive right granted for an invention. The invention can be in the form of a product or a process that usually provides a new way of performing some task or gives a new technical solution to a problem. In order to be patentable, the invention must fulfil certain conditions. A patent provides protection for the invention to the owner of the patent. The protection is granted for a limited period, which is usually 20 years.

If an invention is patented, it cannot be commercially made, used, distributed or sold without taking agreement of the owner of the patent. The patent rights are usually enforced in a court and in most systems, the court holds the authority to stop patent violation. In the opposite manner, a legal court can also declare a patent invalid if a third party can successfully challenge it.

Patents provide encouragement to individuals by providing them recognition for their creativity and monetory rewards for their remarkable and marketable inventions. These encouragements inspire innovation, promising that the quality of human life is continuously improved.

A patent is granted by either a national patent office or by a regional office that does the work for a number of countries. For example, European Patent Office and the African Regional Intellectual Property Organisation are regional patent offices. Under regional systems, an applicant can request protection for his or her invention in one or more countries, while each country decides whether it should offer patent protection within its borders or not.

The Patent Cooperation Treaty (PCT) administered by World Intellectual Property Organisation (WIPO)[2] provides a method for the filing of a single international patent application which has the same effect as national applications filed in the designated countries. An applicant who is looking for the protection for his or her

[2] www.wipo.int/

invention may file an application and request for protection in as many signatory states as needed.

7.2.2 Trademark

A trademark is a distinctive sign which identifies certain goods or services as those produced or provided by a specific person or enterprise. Over the years these marks have evolved into today's system of trademark registration and protection. The system helps consumers to identify and purchase a product or service because its nature and quality—indicated by its unique trademark—may meet their needs.

A trademark provides protection to the owner of the mark by ensuring the exclusive right to use it to identify goods or services. The period of protection usually varies, but a trademark can be renewed endlessly for further legal time period on payment of additional fees. Trademark protection is enforced by the courts in which most systems have the right to block trademark violation.

7.2.3 Trade Secrets

Any confidential trade information which provides any company a competitive edge may be considered as a trade secret. Trade secrets usually include manufacturing methods, industrial and commercial information, sales and distribution methods, consumer profiles, advertising strategies, lists of suppliers and clients. As in case of patents and trademarks, trade secrets do not have a well-defined legal protection system. But an unauthorised use of such information by persons or company other than the holder is regarded as an unfair practice and a violation of the trade secret.

The safeguarding of the trade secret is considered as the part of the general concept of protection against unfair competition. Very often, trade secrets are protected using the specific provisions of law for the protection of confidential information.

7.2.4 International Organisations and Treaties for Intellectual Property

A United Nations agency, namely the World Intellectual Property Organisation (WIPO) administers treaties in the field of intellectual property. It is a specialised agency of the United Nations and dedicated for developing a balanced and accessible international intellectual property system which rewards creativity, stimulates innovation and contributes to economic development while safeguarding the public interest.

WIPO was established by the WIPO Convention in 1967 with a mandate from its member states to promote the protection of intellectual property throughout the world through cooperation among states and in collaboration with other international organisations. WIPO has its headquarters in Geneva, Switzerland. In India, the Department of Industrial Policy & Promotion is the nodal department of the Government of India for all matters concerning WIPO.

7·3 PRIVACY AND LAW

We come across the issue of privacy in everyday life. For example, when we go to a hospital for any treatment, we need to give our personal data and we may not like to share this data with others. Similarly, to browse the internet, we need to type our password, or to access our bank account, we have to provide the password or PIN. This information is critical and cannot be shared with others in order to avoid problems. Every institution or organisation has its own privacy rules explaining what type of information can be gathered and tracked, exactly what they plan to do or how they are likely to use the personal information and with whom the information can be shared. It is likely that, every time we do a business with any such company, we need to sign such privacy statements. For example, while opening an account in a bank, one has to sign a privacy statement or in a hospital, while taking its services, one usually signs some statements.

Privacy laws deals with the protection and preservation of the privacy rights of the people. Many government, public and private organisations collect large amount of personal information from several people and use it for a variety of purposes. The privacy law regulates and puts safeguards for the type of information which may be collected and how this information may be used.

7.3.1 Types of Privacy Laws

Privacy laws can be broadly classified into two types: General privacy laws and Specific privacy laws. General privacy laws have an overall influence on the personal data of individuals and affect the policies that control many different domains of information.

Specific privacy laws are conceived to regulate specific types of information. Some examples of specific privacy laws include financial privacy laws, health privacy laws, online privacy laws, communication privacy laws and information privacy laws.

7.3.2 General Information Privacy Practices

Information or data privacy defines the connection between the collection and the dissemination of information. Interest in information privacy exists wherever personally identifiable information is collected from a person or an organisation and is stored in digital form in the computer. Commonly, information privacy policies are concerned with the collection and use of personally identifiable information, public records, cookies, security, website disclaimer, etc.

Federal Trade Commission (FTC)[3] of United States of America provided a set of guidelines titled "Fair Information Practice Principles" in its 1998 report. These guidelines are considered to be representing widely accepted concepts concerning the fair information practices in an electronic marketplace. These are the outcome of the FTC's inquiry into the manner in which online entities collect and use personal information or data, safeguard to assure that practices are fair and provide adequate information about privacy protection. FTC has described the widely accepted and acclaimed fair information practice principles of Notice (awareness), Choice (consent), Access (participation), and Security (integrity). Consumer-oriented web sites that collect personal identifying information from or about consumers online

[3] www.ftc.gov/

would be required to agree to these four fair information practices. These core practices (principles) are described below:

Notice/Awareness The principle of notice tells that consumers should be given notice of the information practices of the entity or organisation before any personal information is collected from them. Websites which are collecting personal information would be required to provide consumers clear notice of their information practices such as:

- what information is to be collected
- how the information is collected (e.g., directly or through non-obvious means such as browser cookies)
- how the information will be used
- who are potential recipients of the information or data
- whether the provision of the requested data is voluntary or necessary
- how they provide Choice, Access, and Security to consumers
- whether they disclose the information collected to other entities
- whether other entities are collecting information through the site
- what is the nature of the data collected and the means by which it is collected
- what are the steps taken by the data collector to ensure the confidentiality, integrity and quality of the data.

Choice/Consent The principle of choice gives options to consumers regarding the way any personal identifying information collected from them can be used, particularly beyond the use for which the information has been provided (e.g., to consummate a transaction). This type of choice would include both internal secondary uses (such as marketing back to consumers, etc.) as well as external secondary uses (such as disclosing data to other entities, etc.). The two standard types of choice models are *opt-in* and *opt-out*. Opt-in requires consent from the consumer to allow the collection and/or use of information whereas opt-out requires consumer's consent to prevent the collection and/or use of such information. Website can choose the default rule when no consent is given by the customer.

Access/Participation The principle of access deals with the ability of an individual to access the data provided by him and contest for the accuracy and completeness of the data. Websites are required to offer consumers reasonable amount of access to the information that it has collected from them, including a reasonable access to review information and to correct inaccuracies or delete information.

Security/Integrity The principle of security is concerned with the security and accuracy of the data. Any entity collecting data must take reasonable measures, such as using only reputable sources of data and cross-referencing data against multiple sources, providing consumer access to data and destroying untimely data. Websites collecting data are also required to take reasonable steps to protect the security of the information that they collect from consumers.

7.3.3 International Safe Harbor Privacy Principles[4]

The Safe Harbor Principles are designed to prevent accidental disclosure or loss of the information and data. These principles are designed by keeping in mind the organisations within the European Union or United States that store customer data. These principles define a process for companies of United States of America to comply with the European Union Directive 95/46/EC on the protection of personal data. This provides companies of United States of America a choice to opt into the program as long as they are ready to bind themselves to the seven principles described in the directive. Seven safe harbor principles are as follows:

Notice An entity or organisation collecting information from consumers must inform them about the collection of information. It must also inform them regarding the purposes for which it is being collected. It should also lay down the ways that one can use to contact the organisation for any inquiries or complaints. The organisation must provide information to consumers about the type of third party with which it can share the information and the choices that the organisation offers to individuals for limiting its use and disclosure.

These notices must be provided in a very clear and candid way at the time of requesting individuals to provide personal information to the organisation or as soon as possible. The organisation should also provide notice before sharing such information with any third party for a purpose other than that for which it has been originally collected.

Choice An entity or organisation must provide individuals the ability to opt out of data collection and transfer or disclosure of personal information to a third party. This should be made very essential where the intended use of the information is incompatible with the purpose for which it has been originally collected. The organisation must provide a very clear, willingly available and affordable way to use this option. For sensitive information—such as medical information, information related to racial or ethnic origin—political opinions, religious and philosophical beliefs must be given affirmative or explicit option.

Onward Transfer An entity or organisation must disclose the consumers' personal information to a third party only when the disclosure is consistent with the principle of notice and choice. Transfer of the data to a third party should only happen when designated organisation also follows the same level of data privacy protection as is required by the relevant safe harbor principles.

Security An entity or organisation which is creating, maintaining, using or disseminating personal information, must take reasonable measures to prevent the loss of collected information. It should also assure the reliability of data and put reasonable safeguards to protect it from misuse, unauthorised access, disclosure, change and destruction.

Data Integrity An organisation must be able to assure that data is complete, accurate, current, relevant and reliable for the purpose that it has been collected. The organisation should take reasonable measures to ensure this.

---

[4] Safe Harbor Privacy Principles, issued by the U.S. Department of commerce on July, 2000.

Access An organisation should provide the right to individuals along with the ability to access their information and correct, modify or delete any portion of it, if required.

Enforcement Each organisation must set up effective policies and practices that enforce the above-stated privacy principles. A privacy protection system must include an effective mechanism for assuring compliance with the safe harbor principles.

7.4 COMPUTER FORENSICS

Computer forensics, also known as *digital forensic*, is a branch of forensic science which is used to investigate the crimes committed with computers by using the legal evidences found in computers and digital storage media. In general, the goal of computer forensics is to explain the current state of a digital artefact such as a computer system, a storage medium (e.g., hard disk, floppy, and CD and DVD disks) or an electronic document (e.g., an email message, computer documents and digital images). Digital forensics is even used to analyse sequence of packets moving over a computer network.

The goal of any computer forensic investigation is to make use of the information available in digital media and to infer the sequence of events responsible for the present situation. It starts with the probe of the available data in the computer to check out happenings in the computer and to identify people responsible for it. The investigation process starts with analysis of the ground situation and proceeds further inside of the computer's operating system.

The main task of computer forensic experts is not only to find the criminal but also to find out the evidences and to present the evidence in a manner that leads to legal action against the accused. Some examples of computer crimes are as follows:

1. Unauthorised use of computers, mainly by stealing a username and password
2. Accessing the someone else's computer via the internet
3. Releasing a malicious computer program (for example, a virus)
4. Harassment in cyberspace
5. E-mail frauds
6. Theft of company documents.

Computer forensic makes it easy to perform an organised and careful way of detecting computer-related crimes and abuse cases. Computer forensics experts are required not only to have the knowledge of software and hardware but also the knowledge regarding the ways of collecting electronic evidences and processing them.

7.4.1 Computer Forensics Branches

Computer forensics can be divided into sub categories depending upon the usage of various computing resources. Few prominent categories are discussed here:

Database Forensics It refers to the forensic study of databases. Common principles used in computer forensics can also be applied to forensic study of the databases. For example, the timestamps showing the update time of a row in a database table can be used for forensic purpose to check and verify the actions carried out by the database user. Database forensics is very helpful in handling the fraud case involving financial transactions.

The forensic study of databases requires knowledge of the standards used in databases to encode the data on the computer disk. Few brands of databases such as Oracle and SQL Server have contributed their documentation of standards to the public domain.

Network Forensics It deals with the forensic study of networks. It is used for capturing, recording and analysing of network happenings, in order to find out the security attacks.

To know the kind of data flowing in the network, data need to be monitored in real-time. There are many tools available for real-time traffic monitoring, but real-time monitoring at any stage requires significant amount of computing resources, and does not scale to networks larger than a single workgroup. It is generally more feasible to archive all traffic and analyse subsets of it whenever necessary. This process is known as network forensics.

Firewall Forensics It monitors incoming and outgoing traffic in a network. Firewall forensics helps to explain the contents of the firewall alerts and logs.

Mobile Device Forensics It refers to the methodology used to examine mobile electronic devices for the data which is critical to security investigations. Analysing the content flowing through mobile devices using mobile device forensics is difficult compared to analysing the computer data. This is because of the fact that computer has limited number of operating systems while there are countless vendors of mobile devices. To complicate the matter further, each mobile device manufacturer may have its own proprietary technology and formats.

7.4.2 Electronic Evidence Used in Computer Forensics

Electronic evidence is the data and information that is stored on or transmitted by an electronic device. This evidence can be used for crime investigation. Such evidences are acquired when data or physical items are recovered from crime scenes and stored for examination purposes. Electronic evidence possesses the following characteristics:

1. Electronic evidence is often latent in the same sense as fingerprints or DNA evidence.
2. Electronic evidence can transcend borders with ease and speed.
3. Electronic evidence is fragile and can be easily altered, damaged, or destroyed.
4. Electronic evidence is sometimes time-sensitive and gets destroyed or changes with time.

Since, electronic evidences are very sensitive and fragile in nature, they should be handled very carefully while acquiring and processing. Some precautions must be taken in the collection, preservation and examination of electronic evidence. Handling electronic evidence at the crime scene normally involves following steps:

1. Recognition and identification of the evidence at the crime scene.
2. Documentation of the evidence obtained at the crime scene.
3. Collection and preservation of the electronic evidence.
4. Packaging and transportation of the electronic evidence.

7.4.3 Collecting Electronic Evidence

Electronic evidence can be acquired from many sources such as computers, cell phones, digital cameras, hard drives, CD and DVD ROM, USB memory devices and so on. Some less commonly known sources include digital thermometers, black boxes of automobiles, RFID tags and web, etc. Most valuable information acquired in a forensic examination comes from the computer user. A proper interview with the user can provide valuable information about the system configuration, application softwares and encryption keys.

Computer evidence, like any other evidence, must be handled carefully and in a manner that preserves its evidentiary value. This does not pertain to the physical integrity of an item or device, but also to the electronic data it contains. Since most electronic information can be easily changed and moreover, once changed, it is usually difficult to detect the change which has taken place or to revert the data back to its original state, it is very important to take special measures while handling computer evidences. To keep track of the modifications in electronic evidences, a common practice is to compute the cryptographic hash of an evidence file and to store it at some other place, so that this information can be used at a later point of time to detect if any modification has been carried out. A cryptographic hash function is a deterministic function that takes an arbitrary block of data and returns a fixed-size bit string, called the (cryptographic) *hash value*. This is defined in such a way that an accidental or intentional change to the data certainly changes the hash value.

Some other specific practices that have been adopted to handle electronic evidence include the following:

1. Making the image of computer media using a write-blocking tool to ensure that no data is added to the suspected device at later point of time.
2. Establishing and maintaining the chain of custody.
3. The tools and methods which have been rigorously tested and evaluated to validate their accuracy and reliability should be used for evidence capturing and processing.
4. Preparing proper documentation of all evidences that are acquired at the crime scene.

7.5 ETHICS AND INTERNET

Internet is growing with a very of fast speed where millions of users are being added every year. Figure 7.1 shows the rapid growth of the internet. The internet and the World Wide Web (WWW) have grown rapidly from a research project into something that involves millions of people all over the world.

The internet has a number of noticeable features. It is fast and almost instantaneous. It has a worldwide reach, distributed, interactive, flexible and adaptable up to a great extent. Much of the usefulness of the internet comes from the fact that it is shared by users and service providers (and many others), in the sense that everyone depends on others and needs to support and help others. It pertains to equal rights in the sense that anyone with the necessary tools and moderate technical qualification can make himself an active participant in cyberspace, broadcast messages to the world and can ask for attention. In the present age, thinking of life without internet technology is almost impossible.

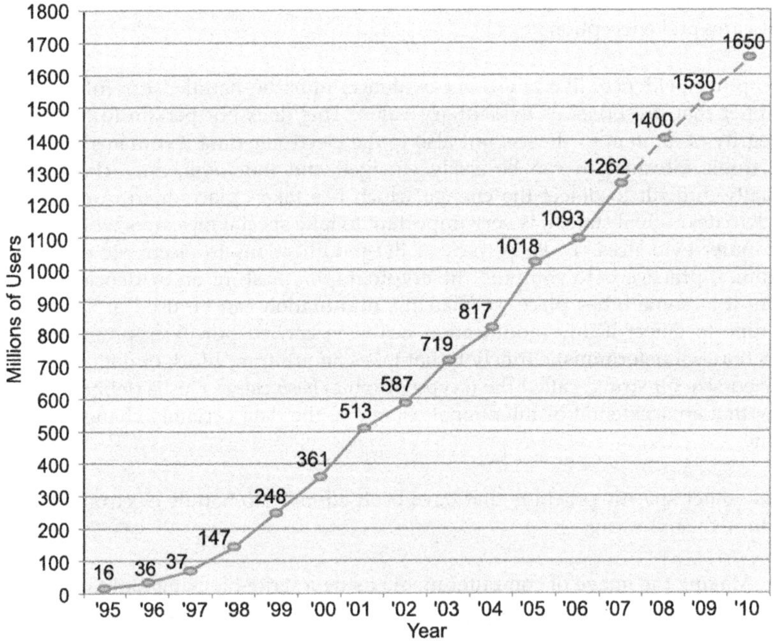

Fig. 7.1 *Internet users in the world growth (1995–2010)*[5]

Note that everything in this world has its own boundaries and limitations. Beyond a certain point, one really cannot stretch the things further any more. We have to stop and draw a margin at some point and one has to be careful not to break laws and

[5] (Source: http://www.internetworldstats.com/, January 2008)

harm others. Similarly, there are limitations on the internet too. There are certain ethics and acceptable behaviour which are expected to be followed by everyone.

The internet being a potential place for abuse of information or damage to resources from malicious use of internet and computer technology, the Internet Architecture Board (IAB)[6] has published a standard titled "Ethics and Internet" which is intended for wide distribution and acceptance from the internet-users' community. It endorses the following activities as unethical and unacceptable:

Unauthorised Access Trying to gain unauthorised access to the resources available in the internet is considered as unethical and unacceptable. Common example of such type of unethical behavior is trying to log on to some computer on the internet by stealing the password. Other instance of such acts could be hacking a web-server and changing its contents.

Interruption in the Use of Internet The act of creating interruption in the intended use of internet is considered unethical. This act can be performed by damaging the internet resources physically or by distributing malicious computer programs.

Misuse of Resources It is also considered to be unethical. Resources can be either human resource or computing resources. For example, misuse of the internet bandwidth is considered as unethical and unacceptable.

Destroying of Information and Data The act of demolishing the integrity of computer-based information is considered as unethical. Logging on to a computer on the internet and damaging its information and data or changing valuable information are the examples of such acts.

Privacy Any individual or organisation has the privilege of maintaining the privacy of data and information. Any compromise with this privacy is always unacceptable and any act of indulging with the privacy of a person or organisation is unethical.

7.5.1 Need for Internet Ethics

The internet blurs the difference between traditional categories of ethics such as *professional* and *non-professional*, *published* and *unpublished* and public and *private*. Therefore, the existing rules of ethical conduct of human beings, which depend on above categories, are difficult to extend to this new era of internet. With good and meaningful information available on the internet, there is a growing possibility of finding unauthenticated, misleading, inaccurate and, many times, dangerous information on the internet. Ethical guidelines can play a role in ensuring people to take full benefit of the internet to improve their lives, without any harm. Ethics standards and guidelines for internet are being developed and promoted by several government organisations and quasi-government agencies. Ethics makes each one of us to realise that the WWW is what we make it. We are the people who use the web, who surf the web and who upload the information on the web.

---

[6] www.iab.org/

7.5.2 Issues Involved in Internet Ethics

There are many issues involved in defining what is ethical and what is not ethical in internet. Few of the reasons for this is discussed below:

A New Tool Internet is relatively a new research tool. It provides a unique and unparalleled research environment.

Public vs. Private It is very difficult to differenciate between the private and public space in the internet.

Availability of Information It is relatively easy to check and collect data on the internet without getting any consent from the author.

No Identity Proof Internet users can easily fake their identities.

7.5.3 Ethical Issues of Internet Privacy

Use of the internet consists of the use of e-mail websites, social networking sites, organisational and institutional websites and browsing of other websites. Internet privacy refers to the control a person has over the information related to him or her and can be considered as a part of computer privacy. It provides a privilege to customers to decide what information they wish to or do not wish to disclose. In simple terms, internet privacy handles the control of access to information over the internet. Few real-life scenarios where internet privacy is of concern are listed below:

1. An example where internet privacy comes into picture is when a website asks users to provide their personal details on the internet.
2. In certain websites which provide online shopping facility, users are asked to give their credit card details, passwords and PINs.
3. Another important privacy concern is whether third parties should be allowed to track the visitors on a website or not.
4. In case of websites providing e-mail facility, there are issues such as whether third parties should be allowed to store or read e-mails without taking the consent of the customers.
5. The other important internet privacy issue is whether the websites collecting users' personal information should be allowed to store or share it.

The efficient sharing of personal identifiable data of users while protecting the private information is the real challenge in the internet. There are two major schools of thought related to internet privacy. One denies the existence of internet privacy while the other advocates the necessity of such privacy. There are growing concerns about the following issues:

- Does internet privacy confirm the privacy of every internet user?
- Does internet privacy suggest that all the information posted on the internet should remain private and confidential?

There are people who avoid using online shopping websites because they have the fear of unauthorised disclosure of their personal identifiable information. In fact, internet privacy is an important issue in the case of disclose of the users' personal identifiable information but it requires to be delimited in cases where privacy puts the internet ethics on risk.

7.6 CYBER CRIMES

Cyber crime or computer crime refers to a criminal activity where a computer or network is used as a medium, target or place for committing the crime. It can be broadly defined as a criminal activity which involves an information technology infrastructure for its execution. Some traditional crimes (such as theft, fraud, blackmail and forgery) in which computers or networks are used, also come under cyber crime. Thus, it has become very important not only to know more about cyber crimes but also to spread awareness among the common people about these crimes. This is because of the fact that in the present time almost everybody is using computers and the new generation is growing up with computers. Conventional crimes such as forgery and extortion are being committed with the help of computers and more importantly, monetory transactions are moving on the internet.

7.6.1 Cyber Crime Categories

Cyber crime is an evil having its origin in the growing dependence on computers in modern life. Certified Information Systems Security Professional (CISSP)—an independent information security certification body—governed by the International Information Systems Security Certification Consortium $(ISC)^2$ classified major cyber crimes in following categories:

Financial Attacks These are attacks targeting banks and other financial institutions for monetory benefits. These include hacking the computer systems, modifying the computer data and tapping the network for stealing the secret password or PIN information.

Business Attacks Illegal accessing of proprietary information for the benefit of one's business comes under business attacks.

Military and Intelligence Attacks This includes all illegal efforts to obtain military and intelligence information.

Terrorist Attacks Making use of computers and networks for carrying out terrorist activities comes under this category.

Grudge and Trill Attacks Grudge attacks are concerned with the act performed by an employee to take the revenge against his company for ill-treatment or for any other reason. Trill attacks, on the contrary, are not for for any revenge but just for fun. Common grudge and trill attacks include hacking the computer, changing information on computer, stealing confidential information, etc.

7.6.2 Common Cyber Crimes

Cyber crime is flourishing at a very high speed and everyday, a new type of cyber fraud is coming into picture. Some of the major-cyber crimes that have been noticed in the past are listed here:

Denial of Service Attack (DoS) It is a type of attack that is designed to bring a network or website down and stop its legitimate access, by flooding it with useless traffic. Common DoS attacks target network bandwidth or connectivity and exploit the limitations of the TCP/IP protocols. Bandwidth attacks try to flood the network with a very high amount of network traffic so that all network resources are consumed and legitimate user requests are prevented from being fulfilled. Connectivity attacks flood a computer with very high volume of connection requests so that available connection limit is reached and the computer can no longer process legitimate user requests. For almost all known DoS attacks, there are software solutions available which system administrators can install in the systems and use them to limit the damage caused by these attacks. Similar to the computer virus, new DoS attacks are continuously being dreamed up by hackers.

A DoS attack which uses multiple computers to launch a coordinated DoS attack against one or more targets is called Distributed Denial of Service attack (DDoS). DDoS attacks usually make use of client/server technology where a *master* program, installed on one computer, communicates over the internet to multiple *agent* programs installed on other computers. After receiving a command from the master, agents initiate the attack.

Software Piracy Software piracy refers to unauthorised copying and duplication of a software. Most of the computer application programs are licensed for use at one computer or for use by only restricted number of users at any time. Usually, a licensed copy of the software has to be purchased to become a licensed user. However, making copies of the program and distributing them to others is not allowed.

Software piracy is very difficult to stop. Originally, companies have tried to stop software piracy by copy-protecting their software. However, this technique could not work well because it was found rather inconvenient by users and is also not totally foolproof. There are many ways that a software piracy is carried out. Few examples include use of a software on computers without providing the appropriate licenses, illegal use of a single-licensed software version on multiple computers, using a key generator to generate a registration key to convert an evaluation version of a software into a full-fledged version, and posting a licensed version of a software product on the internet and making it available for downloading.

7.6.3 Common Software Piracy Terminologies

The following terminologies relate to the illegal use of software by various ways:

Crack A software crack is a working version of software which is obtained illegally by circumventing the software's copyright protection. Software cracking is carried out by modifying the software in order to remove the encoded copy prevention.

Hack It refers to working around the copy protection of an application software, for the purpose of creating an illegal version of the software.

Hardware Locking It refers to a technique of protecting software piracy by locking the software license to specific computer hardware. Hardware locking uses special hardware modules which are called Hardware Locks (also sometimes referred as 'dongles') that connect to the computer and communicate with the software running on the computer. For example, hardware lock can be used to lock the hard drive where the software is installed so that it cannot work on any other computer. Figure 7.2 shows a picture of hardware lock.

Fig. 7.2 *Parallel port hardware lock*

Key Generators Key Generator (also known as 'KeyGen' in short) is a software program which is used to generate an unauthorised but working registration key or serial number for software. It is used to by-pass copy protection and creates an illegal version of a software program.

Serials It refers to a registration or serial key (which is obtained illegally) to unlock an evaluation version of a software.

Phishing Phishing is derived from the word 'fishing'. It refers to the duplication of an existing webpage to attract users, in order to steal their private or financial particulars such as password, bank account information, etc. Fraudsters use this information to carry out funds transfers or to undertake transactions that are billed against original customer. The duplicated webpage, commonly known as spoofed webpage, looks very similar to a real webpage of a genuine institution. For example, if a bank's actual internet URL is **www.mybank.com**, the fraudsters may create a webpage in the fashion **www.mybank.org** or **www.mybank.net**, etc.

Normally, to deceive users, an e-mail containing a web-link is sent to them. The e-mail requests users to click on a link and redirects them to visit a website where they are asked to provide personal information such as password, credit card number and bank account number which are legitimately in use in some organisations. The URL or web-link address of such dummy webpages is created on freely available web-hosting servers and is disguised to appear real. Most of the time, users who submit their personal details are not aware that the information provided by them is being captured in the background by the fraudsters. Such spoofed websites remain active only for a very short time, till the fraudsters have collected the personal information of a number of customers.

Spoofing of Internet Protocol (IP) Addresses IP spoofing refers to sending mails and messages to other users under an incorrect IP address to convince the receiver that sender is someone else. IP spoofing is most frequently used in Denial-of-Service attacks (DoS). As we know, in DoS attacks, the goal of an attacker is to flood the network with overwhelming amount of traffic without bothering about the receiving of the responses to his attack packets; IP spoofing is very much suitable for such attacks. Other services which are vulnerable to IP spoofing includes RPC (Remote Procedure Call services), X window system, R services suite (such as rlogin, rsh, etc.).

Hacking In simple terms, hacking can be defined as an illegal intrusion into a computer system and/or network. The person who breaks into computers is called a hacker. Hackers write a computer programs to attack the target computer. Usually, they possess the desire to destroy the system and get rid of such destruction. Most of the time, hacking is done to get some monetary gains such as stealing credit card information, transferring money from other's bank accounts to their own account, etc.

The term 'hacking' is bit different from 'cracking'. But in the perspective of Indian laws, there is no difference between 'hacking' and 'cracking'. It considers every act committed towards breaking into a computer and/or network as 'hacking'.

Virus Dissemination Computer virus refers to a small computer program which is designed to damage a computer system upon activation. A computer virus can copy itself and infect a computer without the permission or knowledge of the owner. There are many ways by which a virus can spread. Some of the reasons include copying infected files through network, downloading the infected files from the internet, copying the infected files from floppy disk, USB, DVD, etc. Virus dissemination refers to the spreading of the virus programs via the internet to create damage to computer systems.

Cyber Stalking It refers to the use of the internet or other electronic medium to stalk a person. More precisely, it can be expressed as the repeated acts of harassment, intimidation or threatening behaviour of the cyber criminal towards the victim by using internet services. Harassment by following and monitoring the victim, making harassing phone calls, making false accusations, purposefully destroying victim's property, identity theft, and sending messages or articles are considered as the act of stalking.

Rogue Code It refers to software which is used to record the user's key strokes and send the information to the remote server. It sometimes also refers to the activities used to perform undesirable tasks such as deleting files and damaging the operating system and application software.

Child Pornography Recently, it has been seen throughout the world that the internet is being frequently used by abusers to reach and abuse children sexually. Child pornography is one such act which refers to images or films depicting sexually explicit activities involving a child.

Cyber Terrorism As the internet is becoming more and more common in all areas of human activities, few individuals or groups can use the anonymity offered by cyberspace to threaten citizens, specific groups belonging to some particular ethnicity or religious belief, communities or entire countries. Using the internet, these individuals or groups are able to carry out their task without the inherent danger of capture or death to the attacker which would have been the case if the attackers needed to be physically present at the attacking site. Cyber terrorism is a big threat in current times and can have serious influence on large number of people. It can even adversely affect the economy of a country.

Cyber-bullying It refers to an intentional, repeated and unsociable behaviour by an individual or a group to harm others, using the electronics or information technology equipment such as mobile phone, computer and internet. A very simple example of cyber-bullying could be an incident of continuously sending e-mails to a victim who does not want any further contact with the sender.

Review Questions

1. What do you understand by cyber ethics?
2. What is plagiarism?
3. Give five examples of violation of cyber ethics.
4. Discuss Richard Mason's four ethical issues (PAPA) in the information age.
5. What is the meaning of intellectual property? Explain following with respect to intellectual property:
   (a) Patent
   (b) Trademarks
   (c) Trade Secrets.
6. What is the difference between industrial property and copyright? Explain.
7. What are privacy laws? Describe privacy statement of an organisation?
8. Mention various types of privacy laws and discuss information privacy law in detail.
9. Discuss the four important information privacy principles suggested by Federal Trade Commission of United States of America.
10. Briefly describe international Safe Harbor Privacy principles.
11. What is cryptographic hash function and how does it help in electronic forensics evidence preservation?
12. What is computer forensics? What are its main goals?
13. Write short notes on following:
    (a) Database Forensics
    (b) Network Forensics
    (c) Firewall Forensics
    (d) Mobile Device Forensics.
14. What is the difference between computer privacy and internet privacy?
15. What is electronic evidence? How is it collected? How does it help in computer forensics?
16. Describe following terms:
    (a) Phishing
    (b) Denial of service attack

(c) Software piracy
(d) Hacking
(e) Cyber stalking
(f) Cyber terrorism
(g) Cyber bullying

17. Explain the difference between cyber bullying and cyber stalking.
18. Why is it difficult to define ethical parameters in internet ethics?
19. Give examples of some acts which are considered as unethical in internet.
20. Discuss various issues involved in internet ethics.

Emerging Trends in IT

Chapter 8

8.1 INTRODUCTION

Information Technology (IT) plays a major role in today's society. By considering the growth of IT in the past few years, it is possible to reflect its importance in the future. Although different organisations, industries and regions of the world are adopting IT in different ways, it is increasingly penetrating our daily life. In early years, the use of computers was primarily in the field of business and research. However, introduction of cheaper and more versatile computers in the 1980s and 1990s led to increase in the number of users in the offices and at home. The computer plays an important role in various fields like education, health care, hospitals, entertainment, etc. In business, consumers are expected to register themselves, through digital signature and two parties can then start communicating through encrypted secured communication. With the emergence of the electronic commerce and wireless networks, business and trading activities have become much easier.

The advancement in technology has opened many fronts which otherwise would not have been imaginable. Mobile phone is one such example of cutting edge technology. It is a device that was initially used for wireless communication, but mobile phones today have so many functionalities. Nowadays one can play music, take photographs, listen to FM, watch movies, surf the web, send emails and perform many more activities with mobile phones. One can also transfer files to other mobile phones and pertinent devices. The development of mobile phones and similar services, such as smart card and Bluetooth, has enabled people to communicate with each other in every corner of the world. In this chapter, some of the emerging trends like E-Commerce, EDI and GSM network for mobile communication, Bluetooth and infrared technologies have been discussed in detail.

8.2 e-COMMERCE

Traditionally, the word 'commerce' refers to exchange or buying and selling of goods and services. This includes exchange of money and transportation of goods from one place to another. In present times, we can observe, different forms of commercial activities around us. For example, in a grocery store itself, buying and selling are the main activities that form the essence of commerce. With technological advancement, commerce has added a new dimension in the form of digital information (electronic trade), which is more powerful and easier method to perform such type of transactions compared to the traditional commerce system. After the introduction of electronic trade, a revolution has happened in the commercial system which results in most of the business activities being carried out through electronic commerce across the world. In today's lifestyle, where time and money are the prime factors, e-Commerce plays an important role in bridging the gap between buyers and sellers.

Through electronic commerce, business is performed online. It uses the power of digital information for transactions. It understands the requirements and preferences of each customer and each partner to provide products and services for them. E-Commerce delivers the products and services to everyone who is involved in the process as quickly as possible. Automated and personalised system offers business which has potential to increase revenue and lower costs. It also helps to establish and strengthen relationship between customer and partner. It is a powerful technique to maintain the direct relationship between the customers and partners. In order to achieve these benefits, most organisations today makes use of electronic commerce for direct marketing, selling, buying and other customer services. The organisations such as secure information system, online banking and billing, and corporate purchasing are involved in e-Commerce technology.

8.2.1 Types of e-Commerce

e-Commerce can be divided into four main categories, namely Business-to-Business, Business-to-Consumer, Consumer-to-Business, and Customer-to-Customer, as shown in Fig. 8.1.

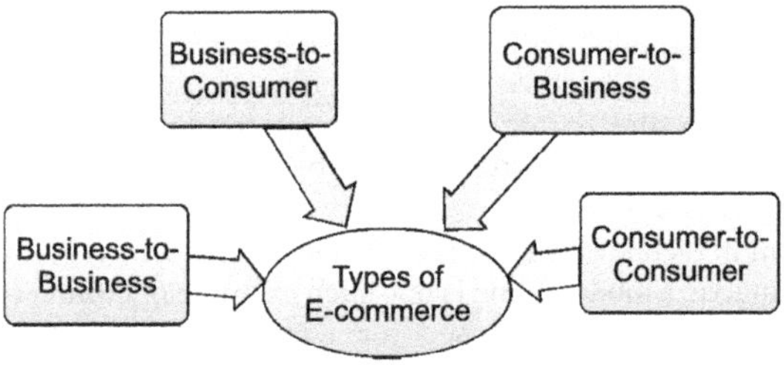

Fig. 8.1 *Types of e-Commerce*

Business-to-Business (B2B) B2B is doing business between companies such as manufacturers selling to distributors and wholesalers selling to retailers. This is between the wholesale and the retail. Pricing is based on quantity of order and is often negotiable. But B2B involves more than this activity, for example, interaction between businesses by chain process or with new trading partners, maintaining detailed information flow among all parties involved in the process. Hence B2B includes widening the circle of suppliers (for safety and competition) and centralising control (for records and discounts).

Business-to-Consumer (B2C) It is a concept of online marketing and distribution of products and services over the internet. For many retailers, this is a stepping process to sell goods directly to the customer. The key features for the success of B2C commerce are reaching more customers, providing better services and increasing sales, while spending less. The importance of e-Commerce is highly important for the consumer as it saves precious time by making transactions sitting at home. Otherwise, one has to spend substantial amount of time by moving from one corner to other to perform business. Also, it enables one to do shopping at any time virtually on the internet and to have goods delivered at the doorstep.

Business-to-Administration (B2A) In B2A system, the interaction between business communities with the public sector happens electronically. B2A includes submission of planning documents, tax returns or patent registration.

Customer-to-Customer (C2C) C2C system enables customers to deal directly each other. This completely excludes the business activities by enabling person-to-person transaction. This refers to an e-Commerce activity which uses an auction-style model. Examples of this type of system are available in **www.ebay.com and www.amazon.com**.

8.2.2 Process Flow in e-Commerce

Figure 8.2 explains the process flow of an electronic commerce system. It consists of several sub-processes where each one is interconnected with other. Every sub-process

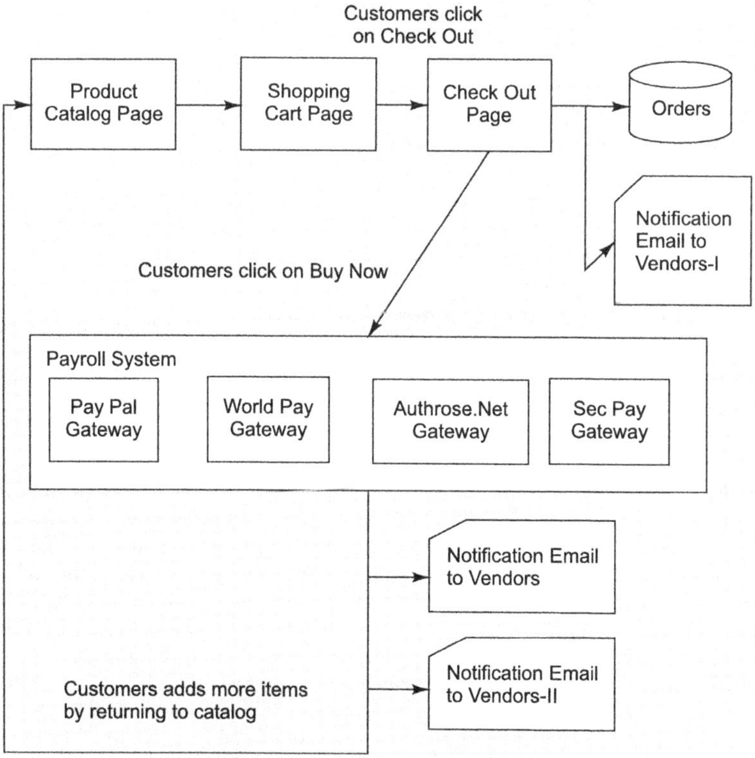

Fig. 8.2 *Process flow in e-Commerce system*

has its own function to execute. The pay roll sub-process consists of payment gateway process and communicates with Customer and Order details to Vendor. Before the customer makes the payment through payment gateway, Vendor has intimated an 'intend to buy' email notification from the e-Commerce system. The payment gateway confirms the transaction to both customer and the supplier when Customer actually makes the payment. The confirmation message carries an order number as a tracking reference number. Vendor has the ability to review and execute the Order in the Order tables, after receiving the confirmation of email.

Check out Page is another sub-process which normally collects the details about the customer such as name, country, email, phone number, etc. In Order sub-process, the e-Commerce system saves the customer and their order details in the database.

Notification Email to Vendors-I is a sub-process through which the vendors receive a notification email with details of the customers and the order, but only for information, since the customer has not yet been through the payment process. The vendor may contact the customer if no actual payment has been confirmed via the payment gateway. The email may include the merchant order number that has been saved on the order table.

The payroll system consists of many payment gateways. The user has to select anyone of them to make the payment. The selected payment gateway is invoked and receives both the order and customer details. The customer does not need to re-enter the information collected on the checkout page.

The payment gateway sub-process sends a confirmation through email, called 'notification by e-mail' to the customer. The email carries the merchant order number available in the orders table as a cross-reference.

Notification Email to Vendor-II is a sub-process through which the payment gateway sends a confirmation to the vendor by email. The email carries the merchant order number that has been saved in the orders table as a cross-reference.

8.2.3 Types of Electronic Payment

e-Commerce is based on the electronic payment mode on the internet of the traditional payment system. Electronic payment systems are based on the digital information. Every transaction takes place in the form of digital string. There are three modes of electronic payment system, namely e-cash, e-cheque and credit card.

E-cash E-cash is one of the commercial transactions in real-time environment on the internet. In e-cash, transactions are carried out in the electronic form. A bank issues a token to the customer for some particular amount of currency. The bank then debits the amount from the customer's account which equals the value of token issued to the customer. The bank then authenticates each token with a digital stamp before transmitting it to the customer. If the customer wants to spend the e-cash, he can transmit the token to the merchant who then approaches the bank for verification. The bank records the serial number of each token that the customer spends in order to avoid fraudulent transactions. If the bank finds that the serial number of the token is already recorded in their database, it sends the intimation to the merchant for its invalidity.

E-cheque e-cheque is similar to a paper cheque. A paper cheque is a kind of message given to a consumer's bank asking them to transfer some amount from one particular account to another. Similarly, e-cheque also issues a request to transfer the fund electronically. The advantage of an e-cheque is that it protects the customer's account details by encoding the account number with the bank's public key. This prevents the merchant from knowing the customer's account details; thereby the chances of fraudulent transactions are eliminated.

Credit Card It is a part of an electronic payment system after a small plastic card has been issued to users of the system. The card holder is entitled to buy goods and services—based on his preliminary proof of the ability to pay—by giving the credit card number to the vendor. The vendor then verifies it from the bank and issues a purchase slip for the customer to approve. The vendor then uses a copy of the purchase slip to collect money from the bank, and in the billing cycle, the consumer receives—at his address—a statement of recorded transaction. As in case of e-cheque, the credit card number is encoded before it gets transmitted over the internet.

8.2.4 Advantages of E-Commerce

The use of e-Commerce technology has a number of advantages. Some of them are highlighted below:

Availability The service availability is 24 × 7. Online business is always ON, as opposed to conventional businesses. Consumers can access these online services at any time they want.

Reduced Cost The product cost is reduced since stages along the value chain are decreased. For example, the company directly sells the product to the customer instead of distributing through a retail store. This process eliminates the intermediaries.

Low Cost Advertising Advertising on the paper is costlier than the advertising on the internet.

Low Start-up Cost Anyone can start a company on the internet. Since there is no need for the capital investment, start-up cost is minimum in e Commerce.

Increased Market Share The power of internet enables business to have access to international markets, thereby increases their market share.

Secure Payment System The advancement in technology makes the payment system secure by enabling an encryption algorithm.

Globally Accessible Consumers can shop anywhere in the world. This also provides wide selection of product and services to the customers.

Lower Cost of Practising Business The cost of practising business is very low since the number of employees is less. It also reduces the cost for purchasing and ordering since costs associated with fax, phone calls, data entry, etc are eliminated. The elimination of physical stores also results in reduced capital investment.

8.2.5 Disadvantages of e-Commerce

The introduction of innovation also brings certain limitations and drawbacks along with it. The same is the case with e-Commerce. The following are some of its disadvantages:

Unable to Examine the Products Online ordering for products through the internet does not allow physical examination of products. Only the images of the products are displayed to the user for viewing. Hence, there is uncertainty regarding the quality of the product.

Need of Specific Setup Specific hardware and software are required to start an e-Commerce company, which increases the cost.

Distribution Setup Efficient distribution is required, especially when supplies are to a global market.

Maintenance of Website It requires regular updates and maintenance, which requires extra labour costs.

Cost Even though it could save money by eliminating middlemen and initial capital investment, other costs may be incurred that include start-up cost of the company (which requires specific hardware, software, training of employees) and the cost to maintain the website and distribution of goods, etc.

Special Training and Maintenance It requires skilled manpower to get themselves trained in order to create, maintain and update the e-Commerce facilities of a company.

Security Risks It exposes itself to security risks and may be vulnerable to confidential data such as transaction information which includes credit card number and personal account details. Possibilities of stealing personal account details are the real threats in e-Commerce activity.

8.3 ELECTRONIC DATA INTERCHANGE

It refers to the transfer of data between different companies with the help of a type of network such as VANs (Virtual Area Network) or the internet. Today, a majority of commercial documents are generated through computer applications. In the past, the information contained in the document was communicated to a business partner, where it was printed and copied. The business partner, in turn, provided all the information available in the paper into another computer application for further processing. Companies found the above process extremely costly, unreliable and slow. The need for cheaper, reliable and faster solution for exchanging commercial data thus became important. For many organisations, these issues made them think about the possibility of Electronic Data Interchange (EDI). As the number of companies connecting to the internet keeps increasing, there is a need of faster but reliable exchange of information. EDI is becoming increasingly important, as it provides an easy mechanism for companies to get information or sell, buy and trade. It is a subset of e-Commerce and is a new way of information management.

At the very basic level, EDI refers to business data transfer between two machines. Specifically, EDI is a standard message format that allows trading partners to exchange data easily, using any electronic message service. Trading partners are customers and vendors involved in data exchange. It provides an application-neutral format for direct computer-to-computer exchange of information. ANSI has approved a set of EDI standards known as the X12 standards.

8.3.1 The Workflow of EDI

Figure 8.3 explains the workflow of EDI. It is a two way working process between a vendor and supplier. Once two EDI enabled partners have agreed to do business, further interaction happens automatically between the two partners. No human interaction is required. EDI translator translates the information from a company-specific format to the structured EDI format and then communicates the EDI message. It also receives the message and translates from standard format to company-specific format. Steps involved in EDI transaction for purchase, shipment and payment are discussed below:

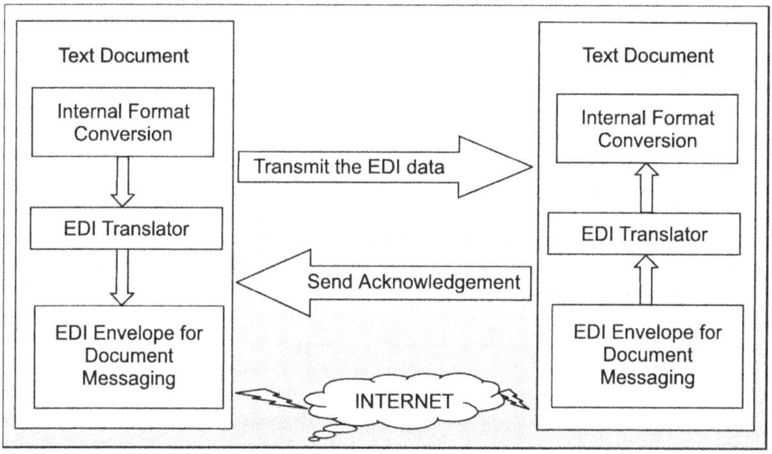

Fig. 8.3 *Workflow of EDI*

EDI translator is available for all types of computers such as mainframes, mini computers and micro computers. To make the system or computer EDI enabled, the system should contain appropriate software and modem to communicate the messages. In addition, the software should be capable of handling and controlling the EDI messages to any number or combination of trading partners. Such software is generally called EDI converter or translator and is totally independent of any computer application that passes data to it or receives data from it. Thus the major functions of the EDI translator are data conversion, data formatting and communicating the EDI messages.

8.3.2 Advantages of EDI

The objective of EDI is to provide a standard format to exchange information in an electronic environment. It is designed mainly for the inter-operability. It solves the problem of sharing data between non-compatible operating systems, applications and computers using a simple standard format, so that every computer connected to the network can exchange data easily. The main advantages of EDI are as follows:

- It eliminates the manual entry of data for analysing and reporting; as a result, it saves time and reduces errors.
- EDI saves money by providing an alternative to paper-based activity that requires a great deal of human interaction and materials such as paper documents, meetings, faxes, etc.
- It increases the speed with which the trading partner receives and incorporates the information into their system, thus greatly reducing cycle times.
- EDI provides a standard format to all contractors to use; hence it eliminates contract-specific data format and data delivery cost.
- Data becomes consistent since the format and the data dictionary follow a standard set of parameters.
- EDI and similar technologies allow a company to take advantage of the benefits of storing and manipulating data electronically, without any cost of manual entry.
- Since EDI is in standard format and is application neutral, it eliminates proprietary software formats and any interfaces for communication.

8.3.3 Disadvantages of EDI

EDI is not a technology but a new way of doing business. Though the implementation cost of the EDI system is low, identifying the benefits of EDI—especially when a company is not using EDI—is difficult. Some of the disadvantages of EDI are given below:

- Existing business processes built around slow paper handling may not be suited for EDI and would require significant changes in order to accommodate automated processing of business documents.
- There is involvement of time and money in the initial set-up. The preliminary expenses and time that arise from the implementation, customisation and training can be costly and may therefore discourage some businesses.

8.4 GLOBAL SYSTEM FOR MOBILE COMMUNICATION (GSM)

It is a globally accepted standard for digital communication. GSM is used by over 3 billion people in more than 212 countries. GSM is the name of a standardisation group established in 1982 to create a common European mobile telephone standard that would formulate specifications for a pan-European mobile cellular radio system. It operates at either 900 MHz or 1800 MHz frequency band. It makes international roaming very common between mobile phone operators, enabling subscribers to use their phones in many parts of the world. GSM has been considered as a second generation (2G) mobile communication system since both signalling and speech channels are digital. It is also built for the easy way of data communication via the mobile system.

8.4.1 The GSM Network

Figure 8.4 describes the GSM network. It consists of three sub-modules—mobile station, base station subsystem and network subsystem. The following sub-section explains each module in detail:

Mobile Station (MS) It consists of two subsystems known as Mobile Equipment (ME) and Subscriber Identity Module (SIM).

Mobile Equipment (ME)

- Different manufacturers produce the mobile equipment.
- It has to obtain the approval from the standardisation body.
- It has to be identified uniquely by an IMEI (International Mobile Equipment Identity)

Subscriber Identity Module (SIM)

- It has to be authorised by the International Mobile Subscriber Identity (IMSI). An example for SIM-based identification is the smart card system.
- It allows the user to send and receive calls. It also enables the user to receive other subscribed services
- It has been encoded by network identification details
- It has been protected by a password or PIN
- It allows transfer from one mobile device to another since it contains key information for activating the phone.

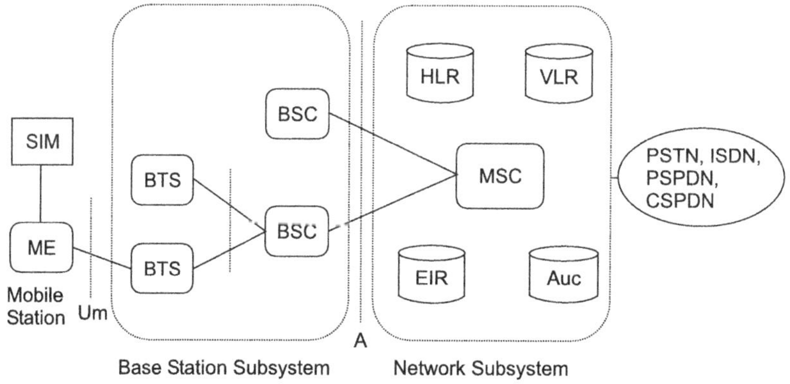

SIM: Subscriber Identity Module
MIE: Mobile Equipment
BTS: Base Transceiver Station
BSC: Base Station Controller
HLR: Home Location Register
VLR: Visitor Location Register
MSC: Mobile service Switching Centre
EIR: Equipment Identity Register
Auc: Authentication Centre

Fig. 8.4 *GSM network*

Base Station Subsystem (BSS) All radio-related functions are performed in the BSS which consists of Base Station Controllers (BSCs) and the Base Transceiver Stations (BTSs).

Base Transceiver Station (BTS) The BTS handles the radio link protocols to the mobile station. The BTS has the radio equipment (transceivers and antennas) needed to provide services to each cell in the network. A group of BTSs is controlled by a BSC. The following are the functions of a BTS:

- Houses the radio transceivers that define a cell
- Records speech and data transmissions from the MS.

Base Station Controller (BSC) The BSC provides all the control functions and physical links between the Mobile Service Switching Centre (MSC) and the BTS. A number of BSCs are served by an MSC. The following are the functions of BSC:

- Manages Resources for BTS
- Configures cell data.
- Handles call set up
- Updates locations
- Handover for each MS.

Network Subsystem The network subsystem is responsible for performing call processing and subscriber-related functions. The network subsystem includes the following functional units.

Mobile Switching Centre (MSC) It performs the telephony switching function of the system such as base station controllers and mobile switching centres. It controls calls to and from other telephone and data systems. It also performs such functions as toll ticketing, network interfacing and common channel signalling. It has three major functions:

- It establishes the calls between sender and receiver
- It collects call details, such as received calls and dialed calls
- It also coordinates the operation of the components in the network.

Home Location Register (HLR) It is a database consisting of information such as subscriber's service profile, location information and activity status. When an individual buys a subscription from one of the PCS operators, he or she is registered in the HLR of that operator. The two major functions of HLR are given below:

- It contains administrative information of each subscriber
- It contains the current location of the mobile.

Visitor Location Register (VLR) It is a database that contains temporary information about subscribers which is needed by the MSC in order to service visiting subscribers. The major function of the VLR is to contain selected administrative information from the HLR. For example, when a mobile station roams into a new MSC area, the VLR connected to that MSC makes a request for data about the mobile station from the HLR. The other major functions of VLR are the following:

- It authenticates the user
- It keeps track of information, such as customers having the phones which are ready to receive a call
- It periodically updates the database regarding which phones are turned on and ready to receive calls

Authentication Center (AUC) It is mainly used for security. It provides authentication and encryption parameters that verify the user's identity and ensure the confidentiality of each call. The AUC protects network operators from different types of fraud found in today's cellular world.

Equipment Identity Register (EIR) It is a database used to track handsets using the IMEI (International Mobile Equipment Identity). This information is used to prevent calls from stolen, unauthorised or defective mobile stations.

8.4.2 GSM Specification

Specification is different for every Personal Communication Service (PCS) among their PCS networks. The following are the specifications of GSM:

Modulation It is a process of transmitting the original signal by varying the carrier frequency. GSM uses Gaussian Minimum Shift Keying (GMSK) technique.

Frequency Band The GSM frequency band is between 1850 to 1900 MHz.

Speech Coder Linear Predictive Coding (LPC) is used in GSM since it reduces the bit rate. Speech is encoded at 13 kbps.

Access Method GSM follows the Time Division Multiple Access (TDMA) concept. It is a channel access method for shared medium networks, in which several different calls may share the same carrier. Each call is assigned a particular time slot.

Channel Separation Channel separation in GSM is 200 kHz.

Transmission Rate The transmission rate in GSM is of 270 kbps

Duplex Distance It refers to the distance between the uplink and downlink frequencies. The duplex distance is 80 MHz

8.4.3 Advantages of GSM

GSM standard has offered several advantages to both consumers and network operators. For the consumers, it provides roaming facility and switching carriers without additional efforts while for the network operators, it allows choice of equipment from any vendor. An alternative to voice call is the Short Message Service (SMS), which is now supported on the other mobile standards as well. Some other advantages of the GSM network are listed below:

- Efficient network design for less expensive system expansion

- Seamless interoperability between networks and handsets
- International roaming capability in over 100 countries
- Efficient use of spectrum
- A wide variety of handsets and accessories
- Ease of use with over-the-air activation, and all account information is held in a smart card which can be moved from handset to handset
- Easy subscription process (SIM-based)
- Global footprint for international roaming, including SMS, data and other value-added services
- Security against fraud and eavesdropping
- Advanced features such as short messaging and caller ID
- High stability mobile fax and data, at up to 9600 baud.

8.5 BLUETOOTH

Bluetooth is the name of a new technology that is now available commercially. It significantly changes the usage of the machines. One can observe that the computer is connected to the keyboard as well as a printer, mouse, monitor and so on. All these peripherals are connected by cables. Cables have become the bane of many offices, homes, etc. Bluetooth is specifically designed to replace the cable by using short range radio links. Figure 8.5 shows the Bluetooth chipboard that is used in a computer system to connect the peripherals without cables. Hence, it is also known as **cable-replacement technology,** which allows users to form wireless connections between devices such as the keyboard, printers, etc.

Fig. 8.5 *Bluetooth chipboard*

It is a standard specification to communicate between small devices. It is a low-cost, short-range radio communication between mobile PCs, mobile phones and other portable devices. The technology allows users to form wireless connections between various communication devices in order to transmit real-time voice and data. Figure 8.6 shows the Bluetooth enabled devices which are connected to each other. Its key features are robustness, compactness, low power and cost, and is designed to operate even in noisy frequency environments.

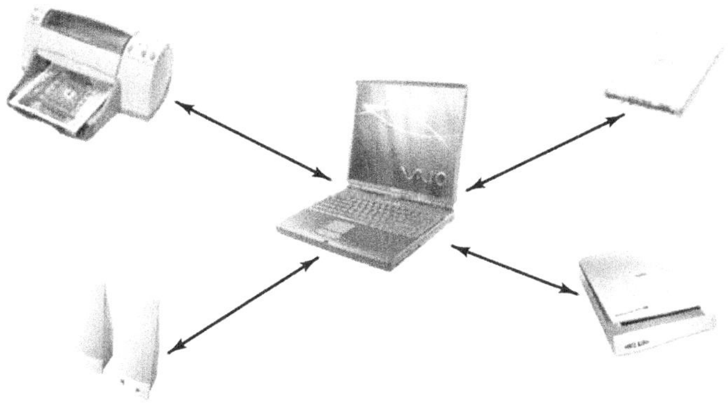

Fig. 8.6 *Bluetooth enabled devices*

8.5.1 Bluetooth—Working Principle

Bluetooth radio operates in the 2.4 GHz band. It is built into a small microchip and operates on a globally available frequency band, ensuring communication compatibility worldwide. It uses a fast acknowledgement and frequency hopping spread spectrum to make the link robust. The standard has been introduced by an electronic group that allows any electronic equipment to connect on its own without wire, cable or any help from a user. Since Bluetooth used spread frequency lopping technique, it is unlikely that there are several devices having the same frequency, it changes its signal 1600 times per second which helps to avoid interception by unauthorised parties. Since every Bluetooth transmitter uses spread spectrum transmitting automatically, it is unlikely that any two transmitters can have the same frequency at the same time. When Bluetooth devices come within range of one another, an electronic communication takes place to determine sand data can be transferred. As the connections are set automatically, a user does not have to manually operate the devices. Once the communication has taken place, devices form a network. Bluetooth systems create a personal area network that allows the devices to communicate with each other.

There are two power levels which depend on the distance of communication. First is the lower power level and second is the higher power level. Lower power level covers the shorter personal area within a room while a higher power level can cover a medium range, say, within a home. This technology uses omni-directional radio waves. It can transmit through walls and other non-metal barriers. However, if there is interference from other devices, the transmission speed decreases but does not stop. It could support both point-to-point (P2P) and point-to-multipoint (P2M) connections. The data rate is up to 720 Kbps within a range of 10 meters (up to 100 meters with a power boost).

In addition, the software is stored on a microchip control which ensures that only those units preset by their owners can communicate. With the current specification, a maximum of seven slave devices can be set to communicate with a master radio in one network, called piconet. Figure 8.7 shows the piconet structure. Piconet follows the master-slave technique to enable the devices to communicate with each other on the net. Several piconets can be linked together to form scatternet which allows communication between other device configurations.

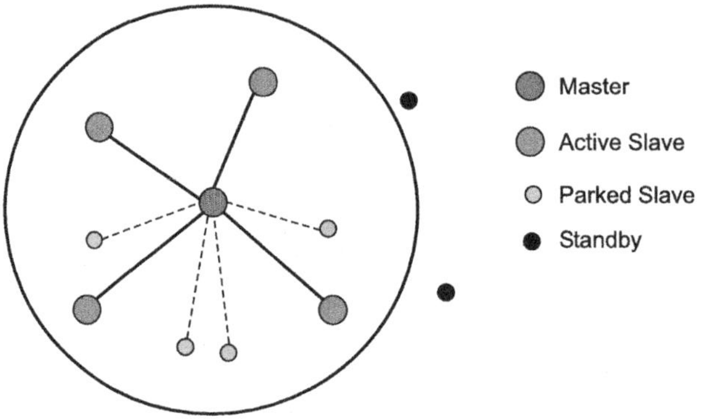

Fig. 8.7 *Piconet structure*

8.5.2 Bluetooth—Applications

Bluetooth has a powerful potential in moving and synchronising information in a localised setting. Since people can now communicate more with those who are close—a natural phenomenon of human interaction—the possibility of Bluetooth applications is enormous. Some applications of Bluetooth technologies are given below:

- In the computer industry, almost all the companies have started using this Bluetooth technology. People who need to transmit data between their laptops or PDAs to their computer, use Bluetooth technology.
- Since Bluetooth supports both point-to-point and point-to-multipoint, it simultaneously creates a virtual link between a number of devices.
- Using Bluetooth technology, it is possible to send still or video images from one location to another, without the hassle of connecting the digital camera to the mobile phone.
- Bluetooth has enabled three different ways of phone connectivity. At home, a phone functions as a portable phone (fixed line charge). When one is on the move, it functions as a mobile phone (cellular charge) and when the phone comes within range of another mobile phone with built-in Bluetooth wireless technology, it functions as a walkie-talkie (no telephony charge).
- In case of urgency, it allows transfer of selected documents instantly with selected participants and exchange of electronic business cards automatically, without any wired connections.
- If the desktop, mobile computer, notebook and the mobile phone are synchronised, the address list and calendar from the notebook are automatically updated to match with the desktop data or vice versa.
- It also supports automatic message delivery. If one sends e-mails on a portable PC while travelling on an airplane, all messages are immediately sent soon after he has landed and switched on his mobile phone.
- It also has support functions, for example, if someone has arrived at home, the door automatically unlocks, the entry way lights switch on and the heat is adjusted to pre-set preferences.

8.5.3 Advantages of Bluetooth

There are many advantages of using Bluetooth wireless technology. The most important is the fact that any two devices can be connected with each other without the use of any cables or wires. Added to that, other benefits of Bluetooth technology are listed below:

- It is an economic wireless solution, both for the data and voice within the short distance.
- It uses global technology specification, i.e., it uses universal radio frequency of 2.4 GHz ISM frequency band.
- It is applicable to both stationary and mobile environments.
- Its devices are automatically connected to themselves. The user does not have to manually operate the devices.
- No specific setup is needed.

8.5.4 Disadvantages of Bluetooth

Even though Bluetooth technology has been highly rated by many analysts in the industry, it has some limitations that must be taken into consideration:

Limited Range The range for this technology is limited to only 30 feet. This limits the Personal Area Network (PAN) and the connection accessibility for the electronic devices to perform an action.

High Chipset Cost Because of its high chipset cost, there exists technology problem in approaching general markets.

Additional Antenna It has led to increased bulk of the portable devices. It requires a larger antenna in portable devices to transmit and receive data through radio waves.

Limited Transmission Capacity Data transmission capacity is limited to 1 Mbps which makes data exchange very slow when handling large size files or folders.

Security Possibility of security threats are more due to the aspect of radio waves. The radio waves may provide others access to the Bluetooth-enabled devices and allow them to break into the network of any organisation from the outside. A Bluetooth chip allows to communicate with any device within 10 metres range. For example, if a mobile call is made using a Bluetooth device, any mobile within the range is capable of picking up the call.

8.6 INFRARED TECHNOLOGY

In recent years, wireless communication has offered an alternative solution to the fixed cable network. Wireless technology is beneficial since it provides mobility and compact devices. In future, the trend in telecommunication may consist of a fibre-optic network and wireless short range access over wireless channels. Presently, wireless technology uses radio waves to communicate which may not be sufficient for fulfilling future needs, since radio communication has several limitations. As a result, every radio communication is being pushed to higher frequencies. In order to overcome this problem, an alternative medium—called infrared wave technology—is becoming available for use as a new medium of communication. Figure 8.8 shows the infrared enabled miniature USB adapter.

Fig. 8.8 *Miniature USB Infrared Adapter*

Infrared (IR) is a wireless technology system that exchanges data through infrared radiation. It is electromagnetic energy with wavelengths somewhat longer than those of red light. It is a technology that allows devices to communicate with each other through short-range wireless signals. With infrared, computers can transfer files and other digital data bi-directionally.

8.6.1 Setup and Usage

Infrared technology uses ports both to transmit and receive data. Infrared adapters are installed in many laptops and handheld personal devices. In Microsoft Windows, infrared connections can be created in the same way as the local area network connections. It supports three different data rates in the following forms:

- IrDA-SIR (slow speed) infrared, supporting data rates up to 115 Kbps
- IrDA-MIR (medium speed) infrared, supporting data rates up to 1.15 Mbps
- IrDA-FIR (fast speed) infrared, supporting data rates up to 4 Mbps

Infrared networks have been designed to support the communication between two computers directly. Two infrared devices are placed within a few meters (not more than 5 meters) of each other, when they are under network. Infrared network signals cannot penetrate walls or other, obstructions, unlike Wi-Fi and Bluetooth technologies. It works only in the direct "line of sight." Infrared communications span very short distances. However, extensions to infrared technology also support more than two computers and semi-permanent networks. Infrared technology is made as simple as possible to reduce the complexity, size and weight of a mobile terminal. For example, powerful algorithms have to be used to transmit high definition video signals to minimise the bandwidth. An infrared wireless communication system has been designed to provide unregulated bandwidth and to offer smaller terminals for mobility.

8.6.2 Applications of Infrared Technology

Infrared communications have many applications. Some of them are mentioned below:

- It is used in every corner of our home since television, air conditioner, computer peripherals, etc. are controlled by infrared-enabled devices.

- It helps to communicate between two buildings, where the cost of cabling between the two buildings is significantly larger.
- Infrared communication is used in sending documents, schedules and books from a hand-held computer to a printer.
- It can also send faxes from a hand-held computer to a distant fax machine.
- Infrared communication is used by business people for exchanging messages, business cards and other information via hand-held personal computers.
- It enables 4 MB per second transfer of digital music, photos, books and other file data to and from MP3 players, cell phones, PDAs and is faster compared to other technologies.

8.6.3 Advantages of Infrared Technology

Infrared technology, as a form of wireless communication, offers several important advantages. The greatest advantage of infrared is being able to use its own receiver with public transmitters (like in movie theatres) and getting the best sound reproduction. Because of their superior sound reproduction, they are often used in movies, plays and musical productions. Some other advantages of infrared technology are listed below:

1. **Simple circuitry:** It can incorporate into the integrated circuit product without any special or proprietary hardware.
2. The infrared enabled devices are portable.
3. **Few international regulatory constraints:** IrDA (Infrared Data Association) functional devices can ideally be used by international travelers, no matter where they may be.
4. **High noise immunity:** It is not as likely to have interference from signals of other devices.
5. **Low circuitry costs:** It requires less cost for the entire coding/decoding circuitry.
6. **Higher security:** Line of Sight (LOS) helps to ensure that data is not leaked or spilled to nearby devices during transmission.
7. It is ideal for laptops, telephones and personal digital assistants because of its low power requirements.

8.6.4 Disadvantages of Infrared Technology

The receivers and transmitters must be in direct line of sight of each other. This reduces the amount of flexibility in movement within the room without interrupting the signal. Unlike FM, one cannot cover the receiver or put it where the direct line of sight can be blocked. Some of the disadvantages are given below:

Short Range Performance is good within a short distance and the performance drops off with longer distances

Light and Weather Sensitive Direct sunlight, rain, fog, dust and pollution can adversely affect transmission.

Blocked by Common Materials People, walls, plants, etc. can block the transmission of data.

Line of Sight Transmitters and receivers must be almost directly aligned (i.e., able to see each other) to communicate.

Speed Data transmission rate is lower than fixed-cable wired transmission.

8.6.5 Comparison of Bluetooth and Infrared Technologies

Bluetooth and Infrared technologies have enabled transfer of data with ease. Infrared technology has certain limitations, such as it requires free line of sight in order to transfer a file. The infrared port should be pointed towards the other phone with which it is to be connected. Also, it should be point-to-point. The other main drawback of infrared technology is that only two devices can communicate at one time. Even USB cables have their constraints. The Bluetooth has overcome the problem of both infrared and USB. Bluetooth is a wireless technology that allows phones, computers and other devices to interact with each other over short distances. It is an economical way of exchanging information between devices. Its priorities include sending photos from mobiles, exchanging business cards, sending voice messages, satellite navigation using **GPS**, etc.

In the case of Bluetooth, the devices need not be in line of sight, it just has to be within the range of each other, say about 10 meters. Bluetooth works by using radio chips. Bluetooth devices frequently change radio frequency, to ensure security and to prevent any eavesdropping. Each device is assigned an individual ID so that, before it can exchange data, the PIN number has to be entered to authorise the connection. This ensures the power of Bluetooth wireless technology. In addition, Bluetooth technology is affordable, energy efficient and it also stands out due to minimal interference, easy automation and compliance with universal standards. Table 8.1 lists the differences between Bluetooth and Infrared wave technologies.

Table 8.1 *Difference between Bluetooth and Infrared Technologies*

S.No.	*Bluetooth*	*Infrared (IR)*
1	Point to multipoint	Point to point
2	Data and voice communication	Intended for data communication
3	Easy synchronisation due to Omni-directional and no LOS requirement	Difficult to synchronise due to LOS (line of sight) requirement
4	It can penetrate solid objects	Cannot penetrate solid objects
5	Both transmitter and receiver can be mobile for synchronisation	Both transmitter and receiver must be stationary for synchronisation
6	The communication range is within 10 m	The communication range is within 1 m

Review Questions

1. Define e-Commerce.
2. What are the different types of electronic commerce technologies?
3. Explain the process flow in electronic commerce system and how is it useful in business activities.
4. What are the different modes of electronic payment system?
5. What are the advantages and disadvantages of electronic commerce system?
6. Mention some applications of electronic commerce system.
7. Explain how electronic commerce technology is used in e-shopping.
8. What is EDI (Electronic Data Interchange)?
9. Explain the workflow of EDI system.
10. What are the advantages and disadvantages of EDI system?
11. Define GSM.
12. What is the frequency band used for the GSM technology?
13. What are the three major subsystems of the GSM network?
14. Mention the activities of BSS (Base Station Subsystem).
15. What are the major functions of MSC (Mobile Switching Centre)?
16. Mention the specifications of GSM network.
17. Give some of the advantages of GSM network.
18. Explain the role of GSM technology and its revolution in mobile communication.
19. What are the disadvantages of GSM technology?
20. What is Bluetooth? How it is different from other wireless technologies?
21. Define the term 'piconet'.
22. What is the working principle of Bluetooth technology?
23. What is the frequency band used for the Bluetooth technology? What is the speciality of Bluetooth frequency band compared to the other technologies?
24. Mention some of the applications of Bluetooth technology and explain how Bluetooth is used in acoustic systems.
25. What are the advantages and disadvantages of Bluetooth technology?
26. Define the term 'Infrared'. How is 'infrared technology' used in data communication?
27. Explain two popular modes of data transfer?
28. What are the different data rates supported by the infrared communication?
29. Mention some of the applications of infrared technology.
30. What are the advantages and disadvantages of infrared technology?
31. Compare Bluetooth and Infrared technologies.

Case Study

Chapter 9

9.1 CASE STUDY OF ASSET NETWORK INCORPORATION

Asset Network Incorporation (hereafter referred as ANI) is an IT organisation which provides services such as e-mail, web hosting, file backup, etc. to its customers. ANI also offers services towards website development, maintenance, management, and administration. ANI's customers are various organisations which like to use external web space for hosting their websites and other related public data.

Regardless of the size of an organisation, considerable amount of money and resources are generally spent in the development of a suitable website that is informative and practical. From an organisation point of view, it is essential to make all public domain information available to the public through their website. So, it is necessary for ANI to take necessary steps to keep the site of each customer up all the time. It is a challenging task for ANI. To run its services smoothly, ANI has set up different departments for each service. For example, e-mail services are managed by one independent department. Similarly, there is a separate department to look after each service.

For smooth functioning of each of these departments, there is a need of a proper management of its infrastructure and activities. This section considers the functioning of ANI and studies various aspects of its activities and infrastructure management. An overview of services offered by ANI is shown in Fig. 9.1.

Through this case study, an attempt has been made to understand the various critical issues involved in managing the activities and infrastructure required for supporting the services offered by ANI. Different services may have their different requirements. For example, in web services, security is a major concern. The organisation needs to look at various security issues while deploying web services. The problems of e-mail services include message overload, tracking of sent mails, privacy concerns, e-mail spoofing, e-mail bombing, maintaining mailing list, spamming and computer viruses. Under most network configurations, user names, passwords, FTP commands and files can be captured by anyone on the network using a packet sniffer while transmission. So file services suffer when unsecure method is used in storing and transferring the files.

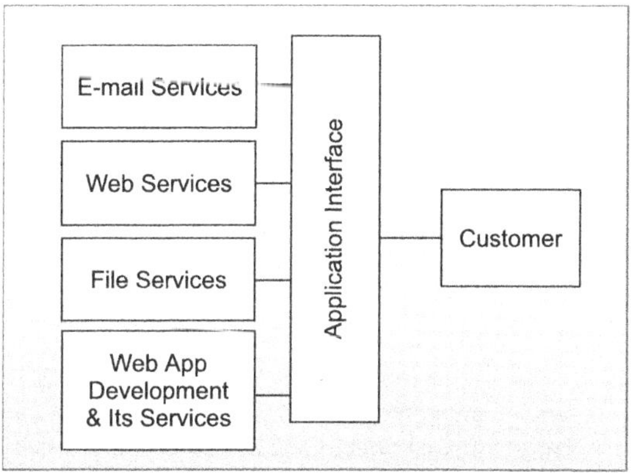

Fig. 9.1 *Different services offered by ANI*

Organisation administration must also be capable to handle issues in workflow such as managing processes and analysing them. It should also be able to plan and define new services, and managing change in any type of environment. Following sections explain the way in which various IT infrastructure management services are being used in running ANI smoothly and efficiently.

9.1.1 IT Service Continuity Management

An organisation is expected to remain operational and provide services to its customers at all times at agreed value. IT service continuity management helps in ensuring that all the services are capable of providing value to the customers at the time of failure of normal availability solutions. It also assists in managing risks to ensure that (i) every offered service is available in case of occurrences of any unlikely or unexpected event and (ii) required IT Infrastructure and services can be restored within desired amount of time if necessary. Absence of services has great influence on customers and can quickly affect the overall reliability of the organisation. IT service continuity management helps in maintaining the services running successfully.

There are many factors that cause unavailability of services. For example, service availability may get interrupted because of hardware failure or human error. A hardware failure may happen on account of broken power supply, failure of disk drives, etc. To handle such problems, ANI maintains dual redundant power supply to minimise the risks of power failure. Moreover, if the power to the whole computer room or data centre fails, then it maintains a battery backup to cover the time needed to start the standby generator. ANI also maintains a contingency plan that describes the countermeasures to handle any availability risk.

9.1.2 Capacity Management

Capacity management helps in planning, analysing, sizing, and optimising capacity requirements to satisfy demand in a timely manner and at a reasonable cost. It also ensures that IT infrastructure of the organisation is used in an efficient manner. Incorrect planning for capacity leads to wastage of resources and results in unnecessary cost or shortage of resources leading to poor performance or/and unavailability of services.

ANI has set up a separate department to look after all capacity-related issues. This department ensures that required capacity for data processing and storage is provided at the right time and in appropriate volume. It continuously tries to optimise existing and future demand and supply of IT resource, and ensures a balance between them. This department proactively adds components, space or people in a cost-effective manner while making sure that the performance is at desired level for new additions and older components.

9.1.3 Availability Management

Availability refers to the ability of a service to perform the function as and when it is desired. Availability management helps to ensure that a given service delivers its functions consistently and cost-effectively. It supports the organisation to deliver a cost-effective and sustainable service availability to meet stringent business objectives.

Availability management ensures that the processes used for the support of critical IT services are mature enough and have the necessary personnel skills and tools to effectively take up their responsibilities. It helps to provide solution even when there is a difference between demand and supply. It also helps to define new services and maintain existing services.

ANI views the accessibility, performance and security of customer's data as critically important for customer as well as its business. It has set up all required network infrastructure, power capacity and physical security a customer would expect. Also, it guarantees the highest quality of service level from each of its customer.

9.1.4 Configuration Management

Configuration management helps in finding out and defining configuration items in a system. It assists in monitoring the status of these items, processing requests for change, and verifying the completeness and correctness of the configuration items. It offers a logical model of the IT infrastructure incorporating hardware, software and associated documentation. It controls the IT infrastructure and ensures that only authorised hardware and software are in use.

To speed up the maintenance and recovery, ANI has identified many configuration items in hardware, software, people and services, and recorded then in Configuration Management Database (CMDB). For example, it has identified the components in file storage system such as hard disks, backup and recovery software, power supply, etc. This helps in keeping track of all the items and makes maintenance fast.

9.1.5 Incident Management

An incident is an event which causes (or may cause) interruption or reduction in quality of service to the customer of an organisation. Incident management helps to restore normal service operations, as quickly as possible with the least possible impact on either the business or the user, in case of an incident. It handles all detected incidents and all service requests that may come from service desk. Incident management usually takes input from users but can also come from other sources like management information or detection systems. The outputs of the process are typically resolved and closed incidents, management information and communication to the customer.

ANI incident management is backed by strong processes that include the ITIL set of standards, ensuring the best service delivered every time. ANI recruits high caliber, skilled people in service desk who can handle most of the customer's problems at service desk level. It also has a team of dedicated experts who work as back end and helps in case service desk is not able to provide the solution. Detected incidents are recorded and classified into one of the types—hardware and application. Incident management team investigates and diagnoses the incident, and tries to recover service as agreed.

9.1.6 Problem Management

Problem management is responsible to ensure that all possible problems and known errors affecting the IT infrastructure are identified and recorded properly. It assists to investigate and resolve the underlying root causes of incidents and prevents incidents of similar nature from occurring again. By removing errors which often require a structural change to the IT infrastructure, the number of incidents can be reduced over a period of time.

In case of web services, the errors are possible for various reasons. ANI uses an exception handler *SOAPFaultException* to fix the errors known as faultcode, faultstring. This exception can give the complete information about the error condition. The faultcode might tell whether the error has happened because of the Server, Client, or something else. For example, in order to access the web services, it requires authentication. If a client does not provide security information such as username and password in the HTTP/SOAP header, it throws an authentication exception. This kind of error is considered to be a Client error. The faultstring contains the corresponding description of the error condition that has happened. This string message is human readable and the developer can easily debug the problem with the help of it.

In case of e-mail services, the possible problems are non-delivery of e-mails, exceeding the e-mail storage quota, exceeding the file attachment size, filling inbox with spam, etc. ANI solves these problems in various ways. Any email message which could not be delivered to receiver has to be notified to the sender. The notification includes the reason for non-delivery of emails. Similarly, if the mail inbox is exceeding the storage quota, the notification has to be sent to the users. ANI efficiently handles the spam mails by using the spam filtering.

9.1.7 Storage Management

The goal of storage management is to define, maintain and track data and data resources in an organisational environment. The important activity of storage management is to take care of the operation and maintenance aspects of storage media. Also, it takes care of the data stored on such media. Backups primarily ensure quick recovery in case of system failure. It is more than just performing data backups and restoration processes in case of a data-related incident. It also covers other important activities such as selecting and maintaining storage media, archiving and tracking the important data of an organisation.

ANI provides larger capacity disk to take backups for window-based file servers and other file servers. It supports backup services to users who have deleted files unknowingly or accidently and requests for file restorations later. ANI sends alert messages to all users like 'if the user has some critical data, it is essential that the user keep their own backups to ensure that such critical data is not lost in case of some unfortunate event'.

Restore ANI User Files ANI provides data restoration facilities in various ways. For example, the process of restoring user files differs depending on how long ago the files have been deleted. If the file has been deleted within 24 hours, the user can probably copy it from the local directory. The local directory contains a complete copy of all the directories, sub directories, and files as they appeared the last time they were backed up. If the file has been deleted beyond 24 hours, the user has to report to the 'help desk' of ANI. Help desk of ANI follows its own rules to restore the data back to users' home directory again. The set of rules followed by ANI can be as follows:

- Only the owner of a file can request for data restoration
- The owner has to submit file restoration requests to the help desk in person or by mail.

Then the help desk service groups notify the user soon after restoration in the corresponding user's home directory. However, some backup tapes are stored offsite which may need longer time to restore back the desired files.

9.1.8 Security Management

Security management prevents unauthorised access of information. It is a significant activity that controls the provision of information. Web servers are often the target of numerous exploit attempts. ANI initiated 'Security Management' in order to train the user about the usage and issues of web services. ANI has prepared a documentation about 'web server security guidelines'. This helps the user to understand the risk involved in unsecure access of web services. The guideline statement includes the user's responsibilities and procedure to be followed by them. In addition, ANI has its own policies to support the web services to users. Some of them are highlighted below.

- ANI installs the web server software on a dedicated host.
- It has enabled necessary web services, applications and disabled all other services.
- It has enabled web authentication and encryption technologies such as SSL/TLS based upon the nature of web server data.
- It performs regular backups of web content and occasional backups of operating system and application configurations.

- It separates the web server content and related subdirectories from operating system and application directories.
- It creates desired log files for further investigations and/or recovery purposes.
- Log files capture failed login attempts, account privilege changes and other potentially suspect activities.

9.1.9 Identity Management

Identity management is a discipline which encloses all tasks required to create, manage and delete user identities in computing environment. It identifies the individuals in a system and restricts their access to the system. Identity management is the most essential component of information protection. ANI uses identity management to automatise the administrative process, such as adding or removing access to specific systems, password reset and change of password. It enforces users for periodic changes of password in order to increase network security. ANI follows its own policies to create the account and set the password to users. Some of its policies are listed below:

- ANI creates the user accounts by following the principle of least-privilege.
- It removes or disables unnecessary default accounts.
- It sets all passwords of account holders appropriately to meet the ANI password guidelines.
- It has enabled that administrators need to monitor appropriate mailing lists and/ or web sites for security-related announcements.
- It always verifies a user's identity before resetting a password. It follows its own steps to confirm the identity of the user. It supports a self-service password reset solution as an effective approach to address password resets.
- It has implemented facilities like automated notification of a password change or reset to the user. In case of self-service password reset/change system, when a user resets changes his password, it automatically sends an email confirmation to the account owner. This provides a confirmation to the user that the change is successful. It also alerts the user in case his password is changed or reset by others.
- ANI follows the policy—'it never asks password from the user'. Often, it scrolls this message to every user's email inboxes to intimate the user not to disclose the passwords to others or any phishing emails.

The ANI has provided guidelines about password management. Some tips from the guidelines are highlighted below:

Enforce Strong Passwords ANI includes a functionality that prevents the user from setting a password that does not meet certain criteria. This functionality is leveraged to ensure only correct passwords are being set.

Do not Use Automatic Logon Functionality ANI instructs the user not to use automatic logon functionality. This is because of the fact that if a malicious user is able to gain physical access to a system that has automatic logon configured, he or she may be able to take control of the system and access potentially sensitive information.

Require Periodic Password Changes ANI forces a user to change the password periodically. ANI system serves a reminder to users and eliminates the human factor in determining whether to change a password. A general rule of thumb is to force a password change every 90 days. The ANI security policy states that "passwords will automatically expire every 90 days" which implies that passwords must be changed every 90 days or less.

Bibliography

1. *Foundations of IT Service Management: based on ITIL*, Jan Van Bon (editor), Van Haren Publishing, 2nd edition, 2005.

2. *Patterns: IT Systems Management and Security*, IBM Redpaper.

3. *IT Service Management—an Introduction: based on ITIL*, Jan Van Bon (editor), Van Haren Publishing, 2nd edition, 2004.

4. *IT Systems Management: Designing, Implementing, and Managing World-Class Infrastructures*, Rich Schiesser, Prentice Hall, 2001.

5. *Patterns for e-Business: A Strategy for Reuse*, Jonathan Adams, Srinivas Koushik, Guru Vasudeva, George Galambos, IBM Press, 2001.

6. *Microsoft Operations Framework*, Microsoft Corporation.

7. *Automating ITSM Incident Management Process*, Rajeev Gupta, K Hima Prasad, and Mukesh Mohania, Proceedings of International Conference on Autonomic Computing, pages: 141–150, 2008.

8. *IT Infrastructure Management and Standards*, Seppo Sirkemaa, Proceedings of the International Conference on Information Technology: Coding and Computing, pages: 201–206, 2002.

9. *Managing the IT Service Processes*, Noel Bruton, Elsevier, 2004.

10. *Wikipedia, The Free Encyclopedia*, www.wikipedia.com.

11. *Multimodal Biometrics System for Efficient Human Recognition*, Phalguni Gupta, Ajita Rattani, Hunny Mehrotra, Anil Kumar Kaushik, Proceedings of SPIE Defense and Security Symposium, Florida, 2006.

Index

Made in the USA
Monee, IL
04 November 2026

67385329R00115